New Casebooks

EMMA

New Casebooks

New Casebooks

EMMA

JANE AUSTEN

EDITED BY DAVID MONAGHAN

MACMILLAN

First published 1992 by
THE MACMILLAN PRESS LTD
Houndmills, Basingstoke, Hampshire RG21 2XS
and London
Companies and representatives
throughout the world

ISBN 0–333–55278–4 hardcover
ISBN 0–333–55279–2 paperback

A catalogue record for this book is available
from the British Library

Typeset by Footnote Graphics,
Warminster, Wiltshire
Printed in Hong Kong

Contents

Acknowledgements

The editor and publishers wish to thank the following for permission to use copyright material:

Nancy Armstrong, extracts from 'The Self-Contained: *Emma*' in *Desire and Domestic Fiction: A Political History of the Novel*. Copyright © 1987 by Oxford University Press, Inc., by permission of Oxford University Press;

J. M. Q. Davies, '*Emma* as Charade and the Education of the Reader', *Philological Quarterly*, 65 (1986), by permission of the author and *Philological Quarterly*;

Alistair Duckworth, '*Emma* and the Dangers of Individualism' in *The Improvement of the Estate: A Study of Jane Austen's Novels* (1971), by permission of The Johns Hopkins University Press;

Paul H. Fry, 'Georgic Comedy: The Fictive Territory of Jane Austen's *Emma*', *Studies in the Novel*, 11 (Summer 1979), by permission of *Studies in the Novel*;

Joseph Litvak, 'Reading Characters: Self, Society, and Text in *Emma*', *PMLA* 100 (1985), by permission of the Modern Language Association of America;

Beatrice Marie, '*Emma* and the Democracy of Desire', *Studies in the Novel*, 17 (Spring 1985), by permission of *Studies in the Novel*;

D. A. Miller, extract from 'Good Riddance' in *Narrative and its Discontents: Problems of Closure in the Traditional Novel* (1981). Copyright © 1981 by Princeton University Press, by permission of Princeton University Press;

Ruth Perry, 'Interrupted Friendships in Jane Austen's *Emma*', *Tulsa Studies in Women's Literature*, 5, no. 2 (Fall 1986). Copyright © 1986 by the University of Tulsa, by permission of the publisher;

Bruce Stovel, 'Comic Symmetry in Jane Austen's *Emma*', *Dalhousie Review*, 57, no. 3 (Autumn 1977), by permission of the author and *Dalhousie Review*;

James Thompson, extracts from 'Intimacy in *Emma*' in *Between Self and the World: the Novels of Jane Austen* (1988), by permission of Penn State Press.

General Editors' Preface

The purpose of this new series of Casebooks is to reveal some of the ways in which contemporary criticism has changed our understanding of commonly studied texts and writers and, indeed, of the nature of criticism itself. Central to the series is a concern with modern critical theory and its effect on current approaches to the study of literature. Each New Casebook editor has been asked to select a sequence of essays which will introduce the reader to the new critical approaches to the text or texts being discussed in the volume and also illuminate the rich interchange between critical theory and critical practice that characterises so much current writing about literature.

The series itself, of course, grows out of the original Casebook series edited by A. E. Dyson. The original volumes provide readers with a range of critical opinions extending from the first reception of a work through to the criticism of the twentieth century. By contrast, the focus of the New Casebooks is on modern critical thinking and practice, with the volumes seeking to reflect both the controversy and the excitement of current criticisms. Because much of this criticism is difficult and often employs an unfamiliar critical language, editors have been asked to give the reader as much help as they feel is appropriate, but without simplifying the essays or the issues they raise.

The project of New Casebooks, then, is to bring together in an illuminating way those critics who best illustrate the ways in which contemporary criticism has established new methods of analysing texts and who have reinvigorated the important debate about how we 'read' literature. The hope is, of course, that New Casebooks will not only open up this debate to a wider audience, but will also encourage students to extend their own ideas, and think afresh about their responses to the texts they are studying.

John Peck and Martin Coyle
University of Wales, Cardiff

Introduction

DAVID MONAGHAN

According to Adena Rosmarin, criticism of Jane Austen's novels written prior to the 1980s is characterised by a 'consensual blandness'.[1] This is, of course, a sweeping judgement and we need look no further than the essays in David Lodge's 1968 collection on *Emma* to grasp its limitations.[2] However, a broader survey of criticism than Lodge's might suggest that there is some justice in Rosmarin's claim. Indeed much the same comment might be made about literary scholarship in general because, prior to the increasing acceptance of new theories in the last decade or so, critics had a very limited range of approaches available to them. Rosmarin argues that criticism of *Emma* has relied entirely on a mimetic poetics but we should add to this New Critical, literary historical and various author-centred methodologies.

I

The consensus that critics working within these limited critical parameters have reached is that *Emma* is the first great English novel because it is an intricate, complex and perfectly achieved work which takes an apparently trivial subject matter – '3 or 4 Families in a Country Village', in Austen's famous phrase – and makes it a vehicle for the expression of universal truths. The origins of this combination of formal brilliance and significant statement are almost always located in the creative genius of Jane Austen, the Author.

The formal achievement of *Emma*, according to Wayne Booth, is rooted in Austen's development of the technique known as free indirect discourse whereby, in a supremely controlled process, the narrator's often ironic voice slides in and out of the consciousness of various characters.[3] Other critics focus on Austen's ability to structure blocks of narrative material so that they complement and play off against each other. Edgar Shannon, for instance, argues that what he calls the 'rhythm' of *Emma* derives from the weaving of a series of tripartite units into the novel's six major episodes.[4] A third way of demonstrating Austen's technical brilliance is provided by the many critics who have analysed how comparisons and contrasts are created between characters, who thus form an interdependent network, in order to bring the moral and emotional dimensions of individual characters into sharper focus. Both Emma and Mrs Elton, for instance, have acquired a greater complexity from analyses of correspondences between them.[5]

The precise nature of the universal truths to be found in *Emma* has been less clearly defined. It is generally agreed, though, that the truth of the novel can be located somewhere in Knightley's viewpoint, in the story of Emma's education and/or in Austen's use of binary oppositions. The terms of these oppositions have been expressed variously as imagination and reason, heart and head, self and society, inexperience and maturity, change and stability, secrecy and openness, selfishness and duty.

The first essay in this collection, Bruce Stovel's 'Comic Symmetry in Jane Austen's *Emma*' is an excellent example of the type of criticism described above. For Stovel *Emma* is a great novel because it combines a complex and aesthetically pleasing form with an important statement about the human condition. To demonstrate his thesis Stovel makes use of both literary historical and New Critical techniques. Thus he explains the formal perfection of *Emma* partly in terms of its closeness to the patterns of Comedy and partly by means of close readings of such textual details as the recurring use of the word 'friend'. The novel's structure is, according to Stovel, the product of an intricate interplay between its 'three main threads' and 'all the local symmetries' which 'lead to and from these threads in networks which get ever finer as we pursue them'.[6]

However, Stovel is not simply a New Critic interested in formal unity for its own sake; for him, the harmonious integration which characterises the structure of *Emma* is a reflection of its universally significant theme. Like other traditional interpreters Stovel looks for this major theme in the story of Emma's education and in binary oppositions, particularly those developed between the Emma–Knightley and Jane Fairfax–Frank Churchill relationships, between Emma and other characters and within Emma herself. In Stovel's reading of the novel all oppositions finally dissolve as Emma's education is completed and her 'desire to be herself, her desire for Knightley, and her desire to be good all . . . coincide' in such a way that a vision of 'harmony, not sacrifice or division, reigns'.[7]

The staunchly ahistorical character of such Austen criticism was modified during the 1970s by the work of a number of scholars who sought to locate her novels within a social context. Their model was Alistair Duckworth's *The Improvement of the Estate*. For Duckworth Austen is a conservative who, like Edmund Burke in *Reflections on the Revolution in France*, structures her novels around an opposition between conservative stability and radical innovation. Duckworth also finds in Burke a source for the paired metaphors of estate and improvements, house and theatricals, and, in *Emma*, culture and games, by means of which this opposition is expressed. Thus, in the excerpt from his book reprinted here (essay 2), Duckworth explores how the conflict between the predictable gentleman, Knightley, and Frank Churchill, for whom life itself is a game, functions as a metonymy for larger oppositions developed in *Emma* between the ' "open" syntax of morals and of manners' which characterise mainstream conservative culture and the antisocial 'concealment and opacity' of games.[8] Succeeding studies variously recast Duckworth's conservative/radical opposition as anti-Jacobin/Jacobin, gentry/bourgeoisie, conservative/romantic, but almost all agree with his positioning of Austen on the side of the establishment. A number of these studies follow Duckworth still further by seeking in the social dimensions of Austen's fiction an understanding not just of its themes but also of its form. In *Jane Austen: Structure and Social Vision*, for example, I argue that in the six novels the formal social occasion functions as a basic unit of structure as well as a vehicle for developing a Burkeian analysis of the connection between manners and morals.[9]

However, while the social critics of the 1970s undoubtedly expanded the scope of Austen criticism, their approach is, in some important respects, extremely traditional. They appeal repeatedly, for example, to authorial intention and their search for complex coherence not just in Austen's novels but in the ideology which informs them is imbued with the spirit of New Criticism. The tendency of these critics to follow Duckworth in using binary oppositions to define Austen's social values is also, of course, thoroughly consistent with traditional critical practice.

II

There was in fact a more genuinely radical new approach available to Austen scholars during the 1970s. This was provided by structuralism which dismisses the idea that a literary work is the unique product of a specific author and focuses instead on those objective elements of language and literary convention that works share with each other.[10] However, during the 1970s, when it exercised its greatest influence, the structuralist approach failed to attract the attention or interest of Austen's critics. By the time Beatrice Marie's 'Emma and the Democracy of Desire' (essay 3) was published in 1985 the key concepts of structuralism had been seriously undermined by poststructuralist theoreticians. Therefore Marie's article is reprinted in this collection for what it reveals about the possibilities and problems inherent in applying a structuralist methodology to *Emma* rather than as an example of a fully developed critical tendency.[11]

Marie's specific interest as a structuralist is focused on the typology of triangular desire which René Girard identifies in a number of European novels including *Don Quixote, Le Rouge et le Noir, Madame Bovary* and *A La Recherche du Temps Perdu.*[12] According to Marie triangular desire functions in particularly complicated ways in *Emma* because the novel blurs what are for Girard two quite distinct versions of the pattern by shifting the distance between the individual and the mediator of his/her desire at certain crucial points in the action. Nevertheless Marie will not allow that *Emma* escapes the confines of Girard's schema and she attempts to express the novel's complicated network of relationships by a diagram of an intricate series of interrelated triangles. Traditionalists might be offended by the way in which Emma, Knightley and other of Austen's characters are thus reduced to the apex points of triangles and their relationships to the length of the lines that run between these points. Even those more sympathetic to a structuralist approach might suspect that Marie forces both the Girardian model and *Emma* onto Procrustean beds in order to make a fit between them.[13] Nevertheless, by its refusal to put *Emma* on that other Procrustean bed of authorial intention, Marie's article points up the contribution that structuralism might have made to Austen studies.

III

Austen criticism did not actually become receptive to new critical methodologies until the 1980s when scholars began to approach her novels from the perspective offered by poststructuralist theory, the revolutionary potential of which is contained within its conception of language.[14] Traditional critical practice is founded in the essentialist assumption that meanings pre-exist their expression and that, therefore, language in a literary work functions as a more or less transparent medium for the communication of the author's ideas to the reader. Poststructuralism, by contrast, takes as its starting point the view of the influential linguist, Ferdinand de Saussure, that 'there are no pre-existing ideas and nothing is distinct before the appearance of language'.[15] For Saussure language does not develop from an impulse to name things in the world, as common sense might suggest. Rather it is a self-contained system of signs (each comprising a signifier or sound and a signified or concept) in which any given sign acquires an identity only because it is different from other signs. As Saussure puts it, 'in language there are only differences *without positive terms*'. Therefore 'the idea or phonic substance that a sign contains is of less importance than the other signs that surround it'.[16]

Jacques Derrida takes Saussure's theory one crucial step further by arguing that, if indeed there are no origins or ends outside language, then meaning can never be fully present.[17] Consequently the search for meaning will always proceed along a chain of signification made endless by its lack of a final or 'transcendental signified'. Implicit in this conception of language is the proposition that the 'central signified' of any structure 'is never absolutely present outside a system of differences', with the result that 'the domain and play of signification [is extended] infinitely'. By taking this position Derrida runs counter to the mainstream of Western thought, one of the basic assumptions of which is that precisely such a final signified lies at the centre of all structures, where it creates a 'fundamental immobility'. The persistence with which the Western philosophical tradition has clung to the idea of centred structure is, according to Derrida, a testament to the power of what Freud termed 'desire', that is, the unconscious longing to recover the sense of full presence experienced in the pre-Oedipal bond with the mother.[18] These ideas about the nature of language and structure provide the foundation for all poststructuralist theory.

Acceptance of the poststructuralist position clearly has profound implications for the practice of literary criticism. No longer can a piece of literature be expected to yield up a final signified or, to put it in more familiar terms, be approached in the anticipation that it will emerge as a full and coherent expression of the author's intentions. Nor can it be analysed in the expectation of discovering a centred or completely cohesive structure. Roland Barthes is therefore able to announce the death of the Author[19] and to replace the model of the tightly woven and organically structured 'work', which 'closes on a signified', with that of the 'Text', a site for writing which 'practices the infinite deferment of the signified' and thus becomes a 'woven fabric' of 'signifiers', 'an *irreducible* . . . plural' lacking any possibility of 'closure'.[20]

Given their conviction that it is 'language that speaks, not the author',[21] poststructuralist critics inevitably have a particular interest in what they call textuality, that is, in what language does rather than in what meaning is intended (or as Barthes puts it, in the signifier rather than the signified). Related to this interest is a tendency to regard texts, in Barbara Johnson's words, 'as commentaries on their own production or reception through their pervasive thematisations of textuality – the myriad letters, books, tombstones, wills, inscriptions . . . that serve . . . as figures for the text to be deciphered or unraveled or embroidered upon'.[22]

To the extent that they do attend to those 'conspicuously foregrounded statements in a text'[23] upon which the 'thematic paraphrase[s]'[24] of traditional criticism are based, poststructuralists are concerned to seek gaps, indeterminacies, obscurities, incoherences, contradictions, that is, those places where, because of the contradictions introduced by language, a fissure has occurred between what the text says and what the author may have intended. Of all the traditional tactics for covering over textual cracks and thereby halting the free play of the signifier, poststructuralists, picking up on one of Derrida's major objections to structuralist methodology,[25] are particularly suspicious of the static closure and consequent appearance of 'clarity'[26] effected by the use of binary oppositions. As Barbara Johnson puts it, 'deconstruction attempts to elaborate a discourse that says *neither* "either/or", *nor* "both/and" nor even "neither/nor", while at the same time not totally abandoning these logics either'.[27]

IV

Given the profound ways in which poststructuralism challenges traditional critical assumptions, its acceptance by a significant number of Austen critics in the 1980s clearly opened up new avenues for the interpretation of her fiction. *Emma*, the novel with which we are particularly concerned, no longer had to be read as a 'work' to be entered through the narrator's authoritative opening statements about the heroine's educational deficiencies. Instead it could be approached as a 'Text' in which the narrator's comment that 'seldom, very seldom, does complete truth belong to any human disclosure; seldom can it happen that something is not a little disguised, or a little mistaken'[28] assumes Derridean overtones. Richard Patteson, for example, argues that these words both point towards the ambiguities, anxieties and inconsistencies which characterise *Emma* and serve to mock characters, such as Emma and Mr Knightley, and readers who seek determinate readings of the novel.[29] In the selection from *Narrative and its Discontents* included in this collection (essay 4) D. A. Miller also reads the narrator's comment in a Derridean way by suggesting that, at what should be 'a decisive moment of truth ... , there comes a text' which introduces an element of indeterminancy by 'curiously subvert[ing] the completeness of the moment' through its equivocation concerning 'the truth of the proposal scene'.[30]

Poststructuralist critics, as noted earlier, are particularly interested in those parts of a text where language is thematised. Thus, for them, the cruxes of *Emma* are not so much incidents during which the heroine is forced to face up to her imaginative and moral blindness as episodes when the characters either play word games, such as charades, anagrams and riddles, or read and write letters, since these are the occasions on which language itself or, more specifically, the problems of interpreting and producing language become the novel's main concern. The essays by J. M. Q. Davies (5) and Joseph Litvak (6) included in this collection are both particularly concerned with the thematisation of reading.

Davies draws attention to the ways in which the word games in *Emma* test the interpretative abilities of both heroine and reader. He points out, for instance, that Emma has little trouble in arriving at the answer to the novel's first linguistic puzzle, the charade on courtship, but is less successful in interpreting Elton's motives for presenting it to her. Thus Austen subjects her to a series of tests which demand that she solve more and more complicated charades until she is finally equipped to deal with the complexities of life itself. Active readers, according to Davies, may well avoid many of Emma's misinterpretations but their reading skills are even more thoroughly challenged than hers by Austen's most complex charade, the novel itself.

The relationship between word games and reading takes on a rather different form in Litvak's dazzlingly Derridean analysis of *Emma* in which he employs a network of puns, having to do with 'bad handwriting', 'ciphers' and 'deciphering', and 'figures' and 'figuring out', to demonstrate how unstable language is while thematising the interpretative problems posed by the instability of language. The burden of Litvak's argument is carried by a series of disagreements between Mr Knightley and Emma which for him dramatise the conflict between authoritarian and subversive, or what we might call pre- and post-Saussurian, modes of reading. Thus, as a reader, Knightley can tolerate only a 'superficial "depth" ...', a legible illegibility' and he expects 'individuality' to be subordinated to a 'decipherable code' in order to ensure the 'transparency of the self'. Emma, on the other hand, possesses a 'deep superficiality' and, whereas Knightley expects figurative language to be grounded in 'social rules', she sees it as 'inherently ungroundable'. Consequently, for Litvak, her failure to pick up on the evidence of a concern with power and wealth contained in the answer to Elton's courtship charade is less an indication of her immaturity than a productive misreading which discovers that the 'real "jumble" is not so much the riddle as the self'.[31]

Writing has long been a focus of attention for Austen's critics who have frequently put Emma in the role of author, usually as part of a discussion of the dangers posed by her overcharged imagination, and the moral dimensions of authorship continue to be of interest even to poststructuralist critics. Thus D. A. Miller judges that Emma's novelistic sketches, the most wrongheaded of which is her invention of the affair between Jane Fairfax and Mr Dixon, lack 'a moral control'[32] because she is interested in what might be rather than in what ought to be. Similarly Nancy Armstrong chastises Emma for using language to create 'desire where none would otherwise exist',[33] thereby treating matchmaking as simply another form of fiction making.

However, poststructuralist theory has added new dimensions to the topic by switching critical attention from what a character's writing might signify to writing itself, that is, to how or why writing is done. Miller, for instance, argues that, because her 'imagination is a kind of portmanteau of novelistic effects and details', Emma's fiction fails to achieve 'overall coherent structure'[34] and is thus not what Austen would consider a real novel. Litvak also describes Emma as a bad writer who 'enmesh[es]' Harriet Smith in 'flimsy little novels of sensibility'. In his interpretation, though, this bad writing plays an important part in her subversive challenge to Knightley's patriarchal authority because it 'conjoins feminity itself with the disruptive irregularity of figurative language'.[35] While Miller and Litvak restrict their attention to Emma, Thorell Tsomondo, in his article '*Emma*: A Study of Textual Strategies', argues for the presence in the novel of several scriptors who write stories simultaneously and for very different purposes. Thus Emma writes to discover and control, Frank Churchill and Jane Fairfax to conceal, the Westons to fulfil wishes and Mr Knightley to correct and protect. Woven together by the narrator the stories that these characters fabricate and relate produce, according to Tsomondo, the intertextuality that reveals the nature and operation of the novel.[36]

While Derrida's questioning of commonsense ideas about linguistic transparency has had a significant impact on criticism of *Emma*, surprisingly little attention has been paid to the equally important challenge he has offered to traditional assumptions concerning centred structure. A notable exception, though, is D. A. Miller, whose discussion of *Emma* in *Narrative and its Discontents* is concerned above all with the indeterminacies of form and closure he believes are to be found once interpretation is set free from received opinion regarding the novel's organic structure and coherent ending. Earlier I discussed Miller's analysis of the way in which the narrator's 'seldom, very seldom' speech undermines the apparently perfect moment of truth achieved when Knightley proposes to Emma. However, Miller also reads these words as an explanation of how narrative closure actually works not by pulling everything together but by leaving things out. As a result it practises a forcible suppression of the narratable – those potentially inexhaustible instances of disequilibrium from which narratives arises – in order to fabricate the impression that desire can ultimately be directed towards its proper object and a transparent state of affairs be achieved.

V

As outlined so far a poststructuralist approach to *Emma* seems likely to place the novel once again outside history. However, poststructuralism does have its historical dimensions and scholars influenced by Marxist and feminist analyses of ideology as language and by the discourse-based historiography of Michel Foucault have made an important contribution to criticism of *Emma* in recent years.[37]

Marxists view attempts made to historicise Austen's novels during the 1970s as inadequate because they are based on the assumption that a satisfactory account of social reality is to be found in Burke's codification of conservative ideology. In fact, according to the Marxist theoretian Pierre Macherey, all ideology, including that expressed by Burke, is simply a set of practices and discourses by means of which the ruling class seeks to legitimate and thereby secure its position of power. As a result its reflection of actual history is both incomplete and rift with gaps and contradictions. Since, according to Macherey, literature is written in, and even by, the language of ideology, it too inevitably lacks a real centre or a principle of coherence. Consequently concepts such as 'the unity of the text', 'the work' and 'the author' are no less anathema to Macherey than they are to less historically-oriented poststructuralists such as Barthes or Derrida.[38]

Because he accepts these assumptions David Aers can agree with Alistair Duckworth that Austen is a polemical Tory but at the same time object strenuously to a critical procedure which seeks to identify in these ideological roots a structuring principle for her novels. Whereas Duckworth finds nothing problematical in Burkeian ideology, Aers identifies major contradictions in the way Burke posits a society which is at once capitalist and yet stable, traditional and hierarchical. Therefore, to the extent that this ideological perspective is inscribed in the novel, *Emma* is, according to Aers, similarly marked by contradictions and exclusions.[39]

Duckworth also comes under attack from another Marxist critic, James Thompson who, while yet again accepting that Austen is a conservative, argues that she also enacts the bourgeois ideology of the subject. As a result her novels are caught up in the complex ideological turmoil of the time and reveal the contradictions that exist between the gentry's rhetoric of social obligation and the individual's actual solipsistic experience of interiority. However, most of Thompson's actual analysis of ideology in *Between Self and the World* is concerned not so much with conflicts between ideologies as with the ways in which Austen's novels expose the antinomies of bourgeois thought. The section of his book included in this collection (essay 7), for example, focuses on the treatment of the bourgeois idea of marriage as a private experience in *Emma*. Emma's task, according to Thompson, is to learn, in part by experiencing the alternatives of loneliness and solipsism, that only by marrying Knightley can she achieve the true intimacy that provides the 'private "solution" to alienation and the objectification of social relations' inevitable in a capitalist society. Thompson concludes from his analysis that Austen's novels reveal 'romance and reification as two sides of the same coin or two sides'[40] of a contradiction in bourgeois ideology.

Feminists, who began to play an important part in Austen scholarship only after 1980,[41] tend to share with Marxists the conviction that literature is an ideological practice. However, in their view, ideology is important, not so much for what it reveals about class relationships as for the ways in which it serves the interests of a phallocentric society by excluding and silencing women. It is not surprising, therefore, that feminist critics of Austen's novels have located the major flaw in Tory ideology within its endorsement of patriarchal attitudes and have concerned themselves with Austen's ideological affiliations only in so far as they serve as a gauge of her commitment to women.

In their influential study of women's writing in the nineteenth century, *The Madwoman in the Attic*, Sandra Gilbert and Susan Gubar conclude that, in spite of the subversive elements in her work, Austen ultimately accepts patriarchy. Therefore she punishes Emma for her assertiveness by marrying her off to Knightley, who will confine her to a life of service and silence.[42] However, many recent feminist critics argue that Austen distances herself in significant ways from conservative ideology in order to find space for female characters who are neither intellectually nor morally inferior to men to assert themselves. In Claudia Johnson's reading of *Emma*, for instance, Austen subtly corroborates the fitness of Emma's rule and concludes the novel not with an endorsement of patriarchy but with a marriage between equals.[43] Margaret Lenta similarly views Austen's heroines, particularly Emma, as growing into a moral independence that public opinion of their day would have denied them.[44]

Other feminists agree that Austen recognises the oppression inherent in conservative ideology but can find little evidence in her novels that she believes her society gives women any room in which to achieve selfhood. Thus Ruth Perry, whose 'Interrupted Friendships in Jane Austen's *Emma*' is included in this collection (essay 8), identifies a second plot in *Emma* organised around female friendships which are interrupted so that the main marriage plot, in which are embedded conventional ideas about a woman's role, might achieve closure. This second plot serves, according to Perry, to make Austen's slyly subversive but pessimistic point that, in order to sustain itself, a phallocentric society must destroy women's self-sufficiency.

While most feminist criticism of Austen's novels has employed a Marxist social model, Nancy Armstrong turns to Michel Foucault's poststructuralist historiography as a way of redefining the question of where Austen stands as a woman. Armstrong is particularly influenced by Foucault's idea that power does not just operate from the top down, thereby creating a neat opposition between the powerful and the powerless, as both Marxists and feminists tend to suggest, but on all levels of society in the struggle between different discourses for the status of truth or what Foucault would call power-knowledge (*pouvoir-savoir*). For Armstrong precisely such a struggle began early in the eighteenth century when a female discourse, embodied in domestic fiction and the conduct book, mounted a challenge to the dominant aristocratic male discourse. So successful was this enterprise that, according to Armstrong, by the middle of the nineteenth century the feminine ideal was accepted as the truth by men as well as women, with the result that private life became the dominant social reality. Thus, in her reading of that important domestic novel, *Emma*, part of which is reprinted below (essay 9), Armstrong argues that Austen neither betrays women to patriarchy nor slyly asserts their value but valorises a plain style of writing close to speech, particularly female speech such as gossip and conversation, and by so doing makes a vital contribution to the process of redefining the hierarchy of discourse.

VI

Poststructuralist readings of *Emma* are clearly different in some quite fundamental ways from those produced by the author-based, mimetic and New Critical approaches which dominated interpretation of the novel up until the end of the 1970s. However, in two important and rather surprising respects there is something very familiar about this revisionist criticism which raises some questions about how far poststructuralist theory can move literary criticism away from its traditional assumptions and practices.

First, many of the critics who have analysed Austen's novels from poststructuralist perspectives seem unwilling to do away entirely with ideas of origin or authority. There have been a number of studies, it is true, which have redefined the roles of the narrator and of Mr Knightley, both of whom are often viewed as author surrogates by traditional critics. Richard Patteson, for instance, argues that, rather than terminating the play of signification in *Emma*, the narrator's voice is slippery and exposes the content of 'truth' to be 'a tissue of indeterminacy'.[45] Neither will Litvak or Davies allow Knightley to function as the novel's centre. For Litvak Knightley fails in his self-appointed role as master reader because he insists on the transparency of a social text revealed by the novel to be illegible. Davies similarly argues that the reader should not assume that Knightley is always right in his arguments with Mrs Weston and Emma. However, there has been scarcely any questioning of the belief that a literary work can ultimately be explained by reference to the author's intentions.

For example one might expect that, as a reader-response critic, J. M. Q. Davies would base his analysis of *Emma* on a conviction that meaning is produced not by the author but by the interaction of reader with text. However, he argues throughout his essay that the textual puzzles which challenge the reader's interpretive skills are deliberately placed there by Austen. Thus, for Davies, *Emma* contains what he calls 'intertextual gaps'[46] which the reader can fill in with the correct answers if s/he is clever enough to grasp the author's intentions rather than the 'areas of indeterminacy'[47] which, according to Wolfgang Iser, a leading reader-response theorist, would open up the novel to inexhaustible interpretations.[48]

Many feminist critics of *Emma* are similarly inclined to halt the play of signification which their deconstruction of male authority makes possible by putting female authority in its place. Ruth Perry, for instance, as I noted earlier, posits a subversive second plot concerned with female friendship in order to open up the interpretative possibilities of the main marriage plot of *Emma*, which she sees as pre-shaped by the values of a patriarchal culture. However, she immediately places restrictions on these possibilities by defining the second plot as a vehicle for 'Austen's message', thereby constructing a novel so available to interpretation that its 'layers come away neatly'.[49]

Perhaps most striking of all, however, are those occasions on which Joseph Litvak, who begins 'Reading Characters' by criticising Gilbert and Gubar for implying that the author is 'somehow . . . beyond or above textuality', ascribes what had seemed to be his own playful engagement with the text to authorial intent. In the midst of an ingenious exercise in punning on the word 'cipher', for example, he suddenly comments that 'Austen reminds us of the radical instability of the term'[50] and in the conclusion to his essay states quite categorically that the element of subversion in *Emma* stems from the author rather than from certain textual features.

'Reading Characters' also serves to illustrate the second way in which traces of traditional critical practice have crept into poststructuralist analyses of *Emma*. For much of his essay Litvak plays off Emma's subversive and Knightley's authoritarian social texts against each other in a manner that suggests an acute awareness of Derrida's warning about the tendency of binary oppositions to halt the free play of the signifier. However, his final assertion that society is not a 'legible text'[51] exposes Knightley's wish for total clarity as hopelessly naïve, thereby privileging Emma's position and creating a hierarchy which closes off textual indeterminacy.

Similarly, in *Between Self and the World*, James Thompson tends not so much to explore the contradictions between conservative and bourgeois values which he identifies in Austen's novels as to place them in opposition to each other. His analysis of *Emma*, for example, comes to the conclusion that, because it reflects some of the ways in which marriage was coming under the influence of the bourgeois ideal of private experience at the end of the eighteenth century, the union of hero and heroine must necessarily lack the social dimension accorded it by conservative ideology. In this instance the rigidity of binary thinking not only limits the interpretative possibilities open to Thompson but leads him to the absurd assertion that Emma and Knightley, who intend, of course, to live with Mr Woodhouse after their marriage, are involved in a 'flight from family'.[52]

Clearly, then, poststructuralist criticism of *Emma* has been unwilling or unable to leave behind all traditional assumptions. However, it is probably inevitable that this should happen because, while there may be no final signified, the 'force of . . . desire'[53] for a centre is so powerful, as we have seen Derrida admit, that it will always seek ways of limiting free play. Consequently these two apparently incompatible types of critical practice would seem to be inextricably bound together. The essay which completes this collection (essay 10), Paul Fry's 'Georgic Comedy: The Fictive Territory of Jane Austen's *Emma*', reinforces this point, but from the opposite direction.

In many respects Fry, who indeed refers rather sneeringly to the '*frayages* of deconstruction', is a thoroughly traditional critic. This traditionalism manifests itself in Fry's author-centred approach to *Emma* and in his conviction that Austen's 'ethics . . . , politics' and fictional 'territory' are 'determinate and fixed'. Moreover, like the traditionalist, Bruce Stovel, Fry is concerned with the generic roots of Austen's fiction and makes use of close reading techniques, most notably in his analysis of such words as 'ought' and 'nothing'.[54]

Yet at times Fry's critical sensibility seems closer to Litvak's than Stovel's. He resembles Litvak, for instance, when he plays with language, as in his puns on 'carriage', while exploring the inherent instability of language revealed by the slippage between economic and aesthetic metaphors in *Emma*. Fry also anticipates the interest of poststructuralist critics in those places where the novel's textuality is foregrounded by treating Emma as a 'reader or interpreter' and as a 'plot-maker' of Romantic fictions. Fry's affinities with poststructuralist thought are most evident, though, in his refusal to close off the oppositions between Romance and Georgic Comedy around which his essay is organised. Thus, while arguing that Austen disapproves of Romance, Fry also makes the Derridean assertion that, by allowing potentially romantic characters such as Harriet Smith and Jane Fairfax to occupy a 'necessary outer region of the plot', she 'discredits Romance without discounting it'.[55]

'Georgic Comedy' thus reinforces the point which I have been making in the later parts of this introduction by once again collapsing rigid distinctions between traditional and poststructuralist critical practice. The advances made in criticism of *Emma* during the last ten years or so should not, therefore, be judged as the consequence of a simple displacement of one approach to literature by another. Rather they have come about as the result of an interplay, admittedly not always conscious, between the poststructuralist impulse towards indeterminacy, plurality and infinite play of the signifier and traditional belief in authorial intention, centred meaning and closure on a final signified. To judge one approach as inherently superior to another, as Rosmarin does in the comment with which this introduction begins, simply increases the danger that one type of 'consensual blandness' will be succeeded by another. Even more important, such partisan attitudes make it less likely that critics will gain a clear sense of the contradictory forces at work on them and thus be able to grasp the possibilities open for further developments not just in criticism of *Emma* but in critical practice generally.

NOTES

1. Adena Rosmarin, '"Misreading" *Emma*: The Powers and Perfidies of Interpretive History', *ELH*, 51 (1984), 315.

2. David Lodge (ed.), *Jane Austen: 'Emma'. A Casebook* (London, 1968). Lodge has recently revised this collection and brought it up to 1984.

3. Wayne Booth, 'Control of Distance in *Emma*', in Lodge (above), pp. 195–216.

4. Edgar F. Shannon, '*Emma*: Character and Construction', in Lodge (above), pp. 130–47.

5. See, for example, pp. 30–1 below for Bruce Stovel's comments on the relationship between Emma and Mrs Elton.

6. See pp. 25–6, 22 below.

7. See p. 32 below.

8. See pp. 37, 38 below.

9. David Monaghan, *Jane Austen: Structure and Social Vision* (London, 1980).

10. For a comprehensive introduction to structuralism see John Sturrock, *Structuralism* (London, 1986).

11. D. A. Miller also makes use of Girard's theories of imitative desire. However, his enterprise is poststructuralist rather than structuralist since he is seeking to demonstrate how structure exists only as a violent suppression of narratibility such as that produced by Harriet Smith's mediated desire. See *Narrative and its Discontents: Problems of Closure in the Traditional Novel* (Princeton, 1981), pp. 9–12.

12. René Girard, *Deceit, Desire and the Novel: Self and Other in Literary Structure* (Baltimore, 1965).

13. See pp. 64–5 below for further comment on this point.

14. I am using the term poststructuralism because it has broader connotations than the term deconstruction. Thus poststructuralism should be taken as referring to a range of critical practice influenced by Saussure's theories of language which includes deconstruction, Marxism, Feminism, Foucauldian historiography and reader response. For introductions to poststructuralism see Catherine Belsey, *Critical Practice* (London, 1980); Terry Eagleton, *Literary Theory: An Introduction* (Oxford, 1983); Ann Jefferson and David Robey (eds), *Modern Literary Theory: A Comparative Introduction* (London, 1982); Frank Lentricchia, *After the New Criticism* (Chicago, 1980). For a critique of poststructuralist theory see David Ellis, *Against Deconstruction* (Princeton, 1989).

15. Ferdinand de Saussure, from *Course in General Linguistics*, in Philip Rice and Patricia Waugh (eds), *Modern Literary Theory: A Reader* (London, 1989), p. 8. I refer to this useful anthology of primary sources whenever possible for the convenience of readers who might wish to read the essays cited.

16. Rice and Waugh (above), p. 14.

17. For a comprehensive introduction to Derrida, see Christopher Norris, *Deconstruction: Theory and Practice* (London, 1982).

18. Jacques Derrida, 'Structure, Sign and Play in the Discourse of the Human Sciences', in Rice and Waugh (above), pp. 152, 151–2, 150.

19. See Roland Barthes, 'The Death of the Author', in Rice and Waugh (above), pp. 114–18.

20. Roland Barthes, 'From Work to Text', in Rice and Waugh (above), p. 168.

21. Roland Barthes, 'The Death of the Author', in Rice and Waugh (above), p. 115.

22. Barbara Johnson, *A World of Difference* (Baltimore, 1987), p. 18.

23. Ibid, p. 17.

24. J. Hillis Miller, *Fiction and Repetition: Seven English Novels* (Oxford, 1982), p. 3.

25. See Derrida's discussion of the opposition between nature and culture in the work of Claude Lévi-Strauss in his essay 'Structure, Sign and Play in the Discourse of the Human Sciences', in Rice and Waugh (above), pp. 154–65.

26. Barbara Johnson, *A World of Difference* (Baltimore, 1987), p. 13.

27. Ibid, p. 12.

28. *Emma*, in R. W. Chapman (ed.), *The Novels of Jane Austen*, 5 vols (London, 1932–34), IV, 431.

29. Richard F. Patteson, 'Truth, Certitude and Stability in Jane Austen's Fiction', *Philological Quarterly*, 60 (1981), 455–69.

30. See p. 69 below.

31. See pp. 95–8, 94, 98, 99, 102 below.

32. D. A. Miller, *Narrative and its Discontents: Problems of Closure in the Traditional Novel* (Princeton, 1981), p. 18.

33. Nancy Armstrong, *Desire and Domestic Fiction: A Political History of the Novel* (New York, 1987), p. 143.

34. *Narrative and its Discontents*, p. 18.

35. See pp. 98, 100 below.

36. Thorell Tsomondo, '*Emma*: A Study in Textual Strategies', *English Studies in Africa*, 30 (1987), 69–82.

37. A thorough introduction to modern Marxist theory and practice is

provided by Terry Eagleton, *Criticism and Ideology: A Study in Marxist Literary Theory* (London, 1976). Although less explicit about her approach, Catherine Belsey's perspective is also essentially Marxist in *Critical Practice* (London, 1980). For a critical survey of feminist theory see Toril Moi, *Sexual/Textual Politics: Feminist Literary Theory* (London, 1985). Probably the best introduction to Foucault is provided by Frank Lentricchia, *After the New Criticism* (Chicago, 1980), pp. 189–209.

38. E. Balibar and P. Macherey, from 'Literature as an Ideological Form', in Rice and Waugh (above), pp. 62–70.

39. David Aers, 'Community and Morality: Towards Reading Jane Austen', in David Aers, Jonathan Cook and David Punter (eds), *Romanticism and Ideology: Studies in English Culture, 1765–1830* (London, 1981), pp. 18–36, 184–6.

40. See p. 122 below.

41. Notable exceptions to the lack of substantial feminist criticism of *Emma* prior to the 1980s are Patricia Mayer Spacks, *The Female Imagination* (New York, 1975), particularly pp. 121–34, and Allison G. Sulloway, 'Emma Woodhouse and *A Vindication of the Rights of Woman*', *The Wordsworth Circle*, 7 (Autumn 1976), 320–32.

42. Sandra M. Gilbert and Susan Gubar, *The Madwoman in the Attic: The Woman Writer and the Nineteenth-Century Literary Imagination* (New Haven, 1979), pp. 157–61.

43. Claudia L. Johnson, *Jane Austen: Women, Politics and the Novel* (Chicago, 1988), pp. 122–42.

44. Margaret Lenta, 'Jane Austen's Feminism: An Original Response to Convention', *Critical Quarterly*, 23 (Autumn, 1981), 27–36.

45. Richard F. Patteson, 'Truth, Certitude and Stability in Jane Austen's *Emma*', *Philological Quarterly*, 60 (1981), 465.

46. See p. 85 below.

47. Wolfgang Iser, from 'The Reading Process', in Rice and Waugh (above), p. 81.

48. For a comprehensive introduction to reader theory see Elizabeth Freund, *The Return of the Reader: Reader-Response Criticism* (London, 1987).

49. See pp. 135, 129 below.

50. See pp. 89, 96 below.

51. See p. 103 below.

52. See p. 111 below.

53. Jacques Derrida, 'Structure, Sign and Play in the Discourse of the Social Sciences', in Rice and Waugh (above), p. 150.

54. See pp. 182, 181, 177 below.

55. See pp. 166–7, 171, 170 below.

1

Comic Symmetry in Jane Austen's 'Emma'

BRUCE STOVEL

I

'If any work belong unequivocally to any genre,' Laurence Lerner remarks, '*Emma* is a comedy.'[1] Lerner's insight suggests that it might be profitable to ask what makes the novel seem such a classic comedy. To approach *Emma* as a comedy is to think of it, not in the usual context of nineteenth-century fiction, but rather in conjunction with *Much Ado About Nothing, The Way of the World, Tom Jones.* In such comedies, the conflicts and characters are simple and fixed: what interests us is the intricate design, the complex and surprising pattern, into which these elements fall. In fact, the simple constituents are necessary for the intricate design of the whole. Suppose, for instance, that we allow ourselves to doubt Emma's conviction that Mr Elton's motives in courting her were merely greed and vanity – after all, that conviction is comforting, since it removes any doubt or remorse she might feel about her abrupt dismissal of her first suitor. But the gain in psychological irony, in inner complexity, would slow and blur another set of complex ironies, those emerging from the comic action itself.

Reginald Farrer described the way this comic design works some fifty years ago: 'Only when the story has been thoroughly assimilated can the infinite delights and subtleties of its workmanship begin to be appreciated, as you realise the manifold complexity of the book's web, and find that every sentence, almost every epithet, has its definite reference to equally unemphasised points before and after in the development of the plot.'[2] Farrer's remark suggests that an alert reader of the novel – even an alert first reader – will constantly be thinking backward and forward from the dramatic present as he reads: we are kept from immersing ourselves in the moment by becoming aware of the pattern it contains. Farrer also points out that the comic pattern, if precise, is also 'unemphasised' – implicit, sly, for us to find.

What is essentially comic in *Emma*, then, lies in its design. But since that design is presented ironically, an accurate account of it can be reached only after a great deal of observation and reflection. In fact, the novel is so subtly symmetrical, so mined with interconnected details, that criticism has, I think, yet to define its structure adequately. An instance of sly patterning which has not been noticed by Jane Austen's critics will illustrate the point.

When we, along with Emma, first meet Harriet Smith in chapter iii, we are told of Harriet, 'She was a very pretty girl, and her beauty happened to be of a sort which Emma particularly admired. She was short, plump and fair, with a fine bloom, blue eyes, light hair, regular features, and a look of great sweetness.'[3] This seems innocuous enough, but we learn from Mrs Weston's praise of Emma in chapter v that Emma herself is tall and elegant, with hazel eyes (p. 28). Emma particularly likes Harriet's style of appearance, just as she likes Harriet's style of personality, because it poses no threat to Emma's own – in fact, it forms a perfect foil for Emma's charms. Furthermore, when Emma paints Harriet's portrait in chapter vi, we find that she makes Harriet appear taller and more elegant than she actually is. Emma creates an image of Harriet much more like Emma herself than Harriet really is. The symbolism here not only presents Emma as the artist moulding nature into new and more pleasing shapes, as several critics have pointed out; even more precisely, the portrait epitomises what Emma does to Harriet in general: she transforms Harriet's actual self into a monstrous new identity fashioned in the image of Emma herself. And in this respect, as in so many others, the outing to Box Hill recapitulates the action of the novel. There, Frank Churchill playfully commissions Emma to produce a wife for him when he returns from abroad: 'Find somebody for me. I am in no hurry. Adopt her, educate her.' Emma, thinking of Harriet, coquettishly replies, 'And make her like myself' (p. 292).[4] And so it is appropriate that, like a comic Frankenstein's monster, Harriet eventually turns unwittingly on her maker, forcing Emma to realise what she has created.

My point is that each of these scenes, beginning with Emma's particular admiration of Harriet's sort of beauty, invites us to see beyond the dramatic moment to the pattern it contains. This pattern, being 'unemphasised', is not fixed. We may also note, for instance, that Jane Fairfax is tall and elegant in appearance, like Emma and unlike Harriet. Joseph Wiesenfarth shrewdly juxtaposes Emma's flattering portrait of Harriet with Robert Martin's having taken the exact measure of Harriet's height[5] – a measurement which, but for Emma, would have brought Harriet and the Martins together again.

Much of the most helpful criticism of the novel, in fact, consists of remarking subtle instances of comic symmetry. But, as Farrer suggests, we grasp more than tissues of related words and incidents: through the 'manifold complexity' we sense 'the book's web', a single comic structure. This deeper, ironic structure is much harder to define. I suggest that Jane Austen's web consists of three main threads, and that all the local symmetries lead to and from these threads in networks which get ever finer as we pursue them. These three lines of action are: the hidden love of Emma and Mr Knightley for each other; the counterpointing of that secret love with the secret engagement of Frank Churchill and Jane Fairfax; the use of the other characters to embody aspects of Emma herself. This attempt to chart the novel's structure will also, I hope, throw some light on the methods and attitudes of comedy itself.

II

Though every one who likes the novel at all must smile at Emma's unrecognised love for Mr Knightley, surprisingly little is said about it by critics of the novel. Howard S. Babb, however, has some suggestive remarks; discussing the issue of Emma's snobbishness, he says, 'The cause of her compulsive disengagement is her inability to recognise and admit what she feels for Mr Knightley. ... It is the novel's major irony that an Emma so frequently wrapped up in herself, and one who cultivates detachment, should so radically misconceive her real attachment.'[6] We can take Babb's point one step further and say that Emma's unrecognised love is the cause of her foolish mistakes over Harriet Smith and Mr Elton, over Mr Dixon and Jane Fairfax, and so on: these mistakings provide a screen of romantic fantasies which disguise her real interest in love from herself. Emma, after all, is preoccupied with affairs of the heart – affairs of other people's hearts, that is; she can see clearly and act decisively when love is not involved.

In Emma's case, then, the course of true love runs in two channels. One, at the visible level, contains Emma's embarrassing errors as an amatory busybody; the other, underground channel, which only surfaces at the novel's climax, contains her real feelings toward Mr Knightley, which become clearer and clearer to us (if not to her) as the action advances. If the hidden stream is the source of the visible one, the latter provides a chart throughout to the depths concealed within the heroine.

The surface action of the novel falls into two successive and similar patterns of comic nemesis. Volume I is a self-enclosed prelude, or image in little, for the main action, which occupies volumes II and III. Though the prelude has a cast of only three and a single broad irony, while the main action is much more varied and convoluted, the pattern is the same in each case: Emma's blunders as the Highbury Cupid become more and more obvious to all but her, until finally circumstances, rebelling against her guiding hand, slap her rudely in the face and wake her up. The comic symmetry is very precise here: just as in volume I she discovers, to her dismay, that she and Mr Elton have both been using Harriet Smith as a pawn to advance Mr Elton's charade of a courtship, so in volumes II and III she finds Frank Churchill and Jane Fairfax have been using her as their 'blind' (p. 335); like Harriet before, she must learn that another woman has been secretly preferred to her. At the surface level, then, the novel has a two-part, beguiler-beguiled structure: Emma finds herself living out a comic form of the Golden Rule. So much is worth spelling out, even if almost every reader must enjoy seeing Emma get hers (as we say), because most recent critics have followed Joseph M. Duffy, who argues that the novel falls into three stages: the Emma–Elton–Harriet fiasco; 'the Emma–Frank Churchill–Jane Fairfax illusion and masquerade' (chs xviii through xlvi (i.e. through III, x)); the relationship between Emma and Mr Knightley (chs xlvii through lxv (i.e. III, xi to xix)).[7]

We can, though, see the two main comic situations – the two successive romantic triangles – as parallel surface actions, displacements caused by and directing us to the real plot, which lies in Emma's relationship with Mr Knightley. Unbeknownst to herself, Emma loves him from the start. After learning that Frank and Jane are secretly engaged, after being shocked by Harriet's hopes into realising that 'Mr Knightley must marry no one but herself!' (p. 320), Emma makes the most surprising discovery of all: 'there never had been a time' when she did not love him (p. 324). She would have been able to understand herself at any point, she thinks, if only it had occurred to her 'to institute the comparison' between him and the man she thought she loved, Frank Churchill. We, however, see a great deal more clearly into Emma's heart than she does herself: the cleverly-scattered clues to her real feelings become more and more insistent. This rising curve of ironic disclosure forms the real plot of the novel; certainly, Jane Austen artfully frames the self-enclosed action of volume I within three increasingly-heated debates between Emma and Mr Knightley, one at the beginning, one at the middle, and one at the end of the volume. This ironic curve is supported by an echoing, if subordinate, curve of clues about the real nature of Mr Knightley's concern for Emma.

Why wouldn't Emma admit her love from the start? Why *didn't* it occur to her to institute the comparison? For one thing, like many heroes and heroines of comedy, she does not want to give up her independent selfhood. She tells Harriet in chapter x, 'Never could I expect to be so truly beloved and important, so always first and always right in any man's eyes as I am in my father's' (p. 65). Certainly, Mr Woodhouse is unlikely ever to be outbid in this sort of affection. But, as with, say, Shakespeare's Beatrice and Benedick, events will not so much conquer as correct Emma's selfhood; Emma not only will shed her barren assumptions about love and her own emotional needs, she will find herself, to her surprise, happy to do so. Emma also fears love because she considers it to be blind. Emma is exquisitely self-contained: the idea of being out of control, of losing her will in the grip of passion, disturbs her. This is why she tells Harriet, in the same scene, that her attachment to her nephews and nieces 'suits my ideas of comfort better than what is warmer and blinder' (p. 66). Similarly, after Harriet has confessed her hopes of Mr Knightley to Emma, Emma thinks that she can have no hopes of her own: '*She* could not. She could not flatter herself with any idea of blindness in his attachment to *her*. She had received a very recent proof of its impartiality' (p. 326). Emma is thinking of his stern rebuke of her treatment of Miss Bates; ironically, of course, that rebuke proves, rather than disproves, his real love for her.

The most important aspect of Emma's fear of love – and one she cannot formulate – is her fear of being hurt. Emma is afraid of being undervalued, of being taken as a fluttery, dependent creature, a female, rather than a person of intelligence and dignity of her own. Listen to her challenging Mr Knightley in their debate over breathless, brainless Harriet Smith: '"To be sure," she cried playfully, "I know *that* is the feeling of you all. I know that such a girl as Harriet is exactly what every man delights in – what at once bewitches his sense and satisfies his judgment. Oh! Harriet may pick and choose. Were you, yourself, ever to marry, she is the very woman for you"' (p. 48). Without realising it, she is asking Mr Knightley to declare that he would marry someone like herself, and not a Harriet, but she must content herself with his vigorous generalisation, 'Men of sense, whatever you may say, do not want silly wives' (p. 48). In her opinionated confusion, Emma thinks of men and women as two completely different species, each having its own sphere, its own special kind of knowledge, its own code of action. Like those who make up personality profile tests, Emma assumes men are primarily interested in objects and abstract ideas, while women have expertise in emotional relationships. After her argument with Mr Knightley about the right man for Harriet, Emma 'still thought herself a better judge of such a point of female right and refinement than he could be' (p. 49).

Emma will discover that men and women have much more in common than she thinks, that they can be friends rather than merely symbiotic opposites. In fact, the action of the novel can be seen as Emma's search for, and triumphant discovery of, a true friend. The impulse that sets the action in motion is Emma's loss of Miss Taylor: in Emma's eyes, at least, 'they had been living together as friend and friend very mutually attached' (p. 1). Emma tries to fill Miss Taylor's place with Harriet Smith, though Mr Knightley tells Emma, in words which ring in her mind (pp. 106, 315), 'You have been no friend to Harriet Smith, Emma' (p. 47). Emma refuses to consider Jane Fairfax for the vacancy, though 'birth, abilities, and education' mark Jane out for it (p. 330), and flirts with the possibility of taking on Frank Churchill as her intimate friend – only to find that her real friend from the start has been Mr Knightley. It is as a friend that he addresses Emma. He warns her that there may be some understanding between Frank Churchill and Jane Fairfax 'as a friend – an anxious friend' (p. 273); he ends his stern remarks to her over Miss Bates with, 'I will tell you truths while I can, satisfied with proving myself your friend by very faithful counsel' (p. 294). And when he is about to reveal his own feelings to Emma, she at first refuses to hear what she thinks will be a confession of infatuation with Harriet; but, after a moment of sympathy and self-discipline, she determines to hear him out 'as a friend'. Mr Knightley at first pauses – 'Emma, that I fear is a word – No, I have no wish' – but then decides to give the word a special meaning: 'Emma, I accept your offer – extraordinary as it may seem, I accept it and refer myself to you as a friend. – Tell me, then, have I no chance of ever succeeding?' (p. 337). Emma has shown herself finally worthy of receiving his proposal that he be her friend for life.[8]

The real plot of the novel, then, lies beneath the complicated surface events. This notion helps explain the response of one group of readers. Many in its original audience, like many undergraduates today, found the novel complicated but trivial, lacking in a unified, dramatic, and significant plot. John Henry Newman, for instance, said in 1837: 'Everything Miss Austen writes is clever, but I desiderate something. There is a want of *body* to the story, the action is frittered away in over-little things.'[9] This response, free of canonical, sophisticated sightlines, points to something real in the novel. There *is* a want of body to the story, since the romantic plots that Emma imposes on the world around her lack substance; she is herself in danger of frittering away her life in over-little things. But underneath the over-little things is a single large one, their cause and successor: her response to Mr Knightley.

III

If Emma is merely an instrument in Frank Churchill's schemes, Jane Austen gives her heroine some recompense by making Frank's plot merely a means of bringing Emma's story to its fruition. As in many traditional comedies, the love story at the work's centre is interwoven with the trials of another pair of lovers, Frank Churchill and Jane Fairfax. The action is neatly contrived, so that the resolution of the Frank–Jane plot brings about, by chain reaction, the resolution of the central plot; further, in the manner of comedy, the two plots are presented in intricate counterpoint to bring out the difference between the two matches, to let each illuminate the other. Both plots turn upon a secret love, but one is secret by conscious deception, the other by unconscious self-deception. One love story, that of Frank and Jane, is resolved wholly by chance, by Mrs Churchill's completely unexpected and very timely death; the other match is achieved by choice, by change, by mutual self-direction.[10]

This counterpoint reaches a wonderful subtlety in the Box Hill episode. Box Hill is the turning point for both love affairs, the occasion for a quarrel which pulls each pair of lovers apart only to bring them back together all the more intimately and for good. Frank's letter of explanation allows us to understand how crucial Box Hill is for Frank and Jane. Frank, piqued at Jane's unwillingness to walk home with him from Donwell Abbey the day before, flirts with Emma in order to taunt Jane, and then uses the departure of the Eltons as a screen for delivering a private insult: women can't be known at Bath, or any public place, he says, but only when you see them in their own homes, among their own set (p. 292). Jane, wounded, answers with veiled bitterness: 'It can only be weak, irresolute characters (whose happiness must always be at the mercy of chance) who will suffer an unfortunate acquaintance to be an inconvenience, an oppression for ever' (p. 292). Frank, highly indignant, leaves Highbury that very afternoon without saying farewell to Jane; that evening, she accepts Mrs Elton's eagerly-offered position with Mrs Smallridge and writes to Frank breaking off the engagement. Chance, however, intervenes; Frank's aunt dies and he is not forced to choose between the two ladies who rule his life. Jane's ultimatum, though, does make it advisable that he go directly to his uncle and ask for his permission to marry Jane; now Mrs Churchill is no more, that permission is quickly granted.

My point is this: we can never be sure Frank Churchill would have been willing to give up his fortune for Jane. He is relieved of the choice. Why, after all, did he insist on keeping their engagement secret? In his letter of explanation, he writes, 'But you will be ready to say, what was your hope in doing this? – What did you look forward to? – To any thing, every thing – to time, chance, circumstance, slow effects, sudden bursts, perseverance and weariness, health and sickness' (p. 343). In more simple terms, he was waiting for his aunt to die – or, failing that, to go through some unpredictable alteration. In either case, Frank could marry Jane *and* retain all his aunt's money and status. The force he relies on does reward him in the end: chance allows him to remain a spoiled child, free of painful choices. He closes his letter by saying that Emma had been right in calling him 'the child of good fortune' (p. 348).[11]

Emma begins as another Frank, another pampered only child in a rich home. But she has a different, more substantial kind of good fortune: she is allowed to choose, to repudiate, to grow, to grow up. Emma and Mr Knightley triumph, not by opportunism, but by stern moral choices. Emma's thoughtless insult to Miss Bates at Box Hill corresponds exactly to Frank's sneer at Jane's domestic circle; Mr Knightley's rebuke, as difficult for him to make as it is for her to receive, is parallel to Jane's ironic reproof of Frank as weak and irresolute, so wounding to his pride. But Mr Knightley's criticism is open, not veiled; unlike Frank, Emma has both the courage and the desire to accept the truth. Emma is so hurt at losing Mr Knightley's good opinion, and at seeming inadvertently to scorn his advice, that, feeling pain of a sort she has never known before, she genuinely wants to change, and does. As a result, when Mr Knightley comes calling, Emma brings on his proposal, as she could not have before, by her quiet self-sacrifice. The happy coming together of Emma and Mr Knightley may lack the dramatic éclat, the spectacular good fortune, of the other couple, but it has the dignity and integrity of something they have made themselves. Mr Knightley's comment after reading Frank's letter has an uncomplacent precision: 'My Emma, does not every thing serve to prove more and more the beauty of truth and sincerity in all our dealings with each other?' (p. 350).

This counterpointing of Frank and Emma becomes explicit in their final meeting. Emma says that she is certain that Frank must have enjoyed deceiving everyone in Highbury, because she knows that she herself would have found great amusement in doing so. 'I think there is a little likeness between us', she says drily, to which he bows acknowledgement. Emma adds that, at the least, she and Frank have the same destiny – 'the destiny which bids fair to connect us with characters so much superior to our own' (p. 376). But this same scene shows that the likeness only brings out the unlikeness between Emma, who raises herself to her husband's moral level, and Frank, who brings his wife down to his. In this final view of Frank, he ecstatically admires the complexion, hair, and eyes of his bride-to-be, 'whispering seriously' to Emma the news that 'my uncle means to give her all my aunt's jewels. They are to be new set. Will it not be beautiful in her dark hair?' (p. 377). Frank ends up with both the aunt's jewels and the beautiful hair, though, as Jane's embarrassed reproach a few minutes later suggests, he does so at the price of remaining the thoughtless boy he has always been. Emma returns home even happier in her happiness with Mr Knightley for 'the animated contemplation of his worth which this comparison produced' (p. 378). She, not Frank, is the lucky one.

IV

The two symmetrical networks I have defined emerge from, and control, the twists and turns of the plot. But our comic detachment also forces on our notice a broader and more static kind of design, that created by character contrasts. Such unchanging patterns are a feature of traditional comedy; throughout *Tom Jones*, for instance, the hero and heroine are poised between Mr Allworthy's theoretical benevolence and Squire Western's animal vigour. Such broad oppositions chart the perfect happiness toward which the comic action moves, and which it finally attains; that happiness is imaged as a midpoint combining the excellence of one-sided extremes. Emma and Mr Knightley, for instance, marry out of motives which fall between, and combine, the self-aware calculation of the Eltons and the romantic feeling which unites Frank and Jane.

These comic oppositions have an important consequence: Emma comes to exist, not only in her own self, but as she is reflected and embodied in the characters around her. This extroversion of psychological conflict frequently occurs in sophisticated comedy: when Tom Jones wins his Sophia, when Millamant accepts her Mirabell, inward changes are delicately conveyed. Had these changes been directly presented, we would lose our comic distance, and so our comic perspective; in this sense, my opening assertion that comic characters are simple and fixed should be qualified. In *Emma*, certainly, the heroine has a many-faceted, self-divided personality, since the major characters surrounding her persistently live a double life – they are both themselves and aspects of Emma. Mr Woodhouse, for instance, embodies one extreme within the unregenerate Emma. He is utterly self-absorbed, so that all events must seem to revolve around his preferences; he resists change or effort of any kind; he is utterly unable to distinguish between his own wishes and what actually is the case.[12]

This notion of alter egos gives a new dimension to the first chapter of the novel. Emma falls into self-pitying loneliness the evening after 'poor Miss Taylor' marries Mr Weston, but she rallies herself to combat the same feelings in her father. When Mr Knightley calls, though, Emma takes the plaintive pose again, but now her own rational position is uncompromisingly urged upon her by Mr Knightley: Emma 'cannot allow herself to feel so much pain as pleasure. Every friend of Miss Taylor's must be glad to have her so happily married' (p. 6).

The chapter suggests that Emma is suspended between a Knightley self and a Woodhouse one. Mr Knightley, in fact, functions as Emma's deepest or true self throughout the novel. For instance, Emma expresses a stern view of Frank Churchill's procrastinations to Mrs Weston, but, a few pages later, she perversely claims more sympathy for Frank than she actually feels; she thus finds herself in the ironic position of 'making use of Mrs Weston's arguments against herself', while Mr Knightley expresses 'her real opinion' (p. 112). Jane Austen tells us that Emma can always find excuses to avoid calling on Miss Bates and her mother, though 'she had many a hint from Mr Knightley, and some from her own heart, as to the deficiency' (p. 117). Mr Knightley embodies, then, Emma's own heart and conscience: this is what makes his rebuke on the subject of Miss Bates so painful.[13] The union of Emma and Mr Knightley is thus, in part, a psychic one: Emma becomes reunited with a part of herself she had renounced. This is why Mr Knightley must wait for Emma to educate herself; she can only come to him when she has come to herself.

All this helps explain the importance of Mr Knightley's polar opposite within Emma, Mrs Elton. By leading Mr Elton on and then rejecting him, Emma has summoned from the depths of Bristol a substitute for herself who embodies, in garish, unmitigated form, all her own complacent, vain, mean, and domineering qualities. The correspondences between Emma and Mrs Elton are precise and ingenious; many of them have been remarked by the critics, but the function of this pairing in the larger design is much less clear.[14] Mrs Elton's appearance in Highbury more than halfway through the novel is actually part of Emma's genuine good fortune, a gift to her from comic providence. For now Emma can make a good choice between her good and her bad angels, between her ideal and her selfish selves. The back-to-back excursions to Donwell Abbey and Box Hill, the only occasions in the novel when we leave Highbury, dramatise this opposition: Mr Knightley refuses Mrs Elton's offer to organise the first expedition and runs it in his own satisfyingly unpretentious way; the Box Hill trip on the following day is, from the start, Mrs Elton's party, though Emma comes home from it under Mr Knightley's influence, having once and for all repented of her insensitive Mrs Elton self.

This comic conflict between the Knightley and the Elton in Emma is enacted and defined at the Crown Inn ball. Mrs Elton, it seems clear, has instigated her husband to spurn Harriet publicly (repeating thereby his earlier spurning of Harriet), but Mr Knightley ruins her scheme with his quick generosity, just as he will later rescue Harriet from the fate Emma's schemes seem to have made inevitable. And, after this comic psychodrama, when Emma confesses the reason for the Eltons' spite, Mr Knightley replies:

> 'I shall not scold you. I leave you to your own reflections.'
> 'Can you trust me with such flatterers? – Does my vain spirit ever tell me I am wrong?'
> 'Not your vain spirit, but your serious spirit. – If one leads you wrong, I am sure the other tells you of it.'
>
> (p. 258)

If Mrs Elton is Emma's vain spirit, there is good reason for the withering dismissal of her in the final paragraph. We learn there that Mrs Elton knows of Emma's marriage only 'from particulars detailed by her husband'; she is not among 'the small band of true friends who witnessed the ceremony' because she embodies a part of Emma herself which has been exorcised, banished to a realm of white satin and staring Selinas.

This extroversion of Emma's conflicts is a familiar device in sophisticated comedy. It is accompanied, however, by a striking innovation; the usual social conflicts of comedy are introverted or internalised. According to theorists such as Suzanne Langer and Northrop Frye, traditional comedy presents the rhythm of life overcoming obstacles and renewing itself; this pattern of upset and regained equilibrium underlies the typical comic plot, in which young lovers overthrow and revitalise a society which obstructs natural energies. In *Emma*, the obstructing society is within Emma herself: it is she who frustrates nature's plans for marriage and erects insuperable barriers between social classes. Any renewal of the novel's society will be the result of a change within Emma herself; Mrs Weston reminds Mr Knightley (and us) at the outset that Emma, accountable to nobody but her father, cannot be stopped from indulging any of her projects 'so long as it is a source of pleasure to herself' (p. 29).

But if Emma contains the obstructing society within herself, she also contains the young lover. She is Millamant as well as Lady Wishfort, Good Heavens Gwendolyn as well as Lady Bracknell. Something within Emma makes Mr Knightley more important to her than anything else. This ability to respond to him, without her knowledge and against her will, is at the heart of the novel's comic perspective: Emma's desire to be herself, her desire for Mr Knightley, and her desire to be good all, finally, coincide. Harmony, not sacrifice or division, reigns. In the same way, we soon grasp that Mr Knightley's concern for principle and for Emma's moral state coincide with his affection for her: to him, she is 'faultless in spite of all her faults' (p. 340). Emma's response, in spite of herself, to Mr Knightley is what enables her to keep our sympathy throughout; it is also what makes her second awakening, unlike that at the end of Book I, final and convincing. Emma forsakes her fanciful schemes, and can see the vain motives which prompted them, only when she discovers the deepest 'source of pleasure to herself' is to be in the real world with the man she respects and loves.

'The perfect happiness of the union', the novel's final words, thus describe a personal integration as well as a wedding. Interestingly enough, it is Miss Bates who defines most precisely the connection between psychological and social union; she says during one of her monologues, as if by accident, 'It is such a happiness when good people get together – and they always do' (p. 134).

From *Dalhousie Review*, 57 (Autumn 1977), 453–64.

NOTES

[By the time this essay was published in 1977, many alternatives had been developed to the New Critical and literary historical principles which guide Stovel. That Stovel is able to function without turning to these alternatives does not so much demonstrate that his approach is outmoded as it testifies to the continuing vitality of traditional critical methods. These methods guide many of Austen's critics even today. Comparisons between Stovel's treatment of friendship as a structuring device and Ruth Perry's (essay 8) feminist approach to the topic and between Stovel and Miller's (essay 4) analyses of closure provide concrete examples of some of the differences between traditional and poststructuralist criticism. Ed.]

1. Laurence Lerner, *The Truthtellers: Jane Austen, George Eliot, D. H. Lawrence* (New York, 1967), p. 96.

2. Reginald Farrer, 'Jane Austen', cited here from *Jane Austen: 'Emma'. A Casebook*, ed. David Lodge (London, 1968), p. 65. Farrer's essay first appeared in *Quarterly Review*, 228 (July 1917), 1–30, and is frequently reprinted.

3. *Emma* (Cambridge, Mass: Houghton, Mifflin, 1957), p. 15. Subsequent references to this convenient edition are included within my text.

4. Darrel Mansell in *The Novels of Jane Austen: An Interpretation* (London, 1973), p. 152, links this remark to Emma's portrait of Harriet, though in somewhat different terms. For acute commentary on Box Hill as microcosm, see Mansell, above, pp. 166–70; Stuart M. Tave, *Some Words of Jane Austen* (Chicago, 1973), pp. 240–6; and Richard Poirier, 'Transatlantic Configurations: Mark Twain and Jane Austen', in *A World Elsewhere: The Place of Style in American Literature* (New York, 1966), pp. 144–207.

5. Joseph Wiesenfarth, *The Errand of Form: An Assay of Jane Austen's Art* (New York, 1967), p. 129.

6. Howard Babb, *Jane Austen's Novels: The Fabric of Dialogue* (Columbus, 1962), p. 180.

7. Joseph M. Duffy, '*Emma*: The Awakening from Innocence', *ELH*, 21 (1954), 39–54. For instance, of the critics cited above, Mansell, Wiesenfarth, and Babb all state that the book has a three-part structure.

8. Surprisingly, this patterned play upon the word, 'friend', has escaped notice. J. F. Burrows is an exception, but he thinks Mr Knightley's recurring use of the term is meant ironically; Mr Knightley considers himself to be acting as Emma's friend, but we know differently (*Jane Austen's 'Emma'* [Sydney, 1968], p. 107).

9. John Henry Newman's comment occurs in a letter reprinted in *Jane Austen: The Critical Heritage*, ed. B. C. Southam (New York, 1968), p. 117.

10. I am pursuing here a point made by W. J. Harvey: 'The world of *Emma* is binary. Around the visible star, Emma herself, circles an invisible planet whose presence and orbit we can gauge only by measuring the perturbations in the world we see. ... The written novel contains its unwritten twin whose shape is known only by the shadow it casts' (*Jane Austen: 'Emma'*, ed. David Lodge [London, 1968], p. 239). Harvey's splendid essay, 'The Plot of *Emma*', first appeared in *Essays in Criticism*, 17 (1967), 48–63.

11. This uncharitable view of Frank, implicit in Mr Knightley's comments upon his letter, is becoming more evident to the novel's readers. See, for instance, W. J. Harvey, above, p. 240; Stuart M. Tave, *Some Words of Jane Austen* (Chicago, 1973), passim; Douglas Bush, *Jane Austen* (New York, 1975), p. 165; and Alistair M. Duckworth, *The Improvement of the Estate: A Study of Jane Austen's Novels* (Baltimore, 1971), p. 178, [Reprinted in this volume – see pp. 47–8. Ed.]

12. That other major characters embody aspects of Emma herself has been noted by some recent critics; Joseph Wiesenfarth, for instance, says of Mr Woodhouse that he 'represents the danger of detachment from reality by way of egoism that she [Emma] is liable to' (*The Errand of Form* [New York, 1967], p. 114). What I am trying to define here is the function of such correspondences in the comic structure.

13. A. Walton Litz says of the rebuke, 'It awakens part of herself, and comes as the voice of her own conscience' (*Jane Austen: A Study of Her Artistic Development* [New York, 1965], p. 141).

14. Some illuminating comparisons between the two ladies are drawn by Darrel Mansell, *The Novels of Jane Austen* (London, 1973), pp. 156–60; Laurence Lerner, *The Truthtellers* (New York, 1967), pp. 100–1; Kenneth L. Moler, *Jane Austen's Art of Allusion* (Lincoln, 1968), p. 177; and Mark Schorer, 'The Humiliation of Emma Woodhouse', in David Lodge (ed.), *Jane Austen: 'Emma'* (London, 1968), pp. 180–1.

2

'Emma' and the Dangers of Individualism

ALISTAIR M. DUCKWORTH

When *Emma*'s comedy of errors becomes, with the arrival of Jane Fairfax and Frank Churchill in volume two, a comedy of intrigue, both the social and epistemological implications of Emma's subjectivism are compounded.[1] If Mrs Elton usurps Emma's social position, then Jane Fairfax pre-empts her intellectual prominence (she is 'the really accomplished young woman, which Emma wanted to be thought herself' [p. 166]), and Churchill takes over her powers of managing and directing. Though in one amusing scene she goes so far as to imagine Churchill in love with her, making his declaration, and being tenderly refused, all such dreaming is without possibility of enactment. For, with Churchill's entrance, Emma is no longer the puppet-mistress of Highbury but instead becomes a marionette in Churchill's more subtle show.

A dramaturgical vocabulary is inevitable with Churchill, for if he reminds us of any other character in Jane Austen's fiction it is the histrionic Henry Crawford. Like that actor, Churchill is an impresario of some ability. When, on his initial walk through the town, he sights the Crown Inn, 'its character as a ball-room caught him; and instead of passing on, he stopt for several minutes . . . to look in and contemplate its capabilities' (pp. 197–8). The last word, of course, alerts us to Churchill's desire to 'improve'. Like Crawford at Mansfield or Sotherton, Churchill wishes to introduce movement and flexibility into a landscape of peace and stability.

It is not sufficient to argue that his schemes are forced on him by the restraints of his dependent social position and the enforced secrecy of his engagement to Jane Fairfax. The secret engagement is important to the novel, but it is not the only, or even the major, reason for Churchill's 'manœuvring and finessing' (p. 146). He delights to play-act. He will, of course, use the secret engagement as his excuse in his late letter of apology: 'you must consider me as having a secret which was to be kept at all hazards' (p. 437). And in his personal apology to Emma, he will say: 'I had always a part to act. – It was a life of deceit!' (p. 459). But there can be little doubt that Jane Austen intended us to see him taking a positive delight in 'disguise, equivocation, mystery' (p. 475). There is something gratuitous about his secrecy. No less than Henry Crawford looking back with pleasure on the play period, Churchill recalls with gratification his Highbury career. At the end of the novel, his claims of honourable expediency merely reveal another pose.

There are no actual theatricals in *Emma*, but the theme is continued in minor key in the preparations for the ball and in the children's games which are a curious feature of the novel. Both aspects of *Emma* invite somewhat detailed attention.

When Emma takes up Churchill's enthusiasm for the ball, plans are immediately made. Randalls is their first choice of location, and they are soon engaged, with the help of Mrs Weston, in the 'interesting employment . . . of reckoning up exactly who there would be, and portioning out the indispensable division of space to every couple' (p. 248). It is at once evident that the number of couples is greater than the room can comfortably hold. In what follows we are reminded of the preparations for the play at Mansfield, as the communal desire of a group of people bent on pleasure is sufficient to overcome material objections to their 'scheme'. Furthermore, something of the ontological subversiveness suggested by the mistreatment of the Mansfield house is here repeated as more and more of the house is appropriated for the ball: 'The doors of the two rooms were just opposite each other. "Might not they use both rooms, and dance across the passage?" It seemed the best scheme; and yet it was not so good but that many of them wanted a better' (p. 248). As the disagreements of the participants in the scheme recall the bickering of the would-be actors in *Mansfield Park*, so the increasing list of couples to be invited reminds us of the plans to invite more and more of the neighbourhood to take part in the play at Mansfield. Finally, when Mr Woodhouse's hypochondriacal objections to the use of more than one room force them to return to the 'first scheme', we are shown how subjective desire may ignore objective facts in the pursuit of its goal. Through Churchill's persuasion, 'the space which a quarter of an hour before had been deemed barely sufficient for five couple, was now endeavoured to be made out quite enough for ten' (p. 249).

Churchill's pre-eminence in the preparations for the ball – his revised plan for holding it at the Crown – reveal how far he has already usurped Emma's powers of directing and organising. But Churchill's real power over Emma, and the nature of his threat in the novel, are more evident in his love of games. Games are not, of course, introduced by Churchill – the amusing episode of the mis-understood charade announces the motif in the first volume (ch. ix); but it is Churchill who initiates the word game at Hartfield (III, v) and the games on Box Hill (III, vii). Moreover, it is Churchill who makes a running game out of his conversations with Emma on the subject of the mysterious piano – at Mrs Cole's (II, viii), for example, and in Miss Bates's parlour (II, x).

Such games need have no meaning in individual instances beyond revealing the characteristic deficiencies of the players. In the episode of the charade, for instance, Harriet's immaturity is evident: 'the only mental provision she was making for the evening of life, was the collecting and transcribing all the riddles of every sort that she could meet with' (p. 69); and her irresponsibility is indicated when she prefers the flowery sentiments of Elton's verse to the 'good sense in a common way' of Martin's letters (p. 76). Beyond this, Elton's charade, 'To Miss —', reveals the characteristic deficiency of Emma's imagi-nation, her preference for believing what she wants to happen rather than what her sense of the probable would indicate. Obviously addressed to her (who but a deluded Emma could imagine 'ready wit' as a description of Harriet?), the charade exists, like the blank of the title, as an empty space to be filled by the imagination. When Emma, thinking further to promote the match between Harriet and Elton, transcribes the verse into Harriet's book, we have a repetition of the sketch episode: each of the three participants misapprehends the real situation, but Emma is responsible for the confusion. Mr Elton is hardly to be blamed if he thinks his suit is progressing well when he hears Emma admire the hidden meaning of his poem (court-ship).

Taken cumulatively, however, games carry crucial meaning in *Emma*; they are Jane Austen's means of conveying her apprehension over the continuity of a public and 'open' syntax of morals and of manners. Whatever Huizinga might argue, games for Jane Austen – at least as she explores the motif in *Emma* – are anti-social, and the 'ludic' personality as exemplified by Churchill is a threat to the structures of society and morality that she affirms.[2] Both play and player are suspect, play because it sets up a world of freedom from the ordinary patterns of existence ('it is . . . a stepping out of "real" life into a temporary sphere of activity with a disposition all of its own'[3]), the player because while playing – for Jane Austen – he is absolved from the rules and requirements of ordinary social discourse.

Even before Churchill's entry upon the Highbury scene, the episode of the charade, in exemplifying the concealment and opacity of a game world, had foreshadowed Churchill's behaviour. With his entry a whole vocabulary of concealment begins: nouns like riddle, engima, conundrum, mystery, equivocation, puzzle, espionage, double-dealing; verbs such as guess, conceal, blind; adjectives such as hypo-critical, insidious, suspicious. There is 'doubt in the case' (p. 120) even of his arrival, and Churchill takes care to maintain a doubt as to his motivations and character, not merely because he is secretly engaged to Jane (a transgression of some magnitude in contemporary terms), but also in order to retain his sense of superior manipulation and secret power. His unpredictability is particularly disliked by Mr Knightley, who considers surprises to be 'foolish things' (p. 228).

In requiring predictability of her exemplary characters Jane Austen reveals an attitude toward behaviour that will be found in many later English novelists of manners, from Trollope and James to Ford and Waugh. Predictability is pre-eminently the mark of the gentleman; further, it points to the existence of a structured society with a large body of shared assumptions, to a world where few situations lack appropriate and public response and where individuals can communicate by means of a common vocabulary of words and gestures. In such a world dramatic tension is to be expected when a character thought to be a gentleman fails to act predictably. In Trollope's *The Last Chronicle of Barset*, the drama of the novel centres on the horrifying possibility that the curate of Hogglestock may have stolen a cheque entrusted to him. In *The Portrait of a Lady*, Madame Merle's claims to the status of lady, and Gilbert Osmond's to that of gentleman, are suddenly put into question when Isabel sees her standing while he sits. In Ford's *The Good Soldier*, the narrator, Dowell, speaks of the 'modern English habit . . . of taking everyone for granted', and much of the irony of the novel stems from the fact that the good soldier, Ashburnham, is incapable of acting like the gentleman he is considered to be.[4] In Evelyn Waugh's fiction, of course, the gentleman, from Tony Last to Guy Crouchback, is doomed to be duped by persons who do not act as they might once have been expected to act.

Given the residual faith in, or nostalgia for, behavioural predictability which these and other novelists exhibit, we may understand more forcibly the importance of the issue in *Emma*. Someone like Frank Churchill, who suddenly goes 'off to London, merely to have his hair cut' (p. 205), poses a threat to the trust and confidence of an ordered world; he drops a 'blot' (p. 205) on the transparency that should characterise his behaviour. This is why Knightley is justified in suspecting Churchill even before he sees him. The point in question is quite clear. Frank's father has married again, and it is his son's duty to call on his stepmother. Though Emma argues that it is 'unfair to judge of any body's conduct, without an intimate knowledge of their situation', Knightley points out: 'There is one thing, Emma, which a man can always do, if he chuses, and that is, his duty; not by manœuvring and finessing, but by vigour and resolution. It is Frank Churchill's duty to pay this attention to his father' (p. 146). And later (after Emma has excused Frank by citing his obligations to his adoptive parents) Knightley adds: 'Respect for right conduct is felt by every body. If he would act in this sort of manner, on principle, consistently, regularly, their little minds would bend to his' (p. 147). Knightley introduces into *Emma* the serious tone and social commitment that are characteristic of *Mansfield Park*. His call for duty, for the observance of certain prior moral and social imperatives, for consistent and predictable action − these mark Knightley as an exemplary gentleman.[5]

The contrast with Churchill is consistently drawn, often in terms that remind us of Fielding's distinction between 'Humour' and 'good Breeding'. While Churchill sees life as a game, Knightley sees it as a serious responsibility; while Churchill is typically described as amiable (or 'aimable') and gallant, Knightley is described as courteous and humane; while Churchill promotes his schemes of secrecy, 'Mr Knightley does nothing mysteriously' (p. 226).[6] Churchill, the 'closed' personality, is a creature of interiors; he prefers the company of women. Knightley, who loves an 'open manner' (p. 260), is a man of the outside, a man's man. At the Coles's, while Mr Knightley stays behind to discuss 'parish business' with the other gentlemen, Churchill is the 'very first of the early' gentlemen to rejoin the ladies (p. 220). And on that later occasion at Miss Bates's, while Churchill plays his double game with Emma and Jane (and before an audience of no less than six ladies), Mr Knightley rides by outside, on an errand of duty, as a reminder of the values of an 'outside' existence. Moreover, when he hears that Churchill is inside, he refuses to come in at Miss Bates's invitation. His refusal is in its implications a refusal to leave an 'open' world of consistency and regularity for the interior existence of variability and process which Churchill stage-manages.

Churchill's game-playing is not to be dismissed as venial. It is symptomatic of a world in which once given certitudes of conduct are giving way to shifting standards and subjective orderings. Churchill rejects an inherited body of morals and manners for a little world he himself creates. He is at home in a world of opacity and of separation, preferring it, indeed, to the older world where communication existed by way of public assumptions, for that world required responsibility and consistency, qualities conspicuous by their absence in his character.

We may now be in a position to understand why all the fuss is made about the 'entirely unexpected' (p. 215) gift of the piano to Jane Fairfax. All the doubt and speculation that occupy the minds of the characters are intentionally introduced by Frank Churchill, when he deposits his gift anonymously in Miss Bates's drawing room. (The piano was of course his real reason for going to London.) The object of the game is known; it is addressed to Miss Fairfax. And there is no secrecy as to what it is: it is a 'very elegant looking instrument – not a grand, but a large-sized square pianoforté' (pp. 214–15). Only its sender is unknown, as if – like another charade – it were 'From—'.

Again it can be argued that Churchill's gift stems from no other wish than to provide his beloved Jane with an instrument for her musical talents. Churchill's schemes, however, are never this simple. In addition to providing a topic for surmise in Highbury, Churchill soon finds that he is able to play a game with Emma. In one of her flights of fancy, 'an ingenious and animating suspicion' (p. 160) enters Emma's brain concerning a possibly illicit relationship between Jane Fairfax and Mr Dixon, the husband of Jane's friend. Thus when Miss Bates and Mrs Cole assume that the pianoforte 'of course ... must be from Col. Campbell' (p. 215), Emma refuses to agree, but instead conveys her suspicions of the 'real' identity of the giver to Churchill. At first pretending to think she means Mrs Dixon, he quickly accedes to Emma's real suspicion of Mr Dixon, and convinces her that he is her secret accomplice in knowledge. Churchill is now in his favoured position of superior awareness and power – and not only with respect to Emma. Jane is almost as powerless as Emma.

Though Emma is vulnerable, since she is being laughed at behind her back, she is invulnerable in that she cannot know until near the end that she is being duped. Jane, on the other hand, presumably discovers from Churchill the nature of Emma's suspicions, but this cannot give her much satisfaction when she sees Churchill taking obvious delight in Emma's company, or when, on Box Hill, he and Emma conduct themselves in a way that 'no English word but flirtation could very well describe' (p. 368).

The Emma–Churchill–Jane triangle provides the structural setting of many of the scenes in the second half of the novel, scenes in which, though Emma remains the centre of attention, the reader increasingly suspects that it is Churchill who is pulling the strings. At the Coles's, for example, the triangular relationship appears as first Emma plays, and is surprised when Churchill accompanies her singing, and then Jane plays, and Churchill sings again (II, viii). Later, at Miss Bates's (II, x), Churchill is again able to play his double game with great enjoyment. Jane and Frank have been left alone with the sleeping Mrs Bates while Miss Bates has gone to invite Emma, Mrs Weston, and Harriet into her house for a brief visit. The chapter opens with the entrance of the ladies at a point just after one of the few moments of intimacy that Frank and Jane have been able to enjoy. The visitors see Mrs Bates slumbering by the fire, 'Frank Churchill, at a table near her, most deedily occupied about her spectacles, and Jane Fairfax, standing with her back to them, intent on her pianoforté' (p. 240). They have no inkling (nor, surely, does the average reader on first reading) that the lovers have just sprung apart. The rest of the chapter is a subtle description of Churchill's expert ability to play a double game with consummate skill. Consider, for example, how in the following passage, as he addresses first Emma and then Jane, he is able to poke fun at both girls while delighting both. (He is speaking of the piano which he himself has introduced into the house):

> 'Whoever Col. Campbell might employ,' said Frank Churchill, with a smile at Emma, 'the person has not chosen ill. I heard a good deal of Col. Campbell's taste at Weymouth; and the softness of the upper notes I am sure is exactly what he and *all that party* would particularly prize. I dare say, Miss Fairfax, that he either gave his friend very minute directions, or wrote to Broadwood himself. Do not you think so?'
>
> (p. 241)

By mentioning Col. Campbell, Churchill seems to be entering into complicity with Emma, to whom at this point he turns 'with a smile'.

This impression can only be reinforced when he seems (to Emma) to make a clandestine reference to Mr Dixon with the phrase, *'all that party'*. And when he next addresses 'Miss Fairfax' by referring to the 'friend' who is supposed to have undertaken the purchase of the piano, Emma still believes that he is teasing Jane about Mr Dixon. She even feels that he is going too far. 'It is not fair,' says Emma in a whisper, 'mine was a random guess. Do not distress her' (p. 241). On a first reading, such an interpretation would be reasonable. But if we now consider how the scene appears to Jane, a very different meaning is evident: to her Churchill's remarks can only appear as an amusing ridicule of Emma, and as a series of embarrassing but touchingly nostalgic remembrances of their shared experiences.[7]

Churchill's games are not always as successful as this. At the ball at the Crown, Emma senses that 'Frank Churchill thought less of her than he had done' (p. 326), and the reason is that his genuine love for Jane, and his frustration at the distance that separates them, lead him to lower his mask of amiability to Emma. If we consider the 'shadow-novel-within-the-novel' of which W. J. Harvey speaks, however, we can infer other reasons for Churchill's diminishing success as player. The time draws near when Jane must decide whether or not to accept the position as governess so officiously arranged for her by Mrs Elton – to place herself in what she regards as slavery; and still Churchill has not committed himself. In this light it is not to be wondered at that Jane should find his continued game-playing repugnant. Certainly in the last two games played in the novel – at Hartfield and on Box Hill – Churchill's attempts to communicate with Jane by the indirect means of a game will be rebuffed.

The two episodes are excellent examples of Jane Austen's ability to carry major themes on apparently trivial vehicles. In the first instance, an insidious note is present from the first sentence of the chapter (III, v): 'In this state of schemes, and hopes, and connivance, June opened upon Hartfield' (p. 343). Soon after, we are witness to Churchill's famous 'blunder', when he asks those assembled 'accidentally' outside Hartfield, 'what became of Mr Perry's plan of setting up his carriage?' (p. 344) This information – it becomes clear from one of Miss Bates's rambling speeches – must have come from his secret correspondence with Jane, and not, as he had thought, from his legitimate correspondence with Mrs Weston. (Whether all readers gather this the first time round is an interesting question; certainly clues as to the secret correspondence have previously been deposited, as in the argument between Mrs Elton and Jane over whether or not she should be permitted to go to the post office in the rain [II, xvi].) Since, as in *Sense and Sensibility*, a correspondence constitutes evidence of engagement, Churchill is anxious to cover up his blunder, and he says that he must have dreamed it. Nevertheless – and here surely we have conclusive evidence for the gratuitous nature of his game-playing – when they enter Hartfield, Churchill invites Emma to join him in a children's game of letters.

The scene is carefully set around the 'large modern circular table which Emma had introduced at Hartfield':[8] 'Frank was next to Emma, Jane opposite to them – and Mr Knightley so placed as to see them all' (p. 347). Knightley's position is especially important, for in this chapter, in one major shift of point of view in the novel – indeed in Jane Austen's fiction – Knightley is granted knowledge given to no other character.[9] Prior to the game we have been informed of Knightley's growing dislike of Churchill, and of his suspicion – started by a 'look' he had seen Churchill give Jane at the Eltons' – of 'some double dealing' (p. 343). Now, as he stands apart from the game, he sees Churchill pass an anagram to Jane, and she 'with a faint smile' push it away. At this point, Harriet steps in to retrieve the word. She is too stupid to solve the anagram, but Mr Knightley, to whom she turns for help, sees that the word is *'blunder'* (p. 348). His thoughts are reported:

> Mr Knightley connected it with the dream; but how it could all be, was beyond his comprehension. ... He feared there must be some decided involvement. Disingenuousness and double-dealing seemed to meet him at every turn. These letters were but the vehicle for gallantry and trick. It was a child's play, chosen to conceal a deeper game on Frank Churchill's part.
>
> (p. 348)

When Churchill continues his 'double-dealing' by now pushing the anagram for *Dixon* to Emma 'with a look sly and demure' (p. 348), Knightley sees that Emma, though she judges it 'proper to appear to censure' it, is in spite of herself seduced by Churchill's cunning and charm. 'Nonsense! for shame!' she answers, as she opposes 'with eager laughing and warmth' (p. 348) his suggestion for now giving the word to Jane. Jane, for her part, is 'evidently displeased', and on seeing Knightley watching her, she says with some anger, 'I did not know that proper names were allowed' (p. 349).

The anagram game repeats Churchill's previous game in Miss

Bates's parlour and anticipates the climactic scene on Box Hill. Inside Miss Bates's house, and with Knightley absent, Churchill had been able to satisfy the vanity and trust of both girls, without betraying either. Knightley could only there serve as a passing reminder of responsible conduct. Here, inside the Hartfield house, and with Knightley present, Churchill's manœuvring is not only a quite voluntary danger to Jane's reputation, but is also a cause of justifiable jealousy, as she sees Frank and Emma indulging in a kind of 'courtship' game.

The scene reveals more. By allowing us access to Knightley's rational consciousness, we are granted an awareness of the permissible use of the imagination. Careful to avoid the errors of the undisciplined imagination (even as he speculates, Knightley reminds himself of Cowper's line, 'Myself creating what I saw'), he is able to intuit a 'something of private liking, of private understanding ... between Frank Churchill and Jane' (p. 344), and the word game confirms and gives substance to his well-grounded suspicions. Secrecy and concealment, the scene allows us to see, are not invulnerable to the intelligent and responsible mind.

But precisely here Emma reveals how far her participation with Churchill has taken her, for when Knightley asks her if she perfectly understands 'the degree of acquaintance' (p. 350) between Churchill and Jane, her confident reply — 'I will answer for the gentleman's indifference' (p. 351) — leads him to assume a much closer relationship between Emma and Churchill than he had ever considered possible, and he 'walk[s] home to the coolness and solitude of Donwell Abbey' (p. 351). In spite of Knightley's judicious assessment of probabilities, that is, Emma's collusion with Churchill has caused further concealment. Because of this, the novel at this point reaches toward solemn possibilities; through the next two chapters, at Donwell and on Box Hill, a satisfactory resolution seems remote. Frank's rash actions have alienated his already nervous confidante, so that she will cut him short on their meeting in Donwell Lane; the vacuous Harriet is lost in her impossible, Emma-inspired dreams of Knightley; and Emma has unwittingly damaged her own best prospects.

It is important to stress that the combined actions of Emma and Churchill have done more than endanger three relationships; whether one calls it a culture, an ethos, or a social disposition, what has been threatened is an entire way of life, and in face of the symbolic resonance of the scenes which follow, it is quite insufficient to argue that 'we do not get from *Emma* a condensed and refined

sense of a larger entity.'[10] Consider, for example, the implications of
the walk taken by most of the major characters in the pleasure
grounds of Donwell (one is reminded of the walk in the wilderness at
Sotherton in *Mansfield Park*):

> It was hot; and after walking some time over the gardens in a
> scattered, dispersed way, scarcely any three together, they insensibly
> followed one another to the delicious shade of a broad short avenue of
> limes, which . . . seemed the finish of the pleasure grounds. – It led to
> nothing. . . .
>
> (p. 360)

The suggestion, even in this brief extract, of a group without sense of
community or feeling ('insensibly' carries due force) is strongly
made, as is the implication that the selfish pursuit of pleasure may,
indeed, lead to nothing. The possibility of social disintegration is
very real at this juncture. But, having made her point, Jane Austen
now posits an alternative hope in her description of the view from
Donwell of the Abbey-Mill Farm, as if to underscore the contrast
between the present fragmentation of the party and the enduring
possibilities of an organic society (p. 360). Emma, who has yet to
commit her grossest act of selfishness, is here provided with her true
'grounds' of moral and social action, though full awareness is still
some way off. A little earlier, like Elizabeth at Pemberley, she had
reached some awareness of the value of Knightley's estate, noticing

> . . . the respectable size and style of the building, its suitable, becom-
> ing, characteristic situation, low and sheltered – its ample gardens . . .
> of which the Abbey, with all the old neglect of prospect, had scarcely a
> sight – and its abundance of timber in rows and avenues, which
> neither fashion nor extravagance had rooted up. . . . [The house] was
> just what it ought to be, and it looked what it was. . . .
>
> (p. 358)

The distrust of fashionable improvements here expressed not only
reminds us of the theme in *Mansfield Park*, but comments, too, on
the recent actions and intentions of the visitors to Donwell – especially, perhaps, on Mrs Elton's attempt to redefine what is 'natural'
by coercing Knightley into giving an alfresco 'gipsy-party', complete
with donkey and 'caro sposo' (pp. 355–6).[11]

Emma not only views Donwell with 'honest pride' (p. 358); her
view will soon include, as Trilling notes,[12] what she has previously
excluded from her outlook: 'at half a mile distant was a bank of

considerable abruptness and grandeur, well clothed with wood; – and at the bottom of this bank, favourably placed and sheltered, rose the Abbey-Mill Farm, with meadows in front, and the river making a close and handsome curve around it' (p. 360). The Martins' farm is indeed 'favourably situated', and Emma's visit to Donwell is followed not only by her discovery of her hidden love for Mr Knightley (and her consequent acceptance of the values which he upholds), but by her admission that now 'it would be a great pleasure to know Robert Martin' (p. 475). As Elizabeth and Darcy 'were always on the most intimate terms' (*Pride and Prejudice*, p. 388) with the Gardiners, so Emma and Knightley will remain the friends of the Martins. And in *Emma*, no less than in *Pride and Prejudice* and *Mansfield Park*, the social gaps which individual actions threatened to widen will be closed around the marriage of the central figures.

Richard Poirier has most clearly understood the importance that such scenes have in promoting Jane Austen's 'positive vision of social experience', and in illustrating her capacity, as contrasted with American writers of the nineteenth century, 'to imagine society as including the threat of conformity and artificiality and as offering, nevertheless, beneficial opportunities for self-discovery.'[13] In a brilliant comparison of the episode on Box Hill and Huck's treatment of Jim in chapter fifteen of *Huckleberry Finn*, he comes to the conclusion that 'the stakes for Jane Austen and her heroine are very high indeed – to prevent society from *becoming* what it is condemned for *being* in *Huckleberry Finn*', and one well appreciates the point. For it is in this famous episode that the novel – and, with it, the games motif – reaches a fitting climax, and here too that the spectre of social fragmentation comes closest to actualisation.

On Box Hill, where, as one eighteenth-century description has it, the mazes make it 'very easy for amorous couples to lose and divert themselves unseen',[14] a 'principle of separation' (p. 367) divides the company into separate groups. There is a 'want of union' (p. 367) which the indiscriminately benevolent Mr Weston is quite incapable of harmonising: 'The Eltons walked together; Mr Knightley took charge of Miss Bates and Jane; and Emma and Harriet belonged to Frank Churchill' (p. 367). Here is Lawrence's 'sharp knowing in apartness', but how greatly is the separation to be deplored, and how appropriately does Jane Austen distinguish between the selfishness of the Eltons, the social stewardship of Knightley – he at least is concerned about the fate of single women in society – and the continued and misguided collusion of Emma and Churchill, with Harriet, as usual, in tow. What follows on the hill is an emblem of a vitiated society where selfishness is uncurbed and no publicly accepted rules of behaviour permit free and 'open' communication.

In Poirier's terms, what Emma does when she so flagrantly insults Miss Bates is to violate a social contract; spurred on by Churchill, she forgets her social obligation (or proper role) and adopts the role of an ironic and theatrical wit.[15] After the insult, and a short-lived attempt to play a conundrum game (the last game of the novel), the group erupts into barely concealed hostility (between Mrs Elton and Emma, between Elton and Churchill, between Churchill and Jane), and were it not for Knightley's fidelity to his social duty and Emma's ability soon after to realise the 'evil' of her words and wit and truly to repent of them, the ultimate social vision of the novel would be bleak. Something of the seriousness of the issue involved is apparent in Knightley's rebuke to Emma: 'How could you be so unfeeling to Miss Bates? How could you be so insolent in your wit to a woman of her character, age, and situation? – Emma, I had not thought it possible' (p. 374). Only in the degree that Emma comes to an awareness of her fault and to an acceptance of the principles by which Knightley lives is a positive social alternative to the game world convincingly affirmed.

Emma's repentance is genuine, and the novel succeeds in achieving, in the end, a positive vision of society. But something of the seriousness of the issues treated is revealed in Jane Austen's careful choice of a religious vocabulary in the closing chapters: we hear, for example, of Emma's 'contrition' and 'penitence' (p. 377). Given the degree of her transgression, moreover, her absolution cannot be immediate; Miss Bates and Jane Fairfax for a long time resist her penitential overtures. But henceforth her sorrow and guilt, unlike her previous temporary resolutions to suppress her imaginative tendencies, are real. Now her eyes are 'towards Donwell' (p. 378), the proper home of her values, and, like Elizabeth before Darcy's portrait at Pemberley, all her actions are now considered in the light of Knightley's imagined regard: 'could Mr Knightley have been privy to all her attempts of assisting Jane Fairfax, could he even have seen into her heart, he would not . . . have found any thing to reprove' (p. 391).

Emma must still come to a recognition of the personal evils of her subjective schemes when Harriet reveals to Emma's momentary horror that Knightley is the unnamed superior she hopes to marry. And she must become aware of the degree to which she has been sucked into the vortex of Churchill's play-acting: 'What has it been but a system of hypocrisy and deceit, – espionage, and treachery? – To come among us with professions of openness and simplicity; and such a league in secret to judge us all? – Here we have been, the whole winter and spring, completely duped . . .' (p. 399). But she will soon agree with Knightley's views on the desirability and 'the beauty of truth and sincerity in all our dealings with each other' (p. 446), and with her marriage to Knightley, Harriet's to Martin, and Jane's to Churchill, society is finally reconstituted as the plot is resolved.

Let it be admitted, however, that the Churchill marriage leaves some 'doubt in the case' even at the end. Had the domineering Mrs Churchill not fortuitously died, would Frank still have married Jane and saved her at the eleventh hour from a life of 'slavery'? It will be said that the question is not legitimate, yet the novel's presentation of Churchill's menace has tended to arouse expectations of a less re-warding fate for Jane. Perhaps we should be satisfied with the cir-cumscriptions of his power which are provided. Churchill's epistolary *apologia pro vita sua* in chapter fourteen of the third volume is followed by Knightley's searching explication of the text in chapter fifteen, and as throughout the novel he has stood as a model of excellence against which the reader may judge Churchill, so now Knightley points out to Emma where in Churchill's excuses the un-thinking act becomes immoral, where undisciplined behaviour be-comes anti-social.

Yet Jane's character and role remain in the memory after the novel ends, and if it is true that another novel 'shadows' the novel we read, it is also true that other possible outcomes shadow the resolution we have. It may be that Jane Austen sensed this herself.[16] At any rate, in *Persuasion* she wrote a novel about a heroine whose predicament is closer to that of Jane Fairfax, and in so doing, defined a new outlook in her fiction.

From Alistair M. Duckworth, *The Improvement of the Estate: A Study of Jane Austen's Novels* (Baltimore, 1971), pp. 162–78.

NOTES

[Duckworth's book has been extremely influential in persuading critics to place Austen's fiction in its historical context. In *Improvement* Duckworth argues that, because of its use of estate and improvement metaphors derived from Edmund Burke's *Reflections on the Revolution in France*, *Mansfield Park* is central to an understanding of the allegiance to the conservative establishment of her time which Austen expresses in all her novels except *Persuasion* and the unfinished *Sanditon*. The parts of the chapter on *Emma* which precede the extract published here deal mainly with Emma in the roles of improver and artist and thus align her with that other dangerous individualist, Frank Churchill. The extent to which Duckworth continues to be guided by traditional critical assumptions despite his unhappiness with their lack of an historical perspective can be gauged by comparing his treatment of games with those of Davies and Litvak (essays 5 and 6) and his approach to ideology with Thompson's (essay 7). All quotations in the essay are from *The Novels of Jane Austen*, ed. R. W. Chapman, 5 vols (London: Oxford University Press, 1932–4). Ed.]

1. For a discussion of *Emma*'s movement from a 'comedy of errors' to a 'comedy of intrigue', see J. F. Burrows, *Jane Austen's 'Emma'* (Sydney, 1968), pp. 34–5.

2. J. Huizinga, *Homo Ludens: A Study of the Play-Element in Culture* (Boston, 1955), esp. chap. 1. Huizinga, in support of his view that 'civilisation arises and unfolds in and as play' (p. ix), insists upon the ethical neutrality of play – 'It lies outside of the antithesis of wisdom and folly' (p. 6). And from Huizinga's point of view, no doubt, even Knightley is a player, if of a different kind from Churchill. But Jane Austen sets culture against play in *Emma* (as in *Mansfield Park*, she sets the estate against theatricality), and invests her games with negative social and moral value. It may be as well to add that I am aware that Jane Austen delighted in domestic games, as in her youth she is said to have delighted in private theatricals. Interested readers are referred to *Charades Etc. Written a hundred years ago By Jane Austen and Her Family* (London, 1895).

3. Huizinga (above), p. 8.

4. The title of the first volume of *Parade's End*, 'Some Do Not. . . .' is of further interest here. Although it has numerous applications in the volume, one implication is that there are certain things that gentlemen do not do.

5. Clearly I do not agree with J. F. Burrows's reading of the debate between Emma and Knightley over Churchill's delay in visiting Randalls (*Jane Austen's 'Emma'* [Sydney, 1968], pp. 55–6). Knightley will himself admit to Emma later in the novel that he was 'not quite impartial in [his] judgement', but he will add that even if Emma had not been 'in the case' he would still have distrusted Churchill (p. 455).

6. Knightley himself sets the contrast in terms of English versus French behaviour: 'No, Emma, your amiable young man can be amiable only in French, not in English. He may be very "aimable", have very good manners, and be very agreeable; but he can have no English delicacy towards the feelings of other people: nothing really amiable about him'

(p. 149). For a discussion of Jane Austen's conception of a 'specifically English ideal of life', see Lionel Trilling, 'Emma and the Legend of Jane Austen', in *Beyond Culture: Essays on Literature and Learning* (New York, 1965), pp. 40–1. For an interesting argument setting the Churchill–Knightley contrast in terms of 'the contrast between Lord Chesterfield's and Dr Johnson's social and ethical points of view', see Frank W. Bradbrook, *Jane Austen and Her Predecessors* (Cambridge, 1966), pp. 32–3. In condemning Churchill, Bradbrook suggests, Knightley 'condemns by implication, the point of view of Lord Chesterfield'.

7. The question arises as to how far Churchill thinks he is keeping Emma in the dark. Soon after this scene (in II, xii), Churchill, before leaving for London, calls on Emma and almost reveals to her the secret of his engagement. She thinks, however, that he is about to propose to her. At the end, in his letter of apology to Mrs Weston, Churchill will say: 'I have no doubt of her having since detected me, at least in some degree – She may not have surmised the whole, but her quickness must have penetrated a part' (p. 438). Whether Churchill was really mystifying Emma or merely conniving with her remains, therefore, in some doubt, but the cruelty to Jane remains, whatever one decides, as does his use of Emma as foil.

8. A nice touch this, when one recalls the dubious significance that is attached both to Marianne Dashwood's wish to give Allenham new furniture in *Sense and Sensibility* and to Mary Crawford's wish to make Thornton Lacey a 'modern' residence in *Mansfield Park*. Why a round table should merit comment is perhaps best indicated in *Barchester Towers* where Archdeacon Grantly says: 'A round dinner-table . . . is the most abominable article of furniture that ever was invented' (ch. 21). For Grantly there is 'something peculiarly unorthodox' in the idea of a round table, 'something democratic and parvenue'.

9. Jane Austen on only one other occasion, and there unsuccessfully, changes her point of view in this radical way. I refer to the curious scene in *Sense and Sensibility* (III, iii) where we are given a conversation between Elinor and Colonel Brandon on the subject of the Delaford living through the misconceiving eyes of Mrs Jennings. She thinks that she is witnessing the Colonel's proposal to Elinor, whereas in fact they are discussing the timing of his gift to Edward Ferrars. Having demonstrated Mrs Jenning's misconception, Jane Austen then repeats the conversation as it really occurred, a narrative device she never repeated.

10. Arnold Kettle, 'Jane Austen: *Emma* (1816)', in *An Introduction to the English Novel*, vol. 1 (London, 1951), p. 93.

11. Knightley, of course, will have nothing to do with Mrs Elton's absurd 'scheme'. As opposed to her plan for gathering strawberries, Knightley's 'idea of the simple and the natural will be to have the table spread in the dining-room' (p. 355).

12. Lionel Trilling, 'Emma and the Legend of Jane Austen', *Beyond Culture* (New York, 1965), pp. 40–1.

13. Richard Poirier, 'Transatlantic Configurations: Mark Twain and Jane Austen', in *A World Elsewhere: The Place of Style in American Literature* (New York, 1966), pp. 144–207.

14. Quoted in G. E. Mingay, *English Landed Society in the Eighteenth Century* (London, 1963), p. 154.

15. Richard Poirier, *A World Elsewhere* (New York, 1966), p. 176. My argument in this paragraph is much indebted to Poirier's reading.

16. According to family tradition, Jane Austen divulged that Jane Fairfax survived her marriage to Frank only nine or ten years.

3

'Emma' and the Democracy of Desire

BEATRICE MARIE

In *Deceit, Desire and the Novel: Self and Other in Literary Structure*. René Girard shows how continental fiction from Cervantes to Proust replicates the tripartite structures of what he calls imitative desire.[1] Love, for Girard, is always a triangle; the passion that possesses the great novelistic heroes and heroines – Madame de Clèves, Julien Sorel, Emma Bovary – is not the spontaneous impulse of one soul toward its double, but a mediated social response that fixes its objects at the dictates of a third. Conspicuously absent from Girard's analysis of love in Western fiction is the English novel. Its great couples are star-crossed, Heathcliff-and-Catherine lovers, whose passion negates society rather than developing within it. Even in the English social novelists – Austen, Eliot, Hardy – true love exists almost by definition in opposition to social convention. Sue and Jude, Ladislaw and Dorothea, Anne Eliot and Frederick Wentworth must win their happiness, if at all, in spite of the social constraints that separate them. Love, in English fiction, is the obverse of social intercourse rather than, as for Girard and the Europeans, its most complex and refined manifestation. But every generalisation generates its own contradictions. Jane Austen's last great comedy, *Emma*, belongs to the class of novels Girard designates as romanesque.[2] Its ironic social game, so different from Austen's characteristic romantic comedy, evolves as Austen combines and recombines her characters in increasingly complex patterns of imitative desire.

Like all Austen novels, *Emma* is a fable of love and marriage in which it is the business of the female characters to find husbands and the business of their male counterparts to serve as partners for the marriageable females. The works address deeper issues – the nature of the relationship between men and women, the possibility of personal happiness in a world of material values – but at the level of the *récit*, an Austen novel resembles a chess board on which the unattached characters are free to interchange themselves within a fixed number of positions. Any young man is a potential husband for any young woman, and play will end when all the players have been appropriately paired. It is the distinguishing characteristic of *Emma* that its groupings are not binary, but triangular. In general, Austen's heroines love romantically, that is, against, rather than according to, the valuation of society. In *Pride and Prejudice*, for example, which may stand as the type of Austen's romantic manner, Elizabeth's and Darcy's initial dislike springs from overpraise of his bearing and her beauty by well-intentioned third parties; the desire, or simulated desire, of others creates a perverse repulsion between the protagonists. *Emma* is the exception to this rule. Not only are the minor figures of the novel caught up in the dynamic of imitative desire, but the heroine herself is subject to its levelling effects.

The novel's opening scenes engage the mechanisms of a triangular rivalry which Emma Woodhouse thinks she commands but which will quickly develop beyond her control. Miss Taylor, Emma's governess and friend, has just married, and Emma plans to fill the gap left in her interests and affections by assuming the role of educator herself. The object of her efforts is to be Harriet Smith, a simple girl of small fortune and illegitimate birth who boards at a local school. Emma's intention is to form Harriet's tastes and opinions by setting her own before her as an example: Harriet is to desire what she desires. In effect, she is consciously offering herself as a model for Harriet's imitation.

Emma is pleased with the disinterestedness of her project, but Austen's rendering of her protagonist's thoughts makes apparent the double nature of her motivation:

> She was not struck by anything remarkably clever in Miss Smith's conversation, but she found her altogether very engaging – not inconveniently shy, not unwilling to talk, and yet so far from pushing; showing so proper and becoming a deference, seeming so pleasantly grateful for being admitted to Hartfield, and so artlessly impressed by the appearance of everything in so superior a style to what she had been used to, that she must have good sense, and deserve encourage-

ment. Encouragement should be given. . . . She would notice her; she would improve her; she would detach her from her bad acquaintance, and introduce her into good society; she would form her opinions and her manners. It would be an interesting and certainly a very kind undertaking – highly becoming her own situation in life, her leisure, and powers.

(pp. 23–4)

'Handsome, clever and rich' (p. 5), Emma enjoys a sense of her own importance which Harriet's inferiority flatters. The role she proposes to herself here is one of what Girard calls external mediation.[3] The external mediator may be real or fictive, the abstraction of society's collective desire (like Amadis of Gaul for Don Quixote) or its concrete expression (like Claire de Beauséant for Goriot's daughters), but he stands in a position of absolute priority to the epigone whose desire he dictates. As model, he occupies the third point of the mimetic triangle, but he does so in a state of detachment which prevents his imitator from becoming his rival. The heroines of romance who initiate Emma Bovary into love are external mediators, and Sir William Lucas tries, with comic unsuccess, to play this role for Darcy at the Netherfield ball. Unlike the internal mediator, actively engaged in the desire he propagates, the external mediator, at once powerful and detached, is the signpost to desire without being its conduit. His priority, whether social, temporal, or metaphysical, makes him invulnerable to reciprocation. Through him, the contagion of mimetic desire spreads only one way.

The detached superiority of the external mediator appeals to Emma more than the emotional engagement of the internal mediator, or rival. In her imagination she repeatedly considers and rejects relationships of equality (friend, wife, mother) for those that leave her at a social and emotional distance (benefactress, daughter, aunt). But Emma's decision to serve as Harriet's model is not without its dangers. The social type of the external mediator is the king, and Emma's pretension to this role inevitably raises social issues both within the novel and within the social context within which the novel was generated.[4] It is no accident that the period when Austen wrote is the focus of Girard's wide-ranging study. The early nineteenth century saw the destruction of the fixed social hierarchy which, until the Revolution, set bounds to ambition and blocked the unlimited proliferation of mimetic desire. The concept of 'la carrière ouverte aux talents' was a product of the Revolution's Napoleonic aftermath; Julien Sorel's social and amorous conquests in 1819 are unimaginable three decades earlier. Emma is Julien's near contemporary, and it is not surprising that Austen, like Stendhal, should reflect post-Napoleonic social dislocations through the unrestricted play of mimetic desire. Emma believes she is immune from the desires of her social inferiors, but, like Stendhal's characters, she will find that the king is dead, and that desire has become radically democratic.

Emma's goal is a good marriage for Harriet, and she constructs the novel's paradigmatic triangle between herself, her protégée, and Highbury's young vicar, the Reverend Mr Elton, whom she designates to Harriet as an appropriate object of desire. Harriet's malleability before her social superiors makes her an innocent caricature of desire's innate snobbishness. She abandons her first suitor to fall in love with the clergyman at Emma's dictates, and Elton's frequent visits leave Emma in no doubt that she can direct his desire as well as that of her pupil. She intends to offer Elton her friend as her substitute; if you admire me, she says in effect, admire my imitation. But Emma has miscalculated. Far from considering her unattainably above him, Elton makes Emma, and her fortune, the object of his desire. The first time Elton finds her alone

> she found her subject cut up, her hand seized, her attention demanded, and Mr Elton actually making violent love to her. . . . It really was so. Without scruple, without apology, without much apparent diffidence, Mr Elton, the lover of Harriet, was professing himself *her* lover. She tried to stop him, but vainly; he would go on and say it all. . . . Accordingly, with a mixture of the serious and the playful . . . she replied, –
> 'I am very much astonished, Mr Elton. This to *me*! You forget yourself – you take me for my friend. Any message to Miss Smith I shall be happy to deliver; but no more of this to *me*, if you please.'
> 'Good heaven!' cried Mr Elton, 'what can be the meaning of this! . . . Miss Smith indeed! O Miss Woodhouse, who can think of Miss Smith when Miss Woodhouse is near?'
>
> (pp. 129–31)

Elton's unwelcome avowal demonstrates the fragility of the triangle of external mediation; already Emma and Harriet are being cast not as model and epigone but as rivals. Nor does Emma's humiliation end with Elton's proposal and the painful explanations that follow. Within a few months she finds herself in competition with Elton's nouveau-riche bride for ascendancy in Highbury society. Mrs Elton is Emma's mimetic double, and Austen's use of their rivalry as a vehicle for social commentary will be discussed in detail later. For the moment we may observe that, despite her reduction from model to rival, Emma rejects the notion of equality with Harriet or with the Eltons, whose desires so much resemble her own.

In her ambition, her conceit, and her determination to exploit social convention to her own ends, Emma is the Austen heroine who most closely resembles the egotistical protagonists of Stendhal. *Le Rouge et le Noir* is a novel of education in which Julien learns the reality of his own desires; and *Emma* is the great English example of this type of *Bildung*. Like her Stendhalian homologue, Emma the tutor must be taught the reality of her desire. The reversal of the triangle with Elton teaches her only her desirability – i.e. that she may be the object of others' desires against her will. Ironically, the overweening nature of her project – to fill the place of the monarch, the subject who dictates the desire of others – is first exposed by George Knightley, the novel's representative gentleman. His advice that Emma relinquish patronage of Harriet for friendship with Jane Fairfax is more than *ancien-regime* snobbery, though it reflects Austen's inherent conservatism. As, behind Emma's show of egalitarianism lies her assumption of her absolute superiority, so, behind Knightley's class-consciousness lies the recognition that in Emma's world absolute hierarchy is no longer possible. One's associates are always one's potential equals, and therefore one's rivals, for in post-revolutionary society, desire is already democratic. Emma dismisses Knightley's warnings, but the reductive mechanisms of mimetic desire will eventually teach her that she is not free not to desire the desire of others.

Emma's first failure, however, only teaches her that love is another name for social ambition. She constructs a second mimetic relationship between herself and Harriet, with Frank Churchill substituted for Elton as the object designated by her to Harriet's desire. Without her knowledge, however, Emma has been designated a player in the game of triangular desire which Frank Churchill plays with the woman he loves. Churchill wants to court Jane Fairfax without exciting the suspicions of his rich aunt. A conspicuous flirtation with Emma, which he knows her conceit will approve, is Churchill's ruse to mask his understanding with Jane while making his beloved as jealous as possible. Emma is thus the internal mediator of the triangle the clever Churchill constructs between himself, Emma, and Jane, while she is – or thinks she is – the external mediator of a triangle between herself, Churchill, and Harriet. Emma's triangle of desire proves an illusion; she fails to dictate Harriet's desire, though, ironically, she succeeds all too well in directing it. Churchill's triangle, on the other hand, functions with the efficiency of a machine. He, not Emma, is the master-manipulator of others' desires. Like Julien Sorel, Emma is a failed narcissist, but Churchill has the true solopsistic self-love that sets all other desire flowing toward him. 'The favourite of fortune', a comic version of Dostoyevsky's Stavrogin, 'he use[s] everybody ill, and they are all delighted to forgive him.'[5]

The irony of the desire Churchill triangulates between himself, Jane, and Emma is apparent mainly in retrospect. It precipitates the third of the mimetic triangles which reduce Emma to the democracy of desire. Harriet, it proves, has learned her lesson too well. Perfecting her imitation of Emma, she loves not the man Emma plays at loving (Churchill), but the man she really loves (Knightley). When his aunt dies and Churchill openly announces his engagement with Jane, Harriet's lack of emotion leads to the explanation that destroys Emma's illusions. With Harriet's confession of her love for Knightley and her belief that he loves her in return, Emma's world suffers a total collapse. From being her imitator, Harriet has become Emma's mediator, and her own love for Knightley is revealed to her by her pupil-turned-rival.

This sudden collapse from external to internal mediation, from imitation as a distant ideal to imitation as bitter rivalry, is one of the great comic turns in Austen's fiction. The extent to which Emma has taught Harriet to become her own rival is made clear in the confrontation that takes place between them, and again, it is specifically Harriet as mediator who reveals to Emma the nature and strength of her own desire:

> Harriet was standing at one of the windows. Emma turned round to look at her in consternation, and hastily said, –
> 'Have you any idea of Mr Knightley's returning your affection?'
> 'Yes,' replied Harriet modestly, but not fearfully; 'I must say that I have.'
> Emma's eyes were instantly withdrawn; and she sat silently meditating, in a fixed attitude, for a few minutes. A few minutes were sufficient for making her acquainted with her own heart. A mind like hers, once opening to suspicion, made rapid progress. She touched, she admitted, she acknowledged the whole truth. Why was it so much worse that Harriet should be in love with Mr Knightley than with Frank Churchill? Why was the evil so dreadfully increased by Harriet's having some hope of a return? It darted through her with the speed of an arrow that Mr Knightley must marry no one but herself!
>
> (pp. 407–8)

Harriet's desire can be said to create Emma's where before only feelings of friendship existed. Their rivalry projects from her 'solitary grandeur' (p. 208) into the world of common human conflict, the world of democratic desire. What she will make of it turns on the evolution of the *récit*'s subordinate mimetic structure, a figure of which she is also the pivot. Knightley's implication in the novel's triangular dynamic parallels that of Emma. 'He had been in love with Emma and jealous of Frank Churchill from about the same period, one sentiment having probably enlightened him as to the existence of the other' (p. 432), the narrator reports. Like Emma, he is reduced from aloof social arbiter to jealous lover through the mediation of an erotic rival. When Churchill announces his engagement, Knightley hastens to comfort Emma and finds himself confessing his love. Knightley has been taught to love by his mediator, Churchill, as has Emma by her mediator, Harriet.

If we plot the triangularities of *Emma*'s *récit*, the result looks like this:

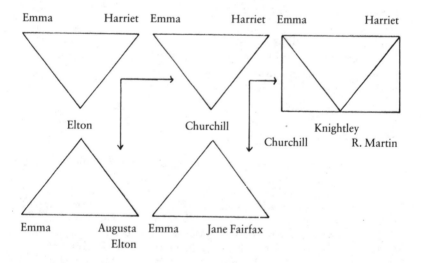

Subordinate figures could be appended – the relationship which Emma's imagination constructs between Jane Fairfax, Miss Campbell, and Mr Dixon, for example – but in their proliferation, these triangles indicate the main movement of the narrative. From the moment Emma substitutes herself for Mrs Goddard's schoolgirls in Harriet's imagination, mimetic relationships replicate until, on Knightley's entry into play, the triangles coincide, and the angles are righted and the figure stabilised. This triangular shape of desire in *Emma* makes Austen's last comedy much more like love novels of the European tradition than her other works. Its recognition of the importance of the third as an impetus to desire relates Austen less to her English predecessors than to contemporary French analysts of the transfiguring passion which Stendhal describes five years later in *De l'Amour*. The fictions of Stendhal and Constant are dramatic, while *Emma* is a comic heroine, but the social nature of love, its ironic definition at the hands of another, is recognised by both.

But *Emma* is more than the history of a young woman's inducement to marry; it is Austen's demolition of the idea of absolute social hierarchy. Recently, Austen critics have taken new interest in the politics of her fiction, and Marilyn Butler argues that her novels depict a stable, hierarchical world reflective of Austen's own Tory values.[6] But whatever Austen's personal views (and available evidence indicates they were conservative), she is too incisive and witty a realist to mistake existing society for a simple reflection of her own ideas. Butler's reading may hold for the early novels, conceived before England had felt the full brunt of Revolutionary turmoil, but it could not be less true of the works that appear at the end of the Napoleonic wars. There, Austen is at one with her European contemporaries in depicting a world revolutionised by the disappearance of social absolutes. *Mansfield Park*, *Emma*, and *Persuasion* all deal with this theme, but *Emma* is the only one to do so comically.[7] Austen's comic device here consists in exposing her heroine's social pretensions through the same triangular dynamic of mimetic rivalry that effects her education in love.

The coincidence of sexual and social desire in Austen has already been noted. Marriage is the Austen heroine's career, and, like Stendhal's heroes, she finds status a magnet to desire. In *Emma*, moreover, objects of ambition, like those of love, are always socially determined; that is, they are designated to the subject by the desire of a third. Harriet is proud to drink tea with Miss Woodhouse because Mrs Goddard's girls envy her, just as she admires Robert Martin because her Highbury friends do. And, in a post-Napoleonic world like that of *Emma*, the final dictators of desire are not an elite, but the majority. An object becomes or remains socially desirable because ordinary people compete to have it. Thus the ironic position, well described by Girard, of the *triste noblesse* around the Marquis de la Mole. These sad aristocrats spend most of their lives trying to distinguish themselves from a middle class their grandparents simply ignored. When a commoner can imitate a gentleman, the position of an elite is always one of similar jeopardy: it must distinguish itself from its inferiors to retain a sense of caste, yet the lower orders *must* strive to imitate it if its privileges are to conserve their glamour. Through the triangular dynamic of mimetic desire, the reactionary nobles of *Le Rouge et le Noir* are paradoxically dependent on the bourgeoisie they detest. They court the emulation of their social inferiors even as they fear their successful rivalry.

This world of democratic desire and universal rivalry is the world of *Emma*, as it is that of Stendhal's characters. Emma means to play the role of arbiter in society and in love; she forgets that in post-Revolutionary society, one's imitators are one's potential competitors. As her rivalry with Harriet reveals Emma's love for Knightley, so the competition of Mrs Elton exposes the reality of Emma's social ambition.[8] 'Self-important, presuming . . . [with] a little beauty and a little accomplishment, but . . . little judgment' (p. 281), Mrs Elton is Emma's double; and Austen's dissection of her heroine's personal and social pretensions through the foil of mimetic rivalry provides some of the subtlest satire in her fiction.

As Emma's successor in Elton's desire, Augusta Elton effects the conversion of the *récit*'s paradigmatic triangle from external to internal mediation. From the first she insists on comparing Emma and her possessions to other people and things, and it is this persistence in discovering equivalence where Emma wants to see only her superiority that earns her the latter's dislike. In fact, the absurd minutiae of Mrs Elton's comparisons should not make us forget that Maple Grove does resemble Hartfield just as she resembles Emma. Specifically, Mrs Elton's character is structured to mirror the defects of Emma's in grosser, more visible form. Above all, she is determined, like Emma, to dictate taste as the first lady of Highbury. The real difference between Mrs Elton and Emma, then, is not one of substance, but of manner. In her vulgarity, Mrs Elton verbalises the attitudes that Emma only thinks, thus making their common prejudices available to Austen's satire.[9] When Emma censures her as 'a vain woman, extremely well-satisfied with herself and thinking much of her own importance' (p. 272), she ironically condemns herself.

Mrs Elton's function in the author's indirect satire of her heroine is of the first importance to the comic *telos* of the novel. Their mirror-image similarity has a second important function, however, which is to constitute Mrs Elton a classic example of the Girardian rival-as-double.[10] The more faithfully an epigone imitates his model, Girard reminds us, the more bitter their rivalry paradoxically becomes; and rivalry with a double is the fiercest of all. Emma's claim to brook no comparison is refuted by the presence of a competitor whose desires reflect her own. The term 'reflect' is not idly chosen; not only does Mrs Elton's ambition generally imitate Emma's; in a number of instances it directly mimes her words or actions.[11] Their rivalry culminates at the Crown ball, where Mrs Elton appropriates Emma's pretension that the dance is given in her honour and succeeds in making herself 'queen of the evening' (p. 329). When Emma must 'submit to stand second to Mrs Elton' (p. 325), literally as well as figuratively, 'the dignity of Miss Woodhouse of Hartfield [is] sunk indeed' (p. 276).

The monarchical figures of language associated with the ball scene are not incidental; they remind us of the political implications of Emma's elitism. It is equally significant that Mrs Elton is pronounced queen of the evening by Miss Bates, Austen's symbol of Highbury society and the Highbury consensus. In her self-effacing ordinariness, Miss Bates is the opposite of Emma's brilliant self-assertion, but it is precisely her mediocrity that makes her representative of her neighbours, so that here, or in her verdict on the preparations for the dance, she is able to speak for all of them. We remember that from her arrival Mrs Elton courts the good opinion of Highbury like a politician, and as a result 'the greater part of her new acquaintance ... were very well satisfied; so that Mrs Elton's praise passed from one mouth to another ...' (p. 281). It is this mouth-to-mouth commendation of the Miss Bateses and Mrs Coles that is the fundamental ground of status in Highbury. Austen permits herself some quiet irony at the expense of Highbury public opinion; like Miss Bates herself, it is 'disposed to commend', and 'not in the habit of judging' (p. 281). But Mrs Elton's triumph at the ball, like the success of the Coles' dinner – another instance in which Emma unsuccessfully pits her prestige against popular opinion – exposes the illusory nature of Emma's notion that she dictates the taste of her inferiors.

Mrs Elton's success as Emma's rival and double, then, has implications that go beyond the reformation of the heroine's individual character. Like Harriet Smith, Mrs Elton mirrors back to Emma her own desires, thus leading her from conceit and illusion to a truer estimate of her relation to others. Mrs Elton's rivalry, however, reduces Emma to the level of her associates in a specifically political as well as a personal sense. Her success in queening it at the ball is in one sense supererogatory; the fact of competition between Miss Woodhouse of Hartfield and the former Miss Hawkins in itself contradicts Emma's claim of absolute superiority. Like Stendhal's aristocrats, Emma is forced to endure comparison with a rival she considers beneath her, and the more she tries to distinguish herself from her double, the more she demonstrates their fundamental similarity. Austen traps her heroine in the paradox of the post-Revolutionary upper classes, eternally engaged in the effort to inscribe a difference between themselves and an emulative bourgeoisie. Mrs Elton does more, however, than reduce Emma from model to rival. By literalising the regal metaphor behind Emma's pretensions – as at the Crown, or in her imitation of Marie Antoinette at the Donwell picnic – she reveals its ridiculous and illusory nature. Indeed, by taking up Emma's conservative social criteria and making them her own, Mrs Elton invalidates a whole set of hierarchical notions that permit her to assert her superiority to the Tupmans as Emma asserts hers to the Eltons. Her condemnation of the Birmingham family mimics Emma's strictures on the Hawkinses and Bristol to devastating satiric effect; read in the light of Mrs Elton's imitation, Emma's judgment can no longer be accepted unironically.

'Snobbery', Girard remarks, 'begins with equality.' Mrs Elton's function as Emma's mimetic double permits her to deconstruct the heroine's Tory ideology from the inside. An incarnation of Girard's epigram, she exposes as contingent and relative the social distinctions Emma supposes are absolute. Emma conceives of her society in terms of rigid inequalities; Miss Woodhouse cannot visit Mrs Martin, the Coles will not presume to invite the Westons, Mr Elton may not aspire to the heiress of Hartfield.[12] But the social hierarchy of England in 1816 is one of open classes, not closed castes. The course of the narrative contradicts these conservative misconceptions in the same way it exposes Emma's errors of personal psychology. This is not to say that the distinction between bourgeoisie and gentry, and between the working and leisured classes generally, is not a real one in *Emma*. For all his gentility of mind, Robert Martin is his landlord's social inferior. But the barrier dividing the classes is not, as Emma imagines it, impassable. It can be and repeatedly is transgressed in the course of the narrative. A poor gentlewoman may fall to be a governess, or see herself confined to two rooms above a shop; the heiress of a great family may marry a captain of militia. On the other hand, a governess may marry into leisure and property, a city businessman may retire to a country estate. An industrious farmer may 'thrive, and become a very rich man' (p. 34), or the son of a middle-class father a scion of the aristocracy through a change of name. To Emma's (and Butler's) illusion of a stratified, stable rural English society, Austen counterposes the narrator's vision of a society stable only in change, in which social status is constantly altered by good fortune and bad, by marriage and by death, by hard work, and, above all, by the passage of time.

The world of *Emma*, then, is a revolutionised world in which traditional notions of rank and caste are challenged by new social forces that express themselves through universal rivalry and Girardian mimesis. In fact, the more closely we analyse the social fabric of *Emma*, the more its first illusion of Burkean stability disappears before a picture of a traditional society in rapid, almost chaotic, flux. The absence or incapacity of fathers, the pointed play with family names, the recurrence of the epithet 'nobody' (applied first and most tellingly to Harriet Smith, then to a range of characters from the Elton family to Mrs Churchill) all suggest that the patriarchal and hierarchical divisions of English country society are in the process of being subverted. Tradition itself becomes relative: the Sucklings look down their noses at the Tupmans on the same principles by which Emma scorns them. Time is repeatedly invoked in favour of traditional prejudices by reactionaries like Mr Woodhouse (who so dislikes change he would stop marriage and generation if he could), but in *Emma*, it paradoxically proves to favour the upstart. Mrs Churchill, *Emma*'s synecdoche for the power of rank, was 'nobody when he married her' (p. 310); twenty years later she 'outChurchills all the Churchills' in arbitrary arrogance. Frank Churchill, the master-manipulator of *Emma*'s erotic triangles, also epitomises, by his ambiguous class status and egotistical pursuit of self-interest, the career of the successful *arriviste*. The confidence in 'chance [and] circumstance' (p. 438) he proclaims in his letter to Mrs Weston is borne out in his Beylian gamble for love and wealth. If Emma's and Knightley's marriage restores an appearance of social stability at the narrative's close, the anticipated marriage of Churchill and Jane is a symbol of the social order's radical contingency.

We need only contrast the marriages which close *Emma* with those that conclude *Pride and Prejudice* to appreciate the difference between Austen's romantic and romanesque manners. In both, gentlemen marry gentlemen's daughters. The romantic quality of the early novel lies less in the disparity of its matches than in the manner in which it brings them about. Jane's union with Bingley and Elizabeth's with Darcy are presented as victories of individual emotion over the obstructive jealousy and snobbery of third parties. The regard of the lovers is conceived and maintained outside the sphere of social influence, with the result that neither romantic nor social conventions are challenged. In *Emma*, love and society relate quite differently. From a Girardian perspective, Austen's last comedy has the effectiveness of a great novel because its erotic and social triangles function together, simultaneously deconstructing the romantic concept of love and the Tory concept of society on which Austen's fiction is based. The dynamic of imitative desire engaged by Emma at the narrative's opening operates to expose all its victims' illusions. Behind their idealistic notions of love and rank, it reveals the determining, dialectical presence of the rival Other. Austen is at her strongest when, as here, she mocks her own conservatism. To Emma's elitist illusions she opposes the ironic yet generous concept of equality in the pursuit of happiness, the democracy of desire. If, like Stendhal's, her characters 'still inhabit the same historical world as we do',[13] it is because in her final novels she is already a novelist of what Girard calls 'the bourgeois interregnum'.

From *Studies in the Novel*, 17 (Spring 1985), 1–13.

NOTES

[Beatrice Marie is the only critic writing on *Emma* whose approach is thoroughly structuralist. It is, therefore, the underlying system rather than the author's unique vision which concerns Marie and her attempt to discover in *Emma* the patterns of triangular desire which René Girard argues are present in a number of major European novels allows her to approach the novel from a refreshingly new angle. Her conclusion that the world of *Emma* comprises 'open classes, not closed castes', for example, challenges readings, such as Duckworth's (essay 2), which find a Burkeian stability in the novel and anticipates Marxist readings such as Thompson's (essay 7). However, problems that Marie experiences in making a fit between *Emma* and Girard's schema call into question the structuralist assumption that systems can be developed of sufficient scope to accommodate a wide variety of literary works. The most important of the several instances where Marie does violence to Austen or Girard is located in her eliding of the vital distinction Girard makes between desire, which he uses in its Freudian sense to mean a longing for a satisfaction which cannot be offered in reality, and love. According to Girard desire is the emotion characteristic of a triangulated relationship; consequently illusion always surrounds the object of desire. True love or passion, on the other hand, because it neither trans-figures nor discovers illusory qualities in the object of desire, occurs only in unmediated relationships. Had Marie retained this distinction, it would have been impossible for her to claim that Emma and Knightley come to realise that they love each other as a result of their involvement in internally-mediated triangles in which Harriet Smith and Frank Churchill respectively function as rivals. Instead she would have been forced into the unlikely conclusion that Emma and Knightley are *vaniteux* who, because they are motivated only by a desire to emulate their rivals, will experience disappointment at the moment of possessing each other. Ed.]

1. I want to thank René Girard for reading and commenting on an earlier version of this paper.

2. Jane Austen, *Emma*, in *The Novels of Jane Austen*, ed. R. W. Chapman (Oxford: Clarendon Press, 1933), vol. IV. All page references in the text are to this edition.

3. For a thorough exposition of the varieties of mediation and their consequences, see 'Triangular Desire', in René Girard, *Deceit, Desire and the Novel*, trans. Yvonne Frecerro (Baltimore, 1976).

4. By definition the absolute monarch cannot become the rival of his subjects; he is exempt from desire, properly so called, because he experiences no delay between the formulation of a wish and its gratification. Girard's discussion of Versailles under Louis XIV (above, pp. 117–19) provides a social model of the external type of triangular mediation and an implicit contrast to the internal mediation characterising the bourgeois society of Stendhal. In general, Girard sees external mediation as proper to feudal or neo-feudal societies characterised by fixed hierarchy in social order and Catholicism in religion, while internal mediation distinguishes modern (i.e. post-Revolutionary) societies in which social mobility replaces fixed social position and atheism or agnosticism replaces Christian belief. See also *Des Choses Cachées depuis la Fondation du Monde* (Paris, 1981).

5. Knightley's description of his rival, p. 428. Emma terms him 'the child of good fortune', or, rather, Churchill borrows these words to designate himself in his letter to Mrs Weston, which we read twice.

6. Marilyn Butler, *Jane Austen and the War of Ideas* (Oxford, 1975). Contributions toward a rebuttal include Warren Roberts, *Jane Austen and the French Revolution* (New York, 1979) and Julia Prewitt Brown, *Jane Austen's Novels: Social Change and Literary Form* (Chicago, 1979). Mary Poovey's *The Proper Lady and the Woman Writer: Ideology as Style in the Works of Wollstonecraft, Shelley and Austen* (Chicago, 1984) considers Austen's politics from a feminist perspective.

7. *Mansfield Park* narrates the threat posed to Mansfield by the irresponsibility of the Bertram children and the Regency mores of Henry and

Mary Crawford; the marriage of Edmund Bertram and Fanny Price which ends the novel resolves the conflict in favour of Mansfield's conservative values. *Persuasion* enacts the figurative and literal displacement of an irresponsible aristocrat by a new, Napoleonic generation of self-made men. Clearly the function and fate of the landed classes was much on Austen's mind in her final novels. That her verdict was not always on the side of the traditional gentry is equally clear.

8. Of course the prospect of Harriet's marriage to Knightley has radically democratic connotations in itself. The moment in which Emma contemplates its possibility is followed by a vision of social and ethical chaos so nihilistic that Austen feels obliged, on theological grounds, to retract it even as she writes it: 'Was it new for anything in this world to be unequal, inconsistent, incongruous, or for chance and circumstance (as second causes) to direct the human fate?' (p. 413). The conflict between an intuition of chaos and an imperative of order illustrated here is more characteristic of the late novels than the unproblematical Toryism posited by Butler.

9. Commentary on Mrs Elton sometimes proposes that she functions to mitigate Emma's faults by drawing the reader's criticism to herself. I suggest that her function is precisely the opposite. Through her repeated mimicry of Emma she becomes Austen's most important device for establishing a critical viewpoint on her heroine in a narrative in which the extensive use of free indirect style encourages the reader's uncritical identification with Emma's opinions. See Marilyn Butler, *Jane Austen and The War of Ideas* (Oxford, 1975), pp. 269–71 and Bruce Stovel, 'Comic Symmetry in Jane Austen's *Emma*', *Dalhousie Review*, 57 (Autumn 1977), 453–65. [Reprinted in this volume – see pp. 20–34. Ed.]

10. Girard investigates the phenomenon of the double in *Violence and the Sacred* (Baltimore, 1976).

11. Like Emma, she takes a protégée, lays claim to Frank Churchill, neglects her music, professes her independence of society, tries to dispose of Donwell. She repeats Emma's remarks on the inconvenience of a Mrs Knightley (p. 469), on the appearance of her name in Frank Churchill's correspondence (p. 308), and on the presumptions of upstarts (pp. 310–11). The episode of the ball at the Crown caps all these similarities.

12. Austen's calculated use of free indirect style gives Emma's opinions a deceptive authority which can trap the unwary reader into repeating her mistakes. However, the narrator's independent comments give ample evidence that Highbury society is different from Emma's vision of a rigidly hierarchical community. For example, the detailed retrospect on Mr Weston's origins which opens chapter 2 of Volume I as well as those on the Coles (II, 7) and the Hawkinses (II, 4) describes a social rise from success in business to integration with the country gentry. Indeed,

Emma's reflections on her own family (I, 16) can be constructed to tell the same story; as Butler herself observes, the Woodhouses do not belong to the traditional landed classes. If Emma's characteristic fault is her failure to check her fixed preconceptions against the evidence of reality, it surely flaws her social as well as her personal perception. See Helen Dry, 'Syntax and the Point of View in Jane Austen's *Emma*', *Studies in Romanticism*, 16 (1977), 87–99.

13. René Girard, *Deceit, Desire and the Novel* (Baltimore, 1976).

4

'Emma': Good Riddance

D. A. MILLER

'Seldom, very seldom, does complete truth belong to any human disclosure; seldom can it happen that something is not a little disguised, or a little mistaken' (*Emma*, p. 431). In the context of our argument, the suggestiveness of this text is obvious. It describes the mechanism of closure *almost* as we have seen it operate: at the moment settlement takes place, something gets left out. *Almost*, for the text does not quite say that disclosure, proceeding by mask and mistake, must forgo its claims to a 'complete truth'; even less does it say that a making or mistaking of the complete truth is a necessary condition if disclosure is to take place at all. This is what it teasingly stops just short of saying, merely claiming that it 'very seldom' happens that a masking or mistaking fails to accompany the truth of a disclosure. However, even if we take the text at face value (even before recognising that its face value is two-faced), it is evident that this reflection about human disclosure in general is itself a disclosure; and that, as such, it puts into question its own status (as a 'truth' being 'disclosed'). To what extent is it subject to the liabilities of human disclosure revealed in it? Does it abide by the general rule that it articulates (and if it does, then what is being disguised or mistaken?), or is it one of those exceptions such as 'very seldom' occur?

The placement of the text, coming as it does at a crucial juncture in *Emma*, seems perversely calculated to raise these questions. We hardly expect reticence, much less suppression, at the supreme moment of mutual recognition uniting heroine and hero. On the contrary, it is at this very moment that Jane Austen's lovers typically indulge 'in those retrospections and acknowledgements, and

68

especially in those explanations of what had directly preceded the present moment' (*Persuasion*, p. 241). Far from telling only and no more than what needs to be told, these conversations are characterised by redundancy and repetitiousness. 'Between [two lovers] no subject is finished, no communication is even made, till it has been made at least twenty times over' (*Sense and Sensibility*, p. 364). In this case, however, 'what had directly preceded the present moment' is precisely what is consciously withheld. Emma's initial reluctance to hear what Knightley has to say and her speedy acceptance of his proposal have produced an 'inconsistency' (*Emma*, p. 431) of conduct. Although Emma could easily have accounted for it (by revealing Harriet's newly revealed attachment to him and her own newly excited fears of his returning it), she chooses to let it stand. In the place where her explanation ought to be, an aphorism announces the omission of explanation.

Thus, at a decisive moment of truth in the novel, there comes a text that curiously subverts the completeness of the moment. The subversion is curious, moreover, not only because it comes unexpectedly, but also because it paradoxically tends to neutralise its own force. By suggesting that such moments of truth are 'very seldom' more complete than this one, might not the text be in effect reinforcing the practical adequacy of the scene (which is, at any rate, as complete as can usually be the case)? For it may be true that at the moment in which truth is being disclosed, something is seldom not a little disguised or mistaken; 'but where, as in this case, though the conduct is mistaken, the feelings are not, it may not be very material' (p. 431). A theoretical distinction is insisted upon, but is oddly denied practical consequence. The text equivocates, both granting and taking away the truth of the proposal scene, simultaneously undercutting it and claiming that this undercutting doesn't much matter. We need to explore the possibility of a sense in which this quasi-proverbial text repeats or perpetuates the very process that it recognises: specifically, a sense in which this discordant relationship between the truth of disclosure and the completeness of truth ('very seldom' obviated) is not a matter of mere probabilities. Might not what is presented as merely likely to occur, happen according to a certain necessity? And if so, then what is gained – or guarded against – by presenting this necessity in the disguised or mistaken form of a generally recurring accident?

Emma's secret is this: not only has Harriet Smith once more remade her object choice, she has attached herself (at Emma's unwitting instigation) to a man who no longer has even the possibility of reciprocating. Why does Emma find it necessary to suppress this information, even in a context of intimacy and unresolve? Why does she decide to continue suppressing it until Harriet's marriage to Robert Martin, when 'all necessity of concealment from Mr Knightley would ... be over' and 'the disguise, equivocation, mystery, so hateful to her to practise, might ... be over' as well (p. 475)? It seems unlikely that she is prompted by feelings of either protectiveness or rivalry toward Harriet (who now is 'nothing'); nor would she need to be, at a moment of guaranteed discretion, moved by loyalty toward her sex – what the novel calls 'the duty of woman by woman' (p. 231). Why does the case of Harriet Smith assume such an importance that Emma feels a need not to betray it? What is the nature of her embarrassment?

We might begin to understand the necessity behind Emma's suppression of the 'complete truth' here by taking up another, less deliberate instance of it in the novel. This is the censorship that she retrospectively imposes on the interest once excited in her by Frank Churchill. Here are the important articulations of that interest *before* Emma discovers her more potent feelings for Mr Knightley. First, at Frank's first departure from Highbury:

> To complete every other recommendation, he had *almost* told her that he loved her. What strength, or what constancy of affection he might be subject to, was another point; but at present she could not doubt his having a decidedly warm admiration, a conscious preference of herself; and this persuasion, joined to all the rest, made her think that she *must* be a little in love with him, in spite of every previous determination against it.
>   'I certainly must,' said she. 'This sensation of listlessness, weariness, stupidity, this disinclination to sit down and employ myself, this feeling of every thing's being dull and insipid about the house! – I must be in love; I should be the oddest creature in the world if I were not – for a few weeks at least.'
>
> (p. 262)

Then, during his absence:

> Emma continued to entertain no doubt of her being in love. Her ideas only varied as to the how much. At first, she thought it was a great deal; and afterwards, but little ... pleasing as he was, she could yet imagine him to have faults; and farther, though thinking of him so much, and, as she sat drawing or working, forming a thousand amusing schemes for the progress and close of their attachment, fancying

interesting dialogues, and inventing elegant letters; the conclusion of every imaginary declaration on his side was that she *refused him*. Their affection was always to subside into friendship. Every thing tender and charming was to mark their parting; but still they were to part. When she became sensible of this, it struck her that she could not be very much in love; for in spite of her previous and fixed determination never to quit her father, never to marry, a strong attachment certainly must produce more of a struggle than she could foresee in her own feelings.

'. . . I do suspect that he is not really necessary to my happiness. So much the better. I certainly will not persuade myself to feel more than I do. I am quite enough in love. I should be sorry to be more.'

(pp. 264–5)

Finally, at the news of his secret engagement to Jane Fairfax:

'That you may have less difficulty in believing this boast, of my present indifference,' she continued, 'I will farther tell you, that there was a period in the early part of our acquaintance, when I did like him, when I was very much disposed to be attached to him – nay, was attached – and how it came to cease, is perhaps the wonder. Fortunately, however, it did cease. I have really for some time past, for at least these three months, cared nothing about him. You may believe me, Mrs. Weston. This is the simple truth.'

(p. 396)

One needn't artificially raise the temperature of a response whose limitations Emma acknowledges almost from the start; one need only note that, however low, it is not at zero degree. If Emma always qualifies the strength or the duration of her attachment in these passages, she never denies its existence. Once she becomes aware of her feelings for Mr Knightley, however, even the seemingly trivial fact that 'for a few weeks at least' Emma was 'a little' in love with Frank begins to be denied.

How long had Mr. Knightley been so dear to her, as every feeling declared him now to be? When had his influence, such influence begun? – When had he succeeded to that place in her affection, which Frank Churchill had once, for a short period, occupied? – She looked back; she compared the two – compared them, as they had always stood in her estimation, from the time of the latter's becoming known to her – and as they must at any time have been compared by her, had it – oh! had it, by any blessed felicity, occurred to her, to institute the comparison. – She saw that there never had been a time when she did not consider Mr Knightley as infinitely the superior, or when his regard for her had not been infinitely the most dear. She saw, that in persuading herself, in fancying, in acting to the contrary, she had been

entirely under a delusion, totally ignorant of her own heart – and, in
short, that she had never really cared for Frank Churchill at all!

(p. 412)

Implicitly, Emma's retrospective here censors and revises the texts
that we have cited preceding it. 'She looked back'; but she doesn't see
what she saw when she was back where she is now looking. One odd
sequitur: Emma now compares Knightley and Frank as they must
have been compared by her at any time in the past (had it occurred to
her then to institute the comparison); and she finds that 'there had
never been a time when she did not consider Mr Knightley as infinitely
the superior'. If it did not occur to her to make the comparison in the
past, how can it be that 'there had never been a time' when she did
not find Mr Knightley winning it? Another: Emma begins by admit-
ting that Frank Churchill had once, for a short period, occupied a
place in her affection, and she concludes that 'she had never really
cared for Frank Churchill at all!' Did she fail to make the comparison, or has she always made it? Did she once care for Frank, or has
she never cared for him? One might account for these discrepancies
by an appeal to common-sensical psychology: now that Emma is
'really' in love, she realises that what she called by that name wasn't
'really' love at all. Yet this view would merely paraphrase Emma's
forgetful revision, without explaining what makes it work, that is,
precisely, the invocation of those 'reallys'. What strategic role do
they play? What do they enforce?

I prefer to see Emma confronting the fact of desire's displacement
(Knightley has succeeded to the place occupied by Frank Churchill)
and then juggling it away (no displacement has ever occurred). Far
from succeeding to Frank's place, as Emma is forced to think at the
start of the passage, Mr Knightley ends up having always occupied it.
The oppositions of appearance versus reality, ignorance versus
knowledge, are invoked, then, to keep desire whole: in one place and
on one track, never divided, never transferred or redirected. The
phenomena of division, transference, redirection come to be seen as
effects of a delusion. Emma has always loved Mr Knightley, but
simply never knew it; she has never loved Frank Churchill, but only
imagined she did. By the time that Mr Knightley arrives to condole
with her over Frank's apparent betrayal, the processes of Emma's
self-revision have fully taken:

'Mr Knightley,' said Emma, trying to be lively, but really confused –
'I am in a very extraordinary situation. I cannot let you continue in

your error; and yet, perhaps, since my manners gave such an impression, I have as much reason to be ashamed of confessing that *I never have been at all attached to the person we are speaking of*, as it might be natural for a woman to feel in confessing exactly the reverse – But I never have.'

(pp. 426–7, my italics)

Her claim blatantly contradicts what she has told Mrs Weston earlier ('there was a period ... when I was very much disposed to be attached to him – nay, was attached'). It would seem as though the psychology of being 'really' in love required such retraction to help sustain itself. 'This time, it's the real thing'; but the reality of the real thing is in part produced by treating previous erotic interest as unreal: inauthentic, delusional, even (as here) non-existent.

In the proposal scene, this closure of desire becomes institutionalised. Desire has recognised its 'proper object' and made itself capable of fixing on it; this recognition can now be incarnated socially, in marriage. Two 'one and onlys' have found each other out: such is the implicit ideology of a romantic proposal, and it is not confined to Emma or Jane Austen or even literary texts. Here, however, there is a double urgency behind affirming the ultimate directedness of desire toward its proper object, since the ideology of romantic love carries the rationale of ending the novel as well. The assumptions under which erotic desire is locked into place – in holy matrimony and wholly in matrimony – also permit a story whose subject this is to come to a complete close. Enshrining the directedness of Emma's desire and *Emma*'s design, the proposal scene is thus doubly a staging of the sacred.

It is also likely to be, as René Girard would tell us, a staging of implicit violence: be it only, in this case, the genteel violence of barring a topic from conversation.[1] In a sense, merely to mention the career of Harriet's desire (at this particular crisis in it) would be an affront to the *vraisemblance* of the proposal scene. Romantic love assumes the existence of a right object, and a desire that transcends whatever contingencies have brought it into being. Harriet's case would put forward the incompatible themes of transference (desire sliding onto yet a new object) and mediation (desire crossed up and attached to somebody else's object). If Emma has needed to deny even what has been a very minor attachment to Frank Churchill, then she might well want to eschew these themes, defining the transcendency of her present attachment by an omission of what it is implicitly defined against. There are more specific reasons for her censorship, however. It is insofar as Harriet is a reminder of some-thing in Emma herself that she must be 'forgotten': banished not merely as an inappropriate reference, but as an embarrassing and potentially unsettling one.

Soon forgetting and soon supplanting its object, Harriet's desire has been a parody of Emma's own wandering fancy. (Consider how Frank Churchill gets displaced: other cares, occupations, feelings crowd him out.) We have already seen, moreover, how the revelation of Harriet's feelings for Mr Knightley has awakened Emma's own. Hence Emma needs to protect her desire for him from resembling that of her protégée, now become her 'monstrous double'. If com-mon sense suggests that the difference is obvious, Emma here is unwilling to trust to common sense. It is as though the mention of Harriet's kind of desire in front of Mr Knightley were felt to hold synecdochal implications for her own, undermining its implied tran-scendency at the very moment that it needs most to be claimed. Suppression is Emma's way to differentiate what might become an insinuated identity, and it will cease only when later developments have made the differentiation secure. When Harriet's desire has found its truth in Robert Martin; when Harriet therefore no longer poses the problem of erotic and imaginative instability; when two husbands and two social standings symbolically articulate the differ-ence between the two women; then and only then will Emma give Mr Knightley 'that full and perfect confidence which her disposition was most ready to welcome as a duty' (p. 475).

On the coextensive level of the novel's own closure, we observe a familiar pattern: at the moment of closure, the novel arranges to put in parentheses the inherent instability or suspense of character and situation that has initiated the narrative movement. The narratable is shown being put *hors de combat*: not merely laid to rest in a settled outcome, or drained of its force by an 'etc principle', but actively suppressed. Now if the narratable belongs to the 'complete truth' of a novel (as it would have to do), then we begin to see why the complete truth 'very seldom' belongs to closural disclosures. Very seldom?

> All Suspense & Indecision were over. – They were reunited. They were restored to all that had been lost.
>
> (*Persuasion*, p. 263)

This is the moment of closure from the original version of *Persuasion*. The closure seems to be a trade-off between two orders or dimensions of the text, each presented as a mutually exclusive totality. *Retrouvé*, 'all that had been lost' comes to supplant 'all Suspense & Indecision'; and inversely, it is only because 'all that had been lost' did get lost that 'all Suspense & Indecision' have been able to crop up in the first place. The closural settlement accommodates the narratable only by changing its status, that is, by putting it in a past perfect tense and declaring it 'over'. Closure can *never* include, then, the narratable in its essential dimension: all suspense and indecision. What made the trial of Job so trying was doubtless the fact that he didn't know that it *was* a trial; as Kierkegaard tells us, 'every explanation was still possible'.[2] Once Job knew, the experience was radically changed. Similarly, the narratable disappears when it is looked back on from the point of view of closure. Its meaning is now perfectly clear – that is to say, its defining character ('every explanation was still possible') is lost.

If complete truth never belongs to novelistic disclosure, then why does Jane Austen's text preserve the possibility that there just sometimes might be a pure disclosure, with nothing to void and no history to hide? This ideal of a transparent state of affairs implicitly refers us to a non-narratable world, where closure is not exclusion because there is nothing to exclude. Even though she finds no motivation for narrative except error, Jane Austen admits no *necessity* for error. If Emma had behaved as she should, Harriet would have done so as well, and there would have been nothing for Mr Knightley to mistake or Emma to disguise. Characters may 'fall' into narrative, but it is also insisted that they are 'sufficient to have stood'.

From D. A. Miller, *Narrative and its Discontents: Problems of Closure in the Traditional Novel* (Princeton, 1981), pp. 89–99.

NOTES

[Miller's book is concerned with the tensions present in the work of Austen, George Eliot and Stendhal between the 'utopic state' to which all three orient their texts and 'the narrative means used to reach it'. More specifically, he finds that each author experiences a 'discomfort with the process and implications of narrative itself' because narrative is always generated by 'an underlying instability of desire, language and society' which is 'inevitably felt to threaten the very possibility of [a] finalising state of affairs' (p. x). For Miller, then, narrative lacks a final signified which will terminate the play of the signifier and, as a result, can never achieve 'total coherence'. This poststructuralist approach to fictional form and closure is, as Miller emphasises himself, very different from that of structuralist narratologists who work on the assumption that 'everything in a narrative exists in view of the hidden necessity determined by its final configuration of event and meaning' (p. xiii). In the first part of his opening chapter, 'The Dangers of Narrative in Jane Austen', Miller explores the waverings, uncertainties and indecisions (of Harriet and Emma's desire, for example) which Austen's narrative mocks but which it needs to achieve narratibility. The discussion included in this collection of the ways in which Austen brings *Emma* to a conclusion by suppressing the narratable is taken from the second part of the chapter, subtitled 'Good Riddance', and is preceded by close readings of how the mechanics of closure work in *Sense and Sensibility* and *Mansfield Park*. All quotations in the essay are from *The Novels of Jane Austen*, ed. R. W. Chapman, 5 vols (London: Oxford University Press, 1932–4). Ed.]

1. René Girard, *La Violence et le sacré* (Paris, 1972).

2. Søren Kierkegaard, *Repetition: An Essay in Experimental Psychology*, trans. Walter Lowrie (New York, 1964), p. 115.

5

'Emma' as Charade and the Education of the Reader

J. M. Q. DAVIES

As Jane Austen's novels do not, like Sterne's or Fielding's, call attention to their own artifice, so that the dominant tendency is to class her with the self-effacing novelists of the later nineteenth century like Flaubert and Henry James, one might legitimately infer that her ideal reader would be closer to the passive, receptive model invoked by Georges Poulet than to the active, creative participant John Preston, Wolfgang Iser and others have shown to be implied in some of the monuments of eighteenth-century fiction.[1] But as Q. D. Leavis perceived, Jane Austen always seems to be 'writing with a side glance' at her readers, aware of 'a critical audience liable to pounce'.[2] And in a letter to her sister Cassandra she herself observed that 'I do not write for such dull elves/As have not a great deal of ingenuity themselves'.[3] All her novels are profoundly concerned with the education of her readers, particularly the young female readers of her time, but nowhere does she make more strenuous demands upon their ingenuity than in *Emma*. Indeed though the rhetorical strategies she developed to involve and mystify her readers in this novel are very different from Sterne's, *Emma* in its playfulness is her most Shandean work and shows her too, for different reasons, quite as concerned to 'do all that lies in my power to keep [their] imagination as busy as my own'.[4] Alistair M. Duckworth has argued persuasively that the charades, conundrums and acrostics in *Emma* occur with sufficient frequency to suggest that they were consciously intended as a structuring device.[5] But to view them as he does in an essentially negative light, as emblems of the dubious and socially disruptive games engaged in by Emma and Frank Churchill, seems less than satisfactory because it ignores precisely this playful element in Jane Austen's own attitude toward the reader. The purpose of this essay is to suggest that the function of the charades is in part rhetorical, and that they provide the key to, and models in miniature for, the relationship between text and reader Jane Austen intended to establish.

The obvious limitation of analogies between *Emma* and gothic fiction or the detective story is that these forms characteristically withhold the key to the mysteries they present until the very end, whereas Jane Austen furnishes enough information for the active, critical reader to perceive the true state of affairs as the story unfolds, and in this respect the novel resembles the charade more closely. Though in practice of course individual readers will penetrate the mystery and perceive the ironies at different points. The narrative principle involved has been succinctly described by Wayne C. Booth, who writes that 'whatever steps are taken to mystify inevitably decrease the dramatic irony, and, whenever dramatic irony is increased by telling the reader secrets the characters have not yet suspected, mystery is inevitably destroyed. ... And we all find that on second reading we discover new intensities of dramatic irony resulting from complete loss of mystery.'[6] Two of the mental operations demanded by such plots are guessing and judging, which in *Emma* are closely associated with imagination and reason and thus with the novel's dialogical relation to Romanticism, and in more abstract form they are also the principles involved in solving charades. They are polarised in the very first chapter, when Mr Knightley responds to Emma's claim to have made a match between the Westons with 'you made a lucky guess', and concludes sententiously that 'a straight-forward, open-hearted man, like Weston, and a rational unaffected woman, like Miss Taylor, may be safely left to manage their own concerns' (p. 44). And subsequently guessing and judging recur as binary terms with the frequency of a leitmotif throughout the novel.

These points of congruence raise the question of whether Jane Austen consciously thought of *Emma* as a sort of extended charade, designed to strengthen young readers' powers of judgment in the way often claimed by those compiling collections of conundrums and charades, and reflected in the increasing adaptation of these forms to a variety of educational purposes.[7] In view of the irony with which

the whole subject of charades is introduced in chapter 9, this seems at
first unlikely:

> It was much easier to chat than to study; much pleasanter [Emma
> found] to let her imagination range and work at Harriet's fortune,
> than to be labouring to enlarge her comprehension or exercise it on
> sober facts; and the only literary pursuit which engaged Harriet at
> present, the only mental provision she was making for the evening of
> life, was the collecting and transcribing all the riddles of every sort that
> she could meet with. ...
> In this age of literature, such collections on a very grand scale are
> not uncommon.
>
> (p. 95)

But the amusing scene that follows, where Emma and Harriet puzzle
over Mr Elton's poem, makes it clear that it is the substitution of
charades for more serious reading rather than the qualities necessary
for solving them that is the object of Jane Austen's satire in this
passage. Harriet guesses wildly 'in all the confusion of hope and
dulness' (p. 97), whereas Emma, who Mr Knightley has earlier remarked had at the age of ten been 'able to answer questions which
puzzled her sister at seventeen' (p. 66), solves the riddle itself at once
and explains it point by point to Harriet. When however it comes to
assessing the 'sober facts' of the situation, Emma is as comically inept
as Harriet, urging her to 'receive it on my judgment' (p. 100) that Mr
Elton's 'court-ship' charade was meant for her. Evidently therefore
there are important differences between solving charades and coping
judiciously with life. And Jane Austen deftly hints at the reason for
Emma's blindness by twice repeating the first line of David Garrick's
charade, which Mr Woodhouse struggles to remember and which is
also appropriate to Mr Elton's imminent disappointment and light-
ning courtship of Augusta:

> Kitty, a fair but frozen maid,
>   Kindled a flame I yet deplore,
> The hood-wink'd boy I called to aid,
> Though of his near approach afraid,
>   So fatal to my suit before.
>
> (p. 104)[8]

Life's difficulties are more complex than the difficulties posed by
conundrums and charades, and require more experience and knowledge of the human heart than the fair but as yet still frozen Emma
possesses. But to Jane Austen's empirical temperament the same

principles of reasoning and judgment based on attention to the sober facts are involved in understanding both.

The key to the relationship of the charades to the artifices of the novel as a whole, and part of the evidence that as in *Northanger Abbey* Jane Austen was again consciously using a minor genre experimentally, comes a little later in this crucial ninth chapter, and characteristically it is unobtrusively presented. When Emma remarks to Harriet that Mr Elton's poem 'is a sort of prologue to the play, a motto to the chapter; and will be soon followed by matter-of-fact prose' (p. 100), she means that it must herald more substantial signs of Mr Elton's regard. But coming after the earlier reference to the charade as a literary form, these metaphors also invite readers to consider the appropriateness of the vicar's charade on courtship as a motto both to the chapter and to the 'matter-of-fact prose' novel they are reading. This interpretation might seem fanciful if the idea of the charade as prologue to a play were not followed immediately by an analogy between the action of the novel and a play:

> There does seem to be something in the air of Hartfield [Emma muses] which gives love exactly the right direction, and sends it into the very channel where it ought to flow.
>
> The course of true love never did run smooth —
>
> A Hartfield edition of Shakespeare would have a long note on that passage.
>
> (p. 100)

Since the line that Emma quotes has the proverbial quality of a motto, and *A Midsummer Night's Dream* is itself a play involving courtship, taken together Emma's literary analogies seem designed to set the active reader speculating as to possible relationships between charade, play and novel. And Shakespeare's maxim, which appears so appropriate as a motto to the novel itself on second reading, also functions as a warning to those avid consumers of romances that Jane Austen delighted in satirising, that the lovers may not pair off quite as Emma forecasts.

Coming at a point in the novel where the reader's curiosity has been thoroughly aroused by Emma's own 'genius for foretelling and guessing' (p. 67) then, the rhetorical purpose of chapter 9, and particularly of these analogies, is, I suggest, to tease readers into the realisation that they too are participating in a sophisticated fictional game. It is a game in which the charade on courtship, the entire Elton episode and the main Jane Fairfax–Frank Churchill mystery are related rather like a set of Chinese boxes, each confronting the reader with successively more complex puzzles. And Emma's explanation of the charade to Harriet is paralleled by her self-scrutiny after Mr Elton's confession, and by Mr Knightley's appraisal of Frank Churchill's letter at the end. Despite the delightful levity of tone moreover, it is a serious game, conducted in the conviction Jane Austen shared with Rousseau that each young reader must learn to judge and reason for him- or herself.[9] And the extent to which he passively takes Emma's point of view in his interpretation of events is a measure of his own deficiencies of reasoning and judgment. It is also a rigorous game, and one in which Susan Greenstein's recent insistence that people normally respond to characters in fiction as if they were real is highly pertinent.[10] And as the reader progresses from simple charade solving to disentangling the complexities of life that are mirrored in the novel as charade, he, like Emma herself, is being weaned away from the protected world of children's games into the adult world. Emma's later reference to Jane as 'a riddle, quite a riddle' (p. 286), the anagrams at Hartfield where Mr Knightley begins to suspect Frank of using a child's game 'to conceal a deeper game' (p. 344) and the conundrum at Box Hill not only help hold the novel together structurally therefore, but also serve the rhetorical function of reminding the reader that he is engaged in a similar activity.

The most obvious obstacle to the reader's arriving at the sober facts, as Wayne Booth recognised, is the way in which events are largely presented from Emma's point of view.[11] Emma, as Harriet discovers to her cost, is not only a charming, witty and intelligent, but a very persuasive personality. She has always been able to get the better of her governess, and she tends to sway the passive or unwary reader too. And even after she has been exposed as fallible, her remorse and the personal honesty of her self-appraisals involuntarily restore the reader's confidence in her. But quite as taxing on the reader's powers of judgment and discrimination are the various discussion sequences, because the arguments on both sides are always made to sound so plausible. In chapter 5, for instance, Mr Knightley undoubtedly presents a strong case against Emma's friendship with Harriet. But he does so with ill-humour as he himself admits, and despite his appreciation of Emma's beauty and interest in her welfare, at this stage in the novel he may well appear censorious. And later on in fact he is willing to concede that Emma has done Harriet some good. Mrs Weston, whom the narrator has earlier described as 'a well-judging and truly admirable woman' (p. 47), is perhaps less forceful, but as Emma's former governess her defence of the friendship and confidence in Emma's good sense carry weight. And when she says, 'Mr Knightley, I shall not allow you to be a fair judge in this case. You who are so much used to live alone, that you do not know the value of a companion; and perhaps no man can be a judge of the comfort a woman feels in the society of one of her own sex, after being used to it all her life' (p. 65) – Jane Austen's young female readers would doubtless have agreed.

Similarly in chapter 18, where Mr Knightley comments on Frank's failure to appear, his strong words of censure seem well founded. But Emma too is right when she says to him that 'you are the worst judge in the world, Mr Knightley, of the difficulties of dependence' (p. 163). She is also right that 'it is very unfair to judge of any body's conduct, without an intimate knowledge of their situation' (p. 164), even though she will almost immediately neglect this principle herself in speculating about Jane. By the end of their heated discussion Emma's verdict that 'we are both prejudiced; you against, I for him' (p. 164) seems incontestable, but the reader has been given a good deal to think about. And it is important to notice how the jealousy that colours Mr Knightley's judgment, like the ill-temper that mars his equally 'penetrating' (p. 154) brother, not only makes for greater realism but is vital to the rhetorical game Jane Austen is playing with the reader. An ideal figure such as Grandison, or a totally reliable reflector would have undermined the need for independent judgment.

The strategy deployed to tease the reader into thought in the Elton sequence and the main Frank Churchill–Jane Fairfax mystery is essentially the same. Both involve one or more initial hints or cautions, followed by playful obfuscation, ambiguity and artfully placed false clues, which are then resolved in a comic peripetia and didactic anagnoresis. With the Elton episode the true situation is relatively easy to predict, since Mr Elton is evidently courting either Harriet or Emma. Mr Knightley's warning that 'Elton may talk sentimentally, but he will act rationally' (p. 92) is followed by the delightful ambiguity of the portrait-sketching episode and the charades. But then Mr Elton's failure to declare himself to Harriet at the vicarage, his reluctance to forego dinner at the Coleses for her sake when she falls ill, and a broad hint to Emma from her brother-in-law, make it clear to everyone but her that she is the woman being courted. The whole sequence occupies a position in relation to the main action analogous to the Sotherton episode in *Mansfield Park*. There Edmund with Fanny on one arm and Mary Crawford on the other, remarking that Mary does not tax his strength as had a drunken Oxford companion, is in the position of Hercules at the crossroads between Virtue and Vice, and his deviation from the 'great path' (p. 122) with Mary and eventual return to Fanny epitomises in miniature the course he is to take in the novel as a whole.[12] But where the Sotherton episode exists in a fictive world set apart behind a proscenium arch in the nineteenth-century manner, the Elton sequence initiates the reader into a game of Shandean sophistication.

The main action as charade is of course more complicated, and its successful solution on first reading is in practice to some degree contingent on the reader's having perceived the rules of the game established in the Elton sequence. Jane Fairfax arrives before Frank, and the reader's impulse to accept Emma's speculations about her is immediately moderated by the narrator's comments on her 'decided superiority both in beauty and acquirements' (p. 178), her understanding, her fortitude and her judiciousness. The section ends on a note, albeit a playfully ambivalent note, of caution to the reader:

> With regard to her not accompanying them to Ireland, her account to her aunt contained nothing but truth, though there might have been some truths not told.
>
> (p. 179)

Frank's own arrival has been preceded by Mr Knightley's disapprobation, and the fact that it is two months late and one day early is itself a comment on his reliability. But though his manners are as ingratiating as Mr Elton's had been, Emma quickly absolves him of insincerity. And on the second morning – 'time enough to form a reasonable judgment' the narrator observes ironically – she 'decide[s] ... that he had not been acting a part, or making a parade of insincere professions; and that Mr Knightley certainly had not done him justice' (pp. 208–9). If the reader is inclined to be swayed, he is almost immediately provided with another hint when Frank evades Emma's question about how well he had known Jane at Weymouth, and then tries to conceal the evasion, prompting Emma to remark: 'Upon my word! you answer as discreetly as she could do herself. But her account of everything leaves so much to be guessed ...' (p. 212). Whereupon the difference between guessing and judging is once again impressed upon the reader in the ensuing conversation, where Emma indulges in a good deal of speculation about Jane and Mr

Dixon, and Frank defers to her judgment on Jane's character and musical attainments.

All these cautionary notes are sounded well before the delightful scene of comic obfuscation, where Emma and Frank play a game of speculation as it were, as to who has sent Jane the piano. Here Emma plays the active part initially, the part of 'wit' in Elder Olson's terminology, but then as Frank warms to the possibilities of the game he takes on the role of wit and she unwittingly becomes his 'butt'.[13] And his attentions to her, of course supported by the Weston's hopes for such a match, create one of the chief obstacles to the passive reader's arriving at the facts. Another is Mr Knightley's regard for Jane, a very effective false clue rendered all the more probable by Mrs Weston's speculations, against which however Emma's 'every feeling revolts' (p. 233). And smaller clues like Frank's trip to London for a haircut are also playfully ambivalent. So that while Frank may feel, as he says in parting, that Emma 'can hardly be without suspicion' (p. 265), for the reader *not* to agree with Emma that 'he had *almost* told her that he loved her' (p. 266) requires penetration and judgment indeed.

After Frank's departure Jane is foregrounded rather more, and though Emma finds her a riddle her conduct provides several clues which are ambiguous only if the reader has accepted Emma's speculations about her – her insistence on collecting her own mail, her decision to postpone taking a position as governess and her declining Mrs Dixon's invitation to Ireland, hardly the action of a jealous wife. But the denouement is delayed by a further round of Shakespearean comedic confusion, which arises out of Mr Knightley's rescuing Harriet from Mr Elton's snub at the ball and Frank's rescuing her from the gypsies. The latter episode rouses the Romantic 'imaginist' (p. 331) in Emma, as Mr Dixon's rescuing Jane while sailing had done earlier, and again she actively interferes in Harriet's life, only to find herself the butt of her own contrivance, 'in love, and in some doubt of a return' (p. 69).

The anagram episode where Mr Weston denies having written to Frank about Mr Perry's carriage, and Frank signals 'blunder' (p. 344) to Jane, then 'Dixon' (p. 345) to Emma to cover his tracks, marks the point where most readers will be able to predict the novel's resolution. For it convinces Mr Knightley that he had not been committing 'any of Emma's errors of imagination' (p. 340) in his 'suspicion of there being something of private liking, of private understanding even, between Frank Churchill and Jane' (p. 341). And with Emma's confident rejection of the idea when he tries to warn her –

as his brother had earlier warned her about Mr Elton – even on first reading mystery begins to give way to irony. Mr Knightley's quite explicit comparison of word-games to the double game that Frank is playing also introduces a note of moral censure, not of children's educational games *per se* but of trifling with people's feelings. The dangers of such trifling are dramatised in the Box Hill episode, where mystification and irony are marvellously blended, and where Mr Weston's conundrum is used to comment on Emma's moral deficiencies, as Garrick's charade had shed light on her psychology. The irony of his associating Emma's name with perfection, coming immediately after her witty but unkind remark to Miss Bates, is underscored by Mr Knightley's caustic remark that '*Perfection* should not have come quite so soon' (p. 365).[14] Though here too conundrums and acrostics are not seen as in themselves reprehensible activities so much, as part of the normal social round like Mr Woodhouse's quadrille and backgammon. But if Emma's rudeness distances the reader from her further, it also serves to divert his or her attention away from the effect her flirtation with Frank is having on Jane and Mr Knightley. For those who have already filled in most of the intertextual gaps, however, the clues are immediately to hand in the ensuing two chapters, where Jane accepts the position Mrs Elton has procured for her, Frank departs for Richmond, and Mr Knightley goes off to stay with his brother in London.

After the crisis has been averted and the tables turned by Mrs Churchill's death, the Shandean fun is kept up to the very last, but largely at the expense of Emma rather than the reader. When she is summoned urgently by Mrs Weston, for instance, and begins to imagine 'Half a dozen natural children, perhaps – and poor Frank cut off!' (p. 385), few readers will overlook the irony. And fewer still will be as surprised as Emma to discover that Frank has been less than frank and she 'completely duped' (p. 390). One of the most delightfully ironic final moments, which balances the comic confusion of the two earlier proposal scenes, occurs when Emma misinterprets Mr Knightley's first advance as an attempt to confess his love for Harriet. And all this helps leaven the serious moral tone of the finale. Frank's confessional letter, like Emma's explanation of the charade to Harriet, confronts readers with their own deficiencies of judgment, and Mr Knightley's appraisal of Frank's conduct underlines the seriousness of such deficiencies. And when he sums up the moral to be drawn from the entire intrigue he is clearly acting as the author's spokesman: 'Mystery; Finesse – how they pervert the understanding! My Emma, does not every thing serve to prove more and more the beauty of truth and sincerity in all our dealings with each other?' (p. 430). For Duckworth, Jane Austen's use of the charades in *Emma* confronts us with 'the paradox of a beloved family recreation becoming an aesthetic expression of dubious social behaviour'.[15] To my mind the paradox is the paradox of high comedy and resides in her use of essentially playful rhetorical strategies, modelled in part on the charades, for the serious purpose not only of warning against such 'dangerous game[s]' (p. 430) and the unrestrained use of the imagination, but of weaning readers from the very errors they are reading of.

To the student of literature, as distinct from the linguist or semiotician, not all texts are fruitful subjects for reader-response analysis, but *Emma* seems genuinely so. And this surely is because of its unique combination of rhetorical daring in the tradition of the great eighteenth-century innovators, and narrative discretion in the later nineteenth-century mode. Iser does not discuss Jane Austen's masterpiece in his pioneering study, but it would be hard to find a more apt description of its rhetorical effect than his comment on *Vanity Fair*, where he feels that 'the key word for the reader is "discover", and the narrator continually prods him along the road to discovery, laying a trail of clues for him to follow'.[16] Stanley Fish has made the point that it is legitimate to analyse an effect which the author may have been unconscious of, and Henry James believed that 'Jane Austen . . . leaves us hardly more curious of her process . . . than the brown thrush who tells his story from the garden bough'.[17] But the internal evidence that she intended the charades in *Emma* to provide a clue to how it should be read seems to me substantial and tends to endorse the current consensus that she was indeed, in A. Walton Litz's words, 'a supremely conscious artist'.[18] If so, their function is more comprehensive than the acting charades in *Jane Eyre*, or the statue scene from *Daniel Deronda*, which are essentially isolated mimetic episodes illuminating the respective heroine's plight and character. To gauge how far these strategies are successful would require controlled experiments, such as those conducted by I. A. Richards or Norman Holland, for every generation.[19] It would be interesting to test the effect of simulating the likely response of Jane Austen's charade-loving readers with a group of contemporary undergraduates by studying the charade as a minor genre immediately before introducing *Emma*.

From *Philological Quarterly*, 65 (1986), 231–42.

NOTES

[Davies is grouped together with the other poststructuralist critics in this collection because, in discussing the word games in *Emma*, he places his emphasis on the ways in which language works, as Litvak (essay 6) does, rather than, as Duckworth (essay 2) does, on what it means. His particular interest in reading and writing is one that is shared by Litvak and Armstrong (essay 9) (also by Miller in parts of his analysis of *Emma* which precede the material reprinted here). However, his version of reader-response criticism is, of all the poststructuralist approaches included in this collection, the most wedded to traditional critical practice because it leans so heavily on the notion of authorial intention. Ed.]

1. Georges Poulet, 'Criticism and the Experience of Interiority', in Jane P. Tompkins (ed.), *Reader Response Criticism* (Baltimore, 1980), pp. 41–9; John Preston, *The Created Self* (London, 1970), pp. 1–7; Wolfgang Iser, *The Implied Reader* (Baltimore, 1974), pp. xi–xiv; Howard Anderson, '*Tristram Shandy* and the Reader's Imagination', *PMLA*, 86 (1971), 966–72. For a full annotated bibliography of reader-response criticism see Jane Tompkins (above), pp. 223–73. Page references bracketed within the text in this essay are to the standard Penguin editions of Jane Austen's novels.

2. Q. D. Leavis, 'A Critical Theory of Jane Austen's Writings I', in F. R. Leavis (ed.), *A Selection from 'Scrutiny'* (Cambridge, 1968), 2:8.

3. R. W. Chapman (ed.), *Jane Austen's Letters to her Sister Cassandra and Others* (London, 1952), p. 298.

4. Laurence Sterne, *Tristram Shandy* (New York: Random House, 1950), p. 110. Jane Austen's allusions to Sterne imply an intimate familiarity with his work. See *Mansfield Park*, pp. 126, 460 and *Jane Austen's Letters*, p. 140.

5. Alistair M. Duckworth, '"Spillikins, paper ships, riddles, conundrums, and cards"; Games in Jane Austen's life and fiction', in John Halperin (ed.), *Jane Austen: Bicentenary Essays* (Cambridge, 1975), pp. 179–97.

6. Wayne C. Booth, *The Rhetoric of Fiction* (Chicago, 1961), p. 255.

7. The 'Preface on the Antiquity of Riddles', to *Riddles, Charades, and Conundrums* (London, 1822), pp. iii–vi for instance makes the connection between allegory and riddles, and emphasises their utility as they have 'a tendency to teach the mind to compare and judge'. *Enigmas and Charades* (London, 1823) has a preface 'illustrative of the advantages derivable by the mind of youth', in which the author condemns 'quick, random guessing' and insists that 'the enigma ought to engage as close attention and circumspection on a young mind as any other species of reading or of problems ...' (p. v). And similar claims are reiterated in a wide variety of such publications, from *Enigmas, Historical and*

Geographical (London, 1839) to *The Riddler's Journal and Fireside Companion* (London, 1869), throughout the nineteenth century as the form diversifies.

8. The full text of Garrick's charade is given in Chapman's edition of *Emma* in *The Novels of Jane Austen* (London: Oxford University Press, 1933), 4: 489–90.

9. See Henri Rousseau, *Emile*, trans. B. Foxley (London: Dent, 1911), 131–4.

10. Susan Greenstein, '"Dear Reader, Dear Friend": Richardson's Readers and the Social Response to Character', *College English*, 41 (1980), 524–34.

11. Wayne C. Booth, *The Rhetoric of Fiction* (Chicago, 1961), pp. 242–66.

12. In his introduction to the Penguin edition of *Mansfield Park* (Harmondsworth, 1966), pp. 25ff, Tony Tanner also draws attention to the way in which Maria's escape round the iron gates into the wider freedom of the park with Henry Crawford emblematically foreshadows her adulterous affair with him.

13. Elder Olson, *The Theory of Comedy* (Bloomingdale, 1968), pp. 21–2, 52ff.

14. See Mark Loveridge, 'Francis Hutcheson and Mr Weston's Conundrum in *Emma*', *Notes and Queries*, 228 (1983), 214–16.

15. Alistair Duckworth, '"Spillikins, paper ships, riddles, conundrums, and cards": Games in Jane Austen's life and fiction', in John Halperin (ed.), *Jane Austen* (Cambridge, 1975), p. 293.

16. Wolfgang Iser, *The Implied Reader* (Baltimore, 1974), p. 111.

17. Stanley Fish, 'Literature in the Reader: Affective Stylistics', in Jane Tompkins, *Reader Response Criticism* (Baltimore, 1980), p. 89. James's remark is quoted in Douglas Bush, *Jane Austen* (London, 1975), p. 30.

18. A. Walton Litz, *Jane Austen: A Study in her Artistic Development* (New York, 1965), p. 3.

19. I. A. Richards, *Practical Criticism: A Study in Literary Judgement* (New York, 1935); Norman N. Holland, *5 Reader's Reading* (New Haven, 1975).

6

Reading Characters: Self, Society, and Text in 'Emma'

JOSEPH LITVAK

In *The Madwoman in the Attic*, Sandra M. Gilbert and Susan Gubar describe the fate of the Austenian heroine as a 'fall into literacy'. To fall into literacy is to 'fall from authority into the acceptance of one's status as a mere character', to be at once silenced and confined – in the words of one chapter title, to be 'Shut Up in Prose'.[1] Yet Gilbert and Gubar show how heroines like Elizabeth Bennet, Emma Woodhouse, and Anne Elliot subvert the patriarchal structures in which they are inscribed, imaging Austen's own quiet subversion of the repressive ideology her novels seem to endorse. In reclaiming authority, both Austen and these characters assert their 'irrepressible interiority' and their 'belief in female subjectivity'.

Austen's novels are indeed subtly subversive, but this subversion does not take place in the name of interiority, subjectivity, or even authority, if authority means nothing more than 'freedom, autonomy, and strength'. These virtues look surprisingly like those of the phallic pen to which Gilbert and Gubar, asking 'with what organ can females generate texts?',[1] seek a feminist alternative. Moreover, despite the acuity of their individual analyses, Gilbert and Gubar force themselves into the peculiar position of implying that authorship – a role superior to that of the 'mere character' – involves a redemption from 'literacy', that the ideal author is somehow external to her text, beyond or above textuality. Significantly, this attitude places them in the unlikely company of certain male critics whose

89

mistrust of 'literacy', or literariness, derives from an ideology with which feminism would seem to have little in common.

In an almost canonical gesture, critics of *Emma* stigmatise linguistic playfulness, or merely a fondness for the written word, as a threat to moral well-being. Marvin Mudrick typifies this stance, indicting in both the novel and its heroine – 'whom', Austen predicted 'no one but myself will much like'[2] – what he calls the 'triumph of surface', where the scandal of 'wit adrift from feeling' finds its objective correlative in Emma's latent lesbianism.[3] Admittedly, Gilbert and Gubar differ from Austen's male critics in their reasons for wanting to separate self and text. Whereas the latter equate literariness with frivolity and narcissism, the former view it as an effect of living in the 'tight place' to which women are condemned.[4] Pushed dangerously close to the contaminating world of signs, the Austenian heroine, like Austen herself, must exercise extraordinary ingenuity to keep her autonomous selfhood intact. Both the feminist critics and the conservatives, however, despite their manifest political differences, subscribe to the ideology of character implicit in Malcolm Bradbury's observation that *Emma* persuades us 'to see the full human being as full, fine, morally serious, totally responsible, entirely involved, and to consider every human action as a crucial committing act of self-definition'.[5]

As. D. A. Miller has noted, Austen's quiet authority tends to intimidate even her shrewdest readers.[6] Yet when characters in her work suggest not the plenitude invoked by Bradbury but, rather, the artifice and materiality of *written* characters, moralism encounters significant obstacles. To locate these linguistic residues, these scandals of 'literacy', is to identify traces of Austen's own rebellion against an overly reassuring moral ideology, traces that intimate a subversiveness far more interesting than that imagined by Gilbert and Gubar.[7]

A brief passage from *Mansfield Park* (1814) will serve as a prelude to the tensions at work in *Emma* (1816) and as proof that, even in what looks like her most authoritarian novel, Austen can disrupt her own orthodoxy. The description concerns Fanny Price's attempt, late in the novel, to introduce her sister to the pleasures of reading.

> . . . after a few days, the remembrance of her books grew so potent and stimulative, that Fanny found it impossible not to try for books again. There were none in her father's house; but wealth is luxurious and daring – and some of hers found its way to a circulating library. She became a subscriber – amazed at being any thing *in propria persona,*

amazed at her own doings in every way; to be a renter, a chuser of books! And to be having any one's improvement in view of her choice! But so it was. Susan had read nothing, and Fanny longed to give her a share in her own first pleasures, and inspire a taste for the biography and poetry which she delighted in herself.

(p. 398)

The exultant tone of Austen's *style indirect libre* imitates Fanny's joy on realising herself as what Bradbury calls a 'full human being'. Yet the giddiness of the passage may also betoken Austen's response to an inconspicuous but 'potent and stimulative' contradiction. For the embarrassing fact that the passage just barely conceals is that Fanny comes into her own only by entering a system of exchange, a circulating library. To be 'any thing *in propria persona*', Fanny must spend her wealth, dispersing it into a larger economy; to consolidate her personhood, she has to insert herself into a constantly fluctuating literary structure. It is precisely her fall into 'literacy', or literariness, that establishes Fanny's selfhood.

This passage merits attention not because it speaks of reading and writing: these themes occur often enough – and often innocently – in Austen's novels. Its interest, rather, lies in the way its literary references hint at some more than merely thematic literariness, some nagging but unspecifiable linguistic opacity in the novel itself. By collapsing the distance, moreover, between self and text – between a saving inwardness and a dangerously verbal sociability – the passage confounds categories that the novel posits elsewhere as opposites.

In *Emma*, this unsettling of polarities finds its wittiest advocate in the heroine herself, who, in a characteristic move, complains that Mr Knightley, the novel's 'normative and exemplary figure',[8] finds their respective judgments 'not near enough to give me a chance of being right, if we think differently' (p. 99). Yet Emma's attempt to substitute difference for opposition is more than just a clever piece of sophistry. Emma is frequently 'wrong' as she is here, but perhaps she is 'right' to question the absoluteness with which Knightley does in fact view the distinction between them. Perhaps, moreover, her 'wrongness' is often closer to being 'right' – that is, to yielding knowledge of the fictions that sustain social existence – than Knightley and his scholarly advocates will admit. Patriarchal criticism of *Emma*, of course, takes Knightley's side, portraying the narrative as a conflict in which 'right' seeks to appropriate 'wrong' and to recast it (her) in its (his) own image. It is possible, however, to pursue an apparently perverse but more critically productive tactic: we can give

Emma some respect and construe the conflict dialectically, treating it less as an opposition and more as a difference.

We might try, then, to read the novel as a contest between Emma and Knightley, a contest between two equally compelling interpretations of the self – especially the female self – and society. Knightley states his views succinctly when he objects to Emma's adoption of Harriet Smith as her protégée: 'I am much mistaken if Emma's doctrines give any strength of mind, or tend at all to make a girl adapt herself rationally to the varieties of her situation in life. – They only give a little polish' (p. 39). Despite the stark opposition that Knightley's terms suggest, the difference between the two implicit pedagogies cannot be simplified as the difference between a serious and a playful education or between a moral and an aesthetic one. For if Knightley's 'strength of mind' borders on the conformist virtue of 'adaptability', Emma's 'polish', while it signals a politics of superficiality, is by no means superficial.

Whenever characters in *Emma* seem merely to be playing with words, the stakes are in fact much higher. One particularly instructive episode revolves around 'puzzles', anagrams that the contestants must unscramble. Here the chief competitors are not Knightley and Emma but Knightley and Frank Churchill, whose recalcitrance, as we will see, Emma refines. Knightley dislikes Frank Churchill, not only because the younger man seems to be a rival for Emma's affections but also because Frank presumes to 'read every body's character' (p. 150). Having just let slip a possible clue to his involvement with Jane Fairfax, and regretting his carelessness, Frank uses the word game as a pretext for apology:

> Frank Churchill placed a word before Miss Fairfax. She gave a slight glance around the table, and applied herself to it. Frank was next to Emma, Jane opposite to them – and Mr. Knightley so placed as to see them all; and it was his object to see as much as he could, with as little apparent observation. The word was discovered and with a faint smile pushed away.
>
> (pp. 347–8)

As Knightley's stance here shows, his resentment of Frank stems in part from his fear that Frank may usurp the role of master reader: it is Knightley alone who shall reserve the right 'to read every body's character', to be 'so placed as to see them all'. Knightley's motives here are typical: if *Emma*, as many critics have noted, is a detective novel, then Knightley, even more than Emma herself, aspires to the role of chief detective. For while Emma is content to fantasise about various romantic scenarios involving Frank Churchill, Knightley will not rest until he has been into the heart of the mystery surrounding Frank and Jane. For Knightley, reading fosters 'strength of mind', but it is also a mode of surveillance.

By acting *un*interested, Knightley would appear *dis*interested as well. But his surreptitious behaviour undermines the notion of disinterested reading. Seeing without appearing to observe, reading without appearing to read, Knightley at once admits and suppresses this duplicity. Later in the novel, the fervour with which he praises the 'disinterestedness' of Jane's love for Frank (p. 428), when in fact her own pecuniary and perhaps erotic interest in that relationship seems considerable, betrays Knightley's extraordinary interest in disinterestedness, a virtue he is apt to see even where it does not exist.[9] Earlier in the novel, the vehemence with which he denounces Frank, whom he does not even know yet, strikes Emma as 'unworthy the real liberality of mind which she was always used to acknowledge in him' (p. 151). Of course, the most memorable illustration of Knightley's partiality is his comically nitpicking reading of Frank's long letter to Mrs Weston, a reading whose reductiveness Emma labours to mitigate. However 'impressive and admirable' Knightley may be,[10] he is hardly an innocent interpreter.[11]

Knightley continues his detective work, recalling the incriminating remark that Frank has tried to explain away by recourse to an alleged 'dream':

> The word was *blunder*, and as Harriet exultingly proclaimed it, there was a blush on Jane's cheek which gave it a meaning not otherwise ostensible. Mr. Knightley connected it with the dream; but how it could all be, was beyond his comprehension. How the delicacy, the discretion of his favourite could have been so lain asleep! He feared there must be some decided involvement. Disingenuousness and double-dealing seemed to meet him at every turn. These letters were but the vehicle for gallantry and trick. It was a child's play, chosen to conceal a deeper game on Frank Churchill's part.
>
> (p. 348)

Joseph Wiesenfarth observes that the 'word "blunder" runs like a discord through the novel, indicating mistakes that are made in the games of words as well as in the more serious and dangerous games of matchmaking'.[12] The recurrence of the word points indeed to the centrality of misinterpretation and misbehaviour in this would-be bildungsroman. Yet the problems that a proper education – or at

least one overseen by Knightley – would corrct may be more fundamental than mere 'mistakes': the discord that runs through the novel
may signify a certain perverse malfunctioning that can be neither
corrected nor even regulated. For what disturbs Knightley here is
that his attempts at interpretive mastery of Frank Churchill's game
meet with resistance; he encounters not just the temporary unintelligibility of scrambled letters but the much greater recalcitrance of
'disingenuousness and double-dealing'. As we have seen, Knightley's
own posture partakes of a certain disingenuousness as well. Yet he
cannot accept Frank's 'puzzles' as more than just structurally puz-
zling. What should have been mere 'child's play' has turned out 'to
conceal a deeper game', and Knightley can tolerate only a socially
sanctioned and therefore superficial 'depth', only a legible illegibility.[13]
The social mechanism favoured by Knightley contains and neutral-
ises subjectivity by encoding it within a cultural alphabet, so that one
may read character by reading the characters, or letters, that a
character forms.

   The first sign of malfunctioning appears when Jane's blush gives
the word *blunder* a 'meaning', but one 'not otherwise ostensible'.
Thus finding the affair 'beyond his comprehension', Knightley experiences the same blockage that awaits the reader who approaches
Jane Austen's novels unprepared for their frequent literariness, expecting only the easeful wisdom of 'gentle Jane'. Frank's 'deeper
game' defies Knightley's authority, refusing to confirm the older man
as the paternal or patriarchical supervisor of children at play. For
such, in Knightley's view, is the purpose of games. Since they pre-
suppose rules, they emblematise the governability of society. To the
extent that they include a moment of limited opacity, games permit
the illusion that each player's individual self possesses a unique
interiority. To the extent that they subordinate this individuality to
an ultimately decipherable code, games ensure the transparency
of the self. The real winner, thus, is the ideology of institutional
control – or what Knightley will refer to euphemistically as the
'beauty of truth and sincerity in all our dealings with each other'
(p. 446).

   At least in this round, however, that ideology loses: the most that
Knightley can infer is 'some decided involvement', probably of Frank
Churchill with Jane Fairfax. Frank would appear triumphant for the
time being despite his blunder, because he has rewritten the rules of
the game so that the game itself is no longer the same. To assume, as
Knightley does, that 'these letters were but the vehicle for gallantry

and trick' is not to understand the new game but, rather, to concede its mystery.

Vehicles and conveyance loom large in the next problematic passage as well. In one of her rare utterances, the shadowy Jane Fairfax, talking with Knightley's brother, delivers a surprisingly impassioned hymn to the postal service:

> 'The post office is a wonderful establishment' said she – 'The regularity and dispatch of it! If one thinks of all that it has to do, and all that it does so well, it is really astonishing!'
> 'It is certainly very well regulated.'
> 'So seldom that any negligence or blunder appears! So seldom that a letter, among the thousands that are constantly passing about the kingdom, is even carried wrong – and not one in a million, I suppose, actually lost! And when one considers the variety of hands, and of bad hands too, that are to be deciphered, it increases the wonder!'
>
> (p. 296)

Certain 'literary' institutions seem to inspire a significant rhetorical excess in Austen's novels: Jane's praise of the post office is as suspiciously feverish as Fanny's delight in belonging to the library. Offering her own version of the Lacanian dictum that 'a letter always arrives at its destination', Jane may very well be denying her fear that letters do not always arrive where and when they should. If Lacan's formulation insists on the inevitability of a certain system or structure, then Jane's hyperbolic encomium both represses and reveals grave doubts about the inevitability of any system or structure whatsoever. We will learn, of course, that Jane is concerned about the 'regularity' of her clandestine correspondence with Frank Churchill and that, indeed, their engagement is broken off as a result of a serious blunder on the part not of the post office but of Frank himself: he simply forgets to mail an all-important letter. Yet the postal service is merely a synecdoche for the much larger system of communication on which the novel centres – namely, the social text in which the characters keep construing and misconstruing one another – so that any anxiety about mail deliveries may be taken as an anxiety about the semiotic efficiency or governability of society as a whole.

Jane's desire, then, that blunders never appear – her need to assert that of all the letters 'constantly passing about the kingdom ... not one in a million [is] actually lost' – originates in the same ideology as does Knightley's impatience with Frank's 'deeper game'. Bad handwriting is to Jane what 'disinterestedness and double-dealing' are to

Knightley: both complicate the operation of 'deciphering', com-
promising any institution that would call itself 'very well regulated'.
Yet Jane has said not that blunders never appear, only that they
'seldom' appear. Even she can acknowledge the possibility of handwriting so bad, so shamefully illegible, that no strategy of deciphering could contain it. Should it 'spread', such handwriting could
eventually disrupt the entire system of coding and decoding, of
writing and reading – in short, of communication – by which a Mr
Knightley might define society.

But what would such handwriting look like? Insofar as it resisted
deciphering, it might be too cipher-bound to admit of interpretation.
What would it mean, though, to be cipher-bound, or even to be a
cipher? Paraphrasing a poem by Anne Finch, Gilbert and Gubar
write: '*all* females are "Cyphers" – nullities, vacancies – existing
merely and punningly to increase male "Numbers" (either poems or
persons) by pleasuring either men's bodies or their minds, their
penises or their pens'.[14] Bad or excessively 'ciphered' handwriting
would thus represent a sort of *degré zéro de l'écriture*, writing so
'ladylike' in its vacuousness that it would refuse to add up to anything like a meaning. It is tempting to view the devaluation of women
as ending up ironically subverting patriarchal arithmetic. Yet just
how would that subversion come about? For answers, we might turn
again to *Mansfield Park*, whose heroine, as Leo Bersani points out,
'almost is *not*'.[15] Fanny's aunt, Lady Bertram, may come even closer
to the conditions of nothingness: one of the other characters refers to
her as 'more of a cipher now' (p. 162) than when her husband, away
on business, is at home. That phrase typifies the sarcasm that Austen
reserves for particularly insipid characters, but it also suggests something more interesting. For how can anyone be more – or less – of a
cipher? Either one is a cipher or one is not. In replacing a definition
of the cipher as a mere zero with an understanding of ciphers as
quantities susceptible of increase and decrease, Austen reminds us of
the radical instability of the term. For ciphers are not just numbers
but figures as well, and the word *cipher* itself imitates the shiftiness of
verbal figures. Just as figures of speech mean something other than
themselves, so ciphers are figures both in the mathematical sense and
in the more elusive rhetorical sense: 'symbolic characters', according
to *Webster's New International Dictionary*, ciphers are letters as
well as numbers, but letters that call their own literality into question. No longer mere zeros, ciphers designate that species of 'bad
handwriting' known as figurative language, which, by exceeding the

literal, may prevent letters from arriving at their destinations.[16] Figurative language marks the blundering that threatens the orderly delivery of messages.

One such subversive slippage from mathematical exactness to rhetorical uncertainty takes up almost all of chapter 9 in the first volume of *Emma*, a chapter that has to do precisely with ciphers. We have seen Knightley criticise Emma's educational principles because 'They only give a little polish', but here we observe the decisive role of ciphers in transforming the curriculum of a finishing school into a politics of superficiality. A moralistic reading will assume that the chapter – not to mention the novel as a whole – has been written from the viewpoint of Mr Knightley, the 'custodian of Jane Austen's judgment'.[17] But a reading more sensitive to Austen's figures will discover elements that evade such deciphering. In the following passage, which describes the academic programme Emma has devised for Harriet, we may discern both authoritarian and subversive discourses:

> Her view of improving her little friend's mind, by a great deal of useful reading and conversation, had never yet led to more than a few first chapters, and the intention of going on tomorrow. It was much easier to chat than to study; much pleasanter to let her imagination range and work at Harriet's fortune, than to be labouring to enlarge her comprehension or exercise it on sober facts; and the only literary pursuit which engaged Harriet at present, the only mental provision she was making for the evening of life, was the collecting and transcribing all the riddles of every sort that she could meet with, into a thin quarto of hot-pressed paper, made up by her friend, and ornamented with cyphers and trophies.
>
> (p. 69)

Knightley has already mentioned Emma's long-standing propensity for drawing up lists of books to read, only to abandon her ambitious plans. 'I have done with expecting any course of steady reading from Emma', he announces, explaining that 'she will never submit to any thing requiring industry and patience, and a subjection of the fancy to the understanding' (p. 37). In acknowledging that Emma and Harriet can never get beyond 'a few first chapters', this later passage seems to confirm his opinion. It supports the numerous interpretations of *Emma* as a negative portrait of the artist, as an exorcism of the 'imaginist' (p. 335) or solipsist in Austen herself.[18] Indeed, the gently mocking description of Harriet's sole 'literary pursuit' seems, more seriously, to indict Emma, who would rather 'let her imagination range and work at Harriet's fortune', enmeshing her in flimsy little novels of sensibility, than develop in both her pupil and herself enough *Sitzfleisch* to follow her ambitious syllabus.

Emma is, admittedly, acting like a bad novelist. Yet the 'badness' of her 'novels' corresponds less to the immaturity and capriciousness of one who has not read enough than to the semiotic aberrance of someone with 'bad handwriting'. For though Emma's curriculum may not involve much reading, she and Harriet spend a great deal of time writing – specifically, 'collecting and transcribing all the riddles of every sort that [Harriet] could meet with, into a thin quarto of hot-pressed paper, made up by her friend, and ornamented with cyphers and trophies'. Here, of course, Knightley could find all the evidence he needs to convict Emma of pedagogical malpractice: not only does the copying of riddles seem like a stultifying waste of time; the very cover of the riddle book emblematises the meaninglessness of mere decoration. But, as we have suggested, while 'cyphers' may escape the stratagems of meaning, they are hardly without significance. We might remember Austen's 'merely' ornamental analogy for her own art – a 'little bit (two Inches wide) of Ivory'.[19] Interestingly enough, the 'cyphers' on Harriet's riddle book exist alongside 'trophies', pictures of prizes. Trophies imply victory – which in turn implies conflict – and relate etymologically to tropes. As we will see, this chapter stages a battle between figurative language and figuring out, between ciphers and deciphering, between Emma's deep superficiality and Knightley's superficial depth.

'Depth', here, signifies subversive complexity, not just 'strength of mind', which, as Knightley intimates, presupposes the ability to 'submit' and 'subject' oneself. Yet if the ciphers on the cover of the riddle book suggest the first kind of depth, they do so otherwise than by pointing to a plot below – and more politically serious than – what Gilbert and Gubar call 'Jane Austen's Cover Story'. For ciphers, as the dictionary reminds us, can be 'texts in secret writing', monograms of some systematically dissimulated referent – in short, riddles. Here one *can* judge a book by its cover: the ciphers on the cover of Harriet's book cover the ciphers inside, which turn out to represent not ultimate truth but merely more covering.

Now, such a conception of the relation between surface and depth may seem less than subversive. In fact, it might appear entirely compatible with Knightley's belief that because games permit illusions of depth they guarantee – in their function as 'child's play' – patriarchal control. How is it, then, that ciphers serve the anti-authoritarian cause? How, in Emma's hands, do they become figures of disruption? How does the play of surfaces in which they are implicated become deep in the subversive sense, rather than in either the authoritarian sense or even the sense that Gilbert and Gubar's notion of a feminist subtext might imply? If the chapter supports authoritarian as well as subversive readings and at the same time dramatises the conflict between them, that conflict is not between figurative language and literal language but between two interpretations of figurative language. Where the 'Knightleian' interpretation grounds figurative language in social rules, the 'Emmaesque' interpretation sees it as inherently ungroundable, even in any politically acceptable subtext. Although Knightley himself does not appear in the chapter, we may identify as his proxy the eligible young bachelor Mr Elton, whom Emma is busy imagining as Harriet's suitor and whose amorous riddle supplies Emma with an irresistible opportunity for creative misreading. Let us look at the pre-text out of which she constructs one of her best 'bad novels':

To Miss—

CHARADE

My first displays the wealth and pomp of kings,
  Lords of the earth! their luxury and ease.
Another view of man, my second brings,
  Behold him there, the monarch of the seas!

But, ah! united, what reverse we have!
  Man's boasted power and freedom, all are flown;
Lord of the earth and sea, he bends a slave,
  And woman, lovely woman, reigns alone.

Thy ready wit the word will soon supply,
May its approval beam in that soft eye!

(p. 71)

The misreading begins even before Emma reads the charade, as soon as she tells Harriet: 'Take it, it is for you. Take your own' (p. 71). Ownership is indeed at issue both in the interpretation of this riddle and in the novel as a whole, and in failing to see herself as the rightful 'owner' of Elton's riddle, Emma is at odds with the novel's ethic of property and propriety.[20] The riddle itself is profoundly concerned with 'wealth and pomp', 'power and freedom'. Announcing his interest in 'courtship', Elton at the same time, as Paul H. Fry cogently notes, betrays a preoccupation with 'Power (court) and

Wealth (naval commerce) ... that prove[s] to the unblindered eye that [he] will never marry Harriet Smith'.[21] A reading less wilful than Emma's would, of course, have paid more attention to the way in which Elton's characters express his character. Yet to be at once a reading and a writing – to exemplify productive error – Emma's reading has to be not only a reading of emblems but also an emblem in its own right. In a sense, Emma reads the riddle all too well. For if Elton's flattering rhetoric hints conventionally at a 'reverse' of conventional power structures, Emma's misreading enacts that very 'reverse', reading his figures unconventionally.

Offering an alternative to the patriarchal view of reading as a regimen for 'strengthening the mind' and forming character, Emma's misreading arises from a radically different understanding of character. Whereas the patriarchal programme would form character by inserting the self into the slots of convention, the subversive counter-programme begins by defining the self as a slot. On the one hand, Elton's caption, 'To Miss —', merely indicates that the whole business of courtship is a sort of prefabricated 'text', a series of conventional performances: if the offering of flirtatious riddles is the first stage of the game, then the rules require that the young riddler honour the modesty topos by leaving the young woman's name blank, as in some contemporary novel, and that she, moreover, regard herself as playing a game, acting a part in a ready-made fiction. According to this view, one forms one's character by recognising one's status as character in a novel not of one's own design.[22] On the other hand, 'To Miss —' could be rewritten figuratively as 'To Miss Blank'. Not only does this rewriting magnify the conventionality – we might even say the 'emptiness' – of Elton's formula, but it also invokes the very sign of emptiness or lack on which the subversive discourse turns. For a blank is a kind of zero or cipher. Yet if a cipher is not just a zero but a sign of figurality as well, then 'To Miss Blank' conjoins femininity itself with the disruptive irregularity of figurative language. From a patriarchal perspective, woman is a zero waiting to fill a blank space; from a subversive perspective, 'Miss Cipher' is the name for the irreducible figurality of the self, whether male or female.

Emma's misreading, then, produces a 'novel' in 'bad handwriting', a 'novel' whose female characters personify this illegibility. Such a reading, however, neither proclaims the 'enigma of woman' nor ascribes to women the power of self-authoring. To appreciate its full force – to know what the association of women with ciphers involves

– we must find out why Emma fills the blank with Harriet's name rather than her own. Why, after she has subjected the riddle to a thorough analysis, does Emma persist in the delusion that it was intended for Harriet? How, in getting part of the riddle 'wrong', does Emma produce an interpretation that is curiously 'right'? If the conventional view of character insists that one accept one's place in a predetermined social text, then the subversive view of the self as a rhetorical figure – not just as a figure or character in a novel – can be charged with narcissistic implications: to see oneself as a trope may be to revel in aesthetic self-admiration. And indeed, precisely this charge has been levelled against Emma. Darrel Mansell, for example, writes that Harriet 'never amounts to much more than a projection of Emma's own personality onto a blank, reflecting surface'.[23] Though Harriet does belong to that group of Austenian characters who, as Leo Bersani would say, almost are not, the mere fact of her blankness does not render Emma's relationship with her narcissistic. Something more complex than narcissism characterises this relationship. For in misreading 'Miss —', Emma at once puts Harriet where she herself should be and assumes Harriet's place. Filling the blank with 'Smith' instead of 'Woodhouse', Emma not only cedes her slot to Harriet but also installs herself in Harriet's habitual position – that of blankness.

The Emma described as 'clever' in the first sentence of the novel thus discloses an element of Harriet in herself. It is almost as if, for a moment, Emma and Harriet had become a composite character, so that Emma's assumption that the riddle was intended for Harriet seems oddly appropriate. We might say that the difference between a rhetorical figure and a figure in a novel is the difference between composite and unitary characters, except that to define the self as a rhetorical figure is to suggest the compositeness – the overdetermination – of all characters. As characters in a novel, Harriet and Emma fall short of uniqueness and unity because, substituting for each other, they 'mean' something other than themselves, just as a rhetorical figure means something other than itself. Even Elton's riddle supports this theory of the overdetermined self, since its closing couplet speaks of the loved one's 'ready wit', clearly an Emma-like attribute, and of her 'soft eye', which, Emma says, is 'Harriet exactly' (p. 72). Now, the incompatibility of these epithets may signal the insincerity, or merely the inaccuracy, that results from 'going by the book', as Elton has done. Later, when Emma has learned Elton's true intentions, she corroborates this view, musing indignantly, 'To be sure, the charade, with its "ready wit" – but then, the "soft eyes" – in fact it suited neither; it was a jumble without taste or truth' (p. 134). Repentant, she seems to disavow her first reading. Yet even in this implicit concession to Knightley – even as she repudiates her 'novel' – Emma articulates the most subversive insight of her misreading. For what that misreading discovers is that the real 'jumble' is not so much the riddle as the self. Now she blames Elton's want of taste for the very fascination that underlies her relationship with Harriet – a fascination not with the self but with the otherness of the self, with the heterogeneity that Emma-as-Harriet and Harriet-as-Emma embody. No wonder Emma realises 'that Mr Knightley must marry no one but herself' (p. 408) only after Harriet has confessed *her* love for Knightley: Harriet's discourse is the discourse of the other, the other lodged within Emma herself.

Occupied by rival ideologies, chapter 9 typifies the ambiguity that unsettles the narrative at several junctures. Read from Knightley's point of view, the chapter demonstrates what can happen without a 'subjection of the fancy to the understanding'. Read from Emma's point of view, it allegorises a theory of the self that rejects the hierarchical terms of the first ideology, organising the self horizontally and contingently rather than vertically and paradigmatically. Moreover, although the Emma–Elton–Harriet imbroglio is exposed fairly early in the novel, the misreading performed in chapter 9 anticipates other setbacks in what looks like Knightley's gradual conquest of Emma. One such instance occurs during the famous excursion to Box Hill, in the course of which Emma insults Miss Bates. There, the politics of superficiality presents itself once again in the form of characters and word games. Amid the general unpleasantness of the outing, Mr Weston offers a conundrum, asking the party, 'What two letters of the alphabet are there, that express perfection?' (p. 371). The answer is 'M. and A. – EmMa', and 'Emma found a great deal to laugh at and enjoy in it' (p. 371). Knightley, however, takes the conundrum as an opportunity to reprove Emma, saying '*Perfection* should not have come quite so soon' (p. 371). With characteristic moral seriousness, he reads the characters to read Emma's character, finding in what Austen calls a 'very indifferent piece of wit' an image for that character's imperfection or incompletion (p. 371). Two letters have been left out of Emma's name, and Knightley wishes to see Emma's character made whole. Yet the badness of the pun partakes also of the 'badness' we have come to associate with figurative language, and it is precisely this 'badness' that Emma 'enjoys'. For Mr Weston has reminded her that character need not be a homogeneous entity, that it is an aggregate of many different characters, that the self is no more a fixed identity than the name, a construct susceptible to fragmentation and re-arrangement.

In recalling the otherness of the self, moreover, Emma sees herself through otherness, as another sees her. What Knightley would chastise as narcissistic self-absorption is in fact an acknowledgement that one is embedded in a 'text' more intricate than one's own name. If Knightley conceives the social text as conferring on the self a pre-determined – hence illusory – subjectivity, Emma's social text figures collective existence as an endless collaborative process of reading and writing, in which the self emerges as a site of overlapping interpreta-tions. Emma's valetudinarian father writes melodramatic letters about her misadventure with the gypsies, for 'if he did not invent illnesses for her, she could make no figure in a message' (p. 336). The social text that Emma inhabits comprises any number of such 'inventions': like everyone else in this world, she is always 'making a figure' in one message or another, because she is always being reinvented, or re-read, both by herself and by other selves.

Even marriage – the apotheosis of the 'beauty of truth and sincer-ity in all our dealings with each other', the paradigm of 'every thing that is decided and open' (p. 460) – is marked by the fictiveness and the evasions of the social. For despite Knightley's declaration that he and Emma have finally arrived at a state of mutual transparency, at the end of the novel she is still practising 'disguise, equivocation [and] mystery' in not revealing that Harriet is in love with him (p. 475). As Mudrick observes, 'There is no happy ending'[24] – at least not if happiness lies in the ideal of society as an ultimately legible text composed of and by a homogeneous set of interpretive conventions. The novel ends instead with a trio of marriages whose unintelligibility not only to outsiders but perhaps even to the part-ners themselves, suggests a densely woven fabric of fictions and misreadings.

Oddly enough, it is Knightley, of all people, who contemplates the need for both fictionality and error. Late in the novel, on one of the few occasions when he praises Emma unreservedly, he also pays the highest compliment to the subversive theory of the self:

> My interference was quite as likely to do harm as good. It was very natural for you to say, what right has he to lecture me? – and I am

afraid very natural for you to feel that it was done in a disagreeable manner. I do not believe I did you any good. The good was all to myself, by making you an object of the tenderest affection to me. I could not think about you so much without doating on you, faults and all; and by dint of fancying so many errors, have been in love with you ever since you were thirteen at least.

(p. 462)

Is this speech merely a display of gallantry on the part of a conqueror whose defeated adversary has shown sufficient signs of humility? While it is possible to dismiss these remarks as Emma's reward for submitting, the last sentence in particular has a concessive force that puts it beyond the less-than-sincere rhetoric of the gracious winner. Knightley, after all, is telling Emma not just that he loves her, 'faults and all', but that he himself has 'fancied' or invented 'many' of those 'errors'. If the narrative has traditionally been conceived as a linear development whereby Emma, changing under Knightley's influence, moves gradually toward a welcoming recognition of that influence now the Pygmalion myth gets a new twist: Knightley is interested less in perfecting the 'object of [his] tenderest affection' than in 'fancying' – at once imagining and liking – her charming imperfections. The dissatisfaction Knightley voices when he criticises Mr Weston's feeble conundrum thus appears in a different light: '*Perfection* should not have come quite so soon' no longer means 'Unfortunately, Emma is not yet perfect'; it might be glossed more accurately as 'Thank you, Mr Weston, but I wish to continue enjoying Emma's imperfections for a while'. Demanding perfection so that he may invent further imperfections, denouncing Emma's errors so that he may fancy more of them, Knightley in fact desires nothing less than an indefinite postponement of that conquest toward which he seems to aspire.

Instead of resolving itself into a linear progression, then, the narrative turns out to be going in circles. Those who bemoan the absence of a 'happy ending' – of more persuasive proof that Emma has been converted – are impatient with precisely this circularity. For the failure of the linear model implies a failure of the unilateral ethical scheme in which a morally superior Knightley transforms a morally inferior Emma. Whereas it was his job to rescue her from literariness and its attendant ethical dangers, now he too appears to be tangled up in that net. Pretending to 'sober and direct' her,[25] he has ended up egging her on to further bouts of misguided fiction making. Knightley's words suggest how complicated the picture has become: 'fancying so many errors', he is no more a mere critic than Emma is a mere fiction maker. His interpretations are flights of fancy, which she must read to produce her little novels of error, to which he in turn takes a fancy, producing additional fanciful interpretations. Austen is at her most subversive, then, not in intimating the anti-social recesses of her heroine's interiority but in locating Emma in this potentially endless circuit of fiction, interpretation, and desire, with its dynamic and reciprocal relations between men and women. When the self is an effect of its over-determined acts and society is not one text but a continuously revolving or circulating library, the descent into literacy becomes a fortunate fall.

From *PMLA*, 100 (October 1985), 763–73.

NOTES

[Apart from a passing comment on 'Seminar on the "Purloined Letter"' by the poststructuralist psychoanalyst, Jacques Lacan, Litvak does not acknowledge any specific theoretical origins. However, more than any other essay in this collection, his is informed by the spirit of deconstruction. Litvak clearly assumes, for example, that the element of free play introduced by the indeterminacies of language allows him space to play with or, in Roland Barthes' terms, to take his pleasure of the text. Thus in his reading of *Emma*, which might equally well be termed a writing, Litvak ignores the obvious or the transparent and lingers instead over the metaphorical possibilities of terms such as vehicle, cipher and figure. The product is ingenious, complex and, at times, not at all easy to understand. The difficulties which 'Reading Characters' poses are particularly pronounced, for example, as the reader tries to follow Litvak while – in order to put Emma, femininity and figurative language in opposition to Knightley's male authority – he constructs a network of connections between Jane Fairfax's comments on bad handwriting, cipher-bound writing and several senses of the word cipher. Occasionally Litvak backs out of the role of writer which he has assumed by referring to Austen's intentions but, taken as a whole, his enterprise is a bold one. However, how useful individual readers will actually find Litvak's approach depends very much on their response to his tendency to base his arguments on assertions that fly in the face of commonsense interpretations of the novel. Those unwilling to abandon the insights of old-fashioned character analysis might, for example, find serious flaws in a reading which begins with the assumption that Frank Churchill's intention in playing the anagram game is to apologise to Jane Fairfax for almost exposing their secret intimacy. All quotations in the essay are from *The Novels of Jane Austen*, ed. R. W. Chapman, 5 vols (Oxford: Clarendon Press, 1932–4). Ed.]

1. Sandra M. Gilbert and Susan Gubar, *The Madwoman in the Attic: The Woman Writer and the Nineteenth-Century Literary Imagination* (New Haven, 1979), pp. 139, 161, 179, 177, 7.

2. J. E. Austen-Leigh, *A Memoir of Jane Austen* (Oxford, 1926), p. 157.

3. Marvin Mudrick, *Jane Austen: Irony as Defense and Discovery* (Princeton, 1952), p. 203. Other influential critics who demonstrate the affinity between a certain ethical conservatism and anti-literariness are A. Walton Litz (*Jane Austen: A Study of Her Artistic Development* [New York, 1965]) and U. C. Knoepflmacher ('The Importance of Being Frank: Character and Letter-Writing in *Emma*', *Studies in English Literature*, 7 [1967], 639–58). Litz says of Emma that 'ultimately she must realise that she has viewed life as a game in which she can display her imagination and powers of perception; it is no accident that Jane Austen uses Emma's fondness for conundrum, charades, and word-games to reveal her errors of imagination' (p. 138). According to Knoepflmacher, Frank Churchill's 'letter-writing is emblematic of a failure to front the responsibilities inherent in rank, family and love, and his persistence in employing the written, rather than the spoken, word to convey his final apologies demonstrates also that he has not benefited from the near-disaster brought about by his previous indirections' (p. 656).

4. *The Madwoman in the Attic*, p. 113.

5. Malcolm Bradbury, 'Jane Austen's *Emma*', in David Lodge (ed.), *Jane Austen: 'Emma'. A Casebook* (Nashville, 1970), p. 231.

6. D. A. Miller, *Narrative and its Discontents: Problems of Closure in the Traditional Novel* (Princeton, 1981), p. 59. My reading is indebted at several points to Miller's. His acute analysis of *Emma* provides a model for reading the novel as a product of conflicting narrative and ideological pressures.

7. I should point out that I do not regard my reading as value-free or as privileged with some special access to the 'purely literary' aspect of Austen's novel. Rather, I intend to show the interpenetration of the literary and the political in the text. But unlike much Austen criticism, which presupposes an unproblematically mimetic relation between text and world, this essay attends to the articulations that both join and separate them. Thus, it considers not only the way in which literary pursuits like reading and writing acquire social significance but also the way in which literary devices like riddles and anagrams transform the very notion of the social. Instead of moving in one direction, from the world and our assumptions about it into the text, I propose to move in both directions, from world to text and back.

8. Alistair M. Duckworth, *The Improvement of the Estate: A Study of Jane Austen's Novels* (Baltimore, 1971), p. 148.

9. It might be objected that, since Knightley thinks well of Jane Fairfax and

ill of Frank Churchill, his attitude should not be characterised as 'patriarchal'. Arguing that his likes and dislikes have nothing to do with gender, one might suggest that Knightley insists not on male supremacy but on the need for the honesty and directness he perceives in Jane (and in himself), as opposed to the manipulativeness he senses in Frank (and in Emma). But everything Knightley disdains in Frank he associates with femininity. Of Frank's handwriting, for example, he says, 'I do not admire it. It is too small – wants strength. It is like a woman's writing' (p. 297). For Knightley, *feminine* and *devious* are synonyms, and moral distinctions keep turning into sexual distinctions.

10. Marvin Mudrick, *Jane Austen* (Princeton, 1952), p. 200.

11. The thematics of power and vision in this episode would lend themselves well to the kind of analysis Jacques Lacan performs in his famous 'Seminar on "The Purloined Letter"' (*Yale French Studies*, 48 [1973], 38–72). If, thus far in the game, Emma sees nothing, Frank Churchill resembles those characters in Poe's story whose 'glance . . . sees that the first sees nothing and deludes itself as to the secrecy of what it hides' (p. 44). Frank may delude himself, but Knightley is deluded as well, in so far as he thinks that his own, third glance, which 'sees that the first two glances leave what should be hidden exposed to whoever would seize it' (p. 44), remains itself unexposed. I am not accusing Knightley of failing to recognise that he is a character in a novel. My point, rather, is that by reading – without feigning disinterestedness – Knightley's own reading, we may be able to glance at the secrets that moralistic interpretation would hide. Needless to say, this fourth glance could claim no mastery either, since it too might easily become one more object in an endless chain of deconstructions.

12. Joseph Wiesenfarth, '*Emma*: Point Counterpoint', in John Halperin (ed.), *Jane Austen: Bicentenary Essays* (Cambridge, 1975), p. 210.

13. Marilyn Butler writes, 'Although so much of the action takes place in the inner life, the theme of the novel is scepticism about the qualities that make it up – intuition, imagination, original insight' (*Jane Austen and the War of Ideas* [Oxford, 1975], p. 273). This comment might serve as an accurate description of Knightley's ideological double bind, but, as I hope to show, the novel itself is not always bound to this contradiction.

14. *The Madwoman in the Attic*, p. 9.

15. Leo Bersani, *A Future for Astyanax: Character and Desire in Literature* (Boston, 1976), p. 273.

16. The word *cipher* appears in three significant places in Austen's work. Besides its occurrences in *Mansfield Park* and in the more complex passage from *Emma* that we are about to discuss, the word has an interesting function in *Northanger Abbey* (composed between 1798 and

1803), Austen's earliest major novel. In the climactic episode of that novel's parody of Gothic fiction, the heroine, Catherine Morland, discovers among other curious objects, a chest engraved with a 'mysterious cypher' (p. 164). The subsequent action constitutes a debunking of Gothic conventions: when exposed to the light of day, for example, what looked like a hidden manuscript documenting torture and madness turns out to be a laundry list. But, despite the pains Austen takes to demystify Catherine's suspicions as so much hocus-pocus picked up from Gothic novels, one detail remains unexplained – namely, the cipher. Its indelibility might represent a grudging and furtive tribute to the tradition that Austen is trying to discredit, or it could indicate, as Sandra M. Gilbert and Susan Gubar argue, that Austen is not really opposed to the Gothic at all, that the novel's subject is the 'terror and self-loathing that results when a woman is made to disregard her personal sense of danger' (*The Madwoman in the Attic*, p. 143). In either case, even in this early novel the word *cipher* figures in a resistance to whatever effacements a complacently thematic reading of Austen would accomplish.

17. A. Walton Litz, *Jane Austen* (New York, 1965), p. 68.

18. In addition to Mudrick, see, for example, John Halperin: 'It is Emma's inability to subject fancy to reason that causes most of her problems and forms the core of the novel's dramatic structure' ('The Worlds of *Emma*: Jane Austen and Cowper', in *Jane Austen: Bicentenary Essays* [Cambridge, 1975], p. 201); Darrel Mansell: 'In *Emma* ... an artist is portrayed in the process of creating art, the art of fiction; and it is tempting to see the heroine as a kind of self-portrait of her author' (*The Novels of Jane Austen: An Interpretation* [New York, 1973], p. 153); Susan Morgan: 'The claim of the novel is that life is interesting, that fact can be as delightful as fiction, that imagination need not be in conflict with reality' (*In the Meantime: Character and Perception in Jane Austen's Fiction* [Chicago, 1980], p. 39).

19. *Jane Austen's Letters to Her Sister Cassandra and Others*, ed. R. W. Chapman, 2 vols (Oxford, 1932), 2: 469.

20. The classic discussion of *Emma*'s emphasis on the 'values of commerce and property, of the counting house and the inherited estate' (p. 99), is Mark Schorer's 'The Humiliation of Emma Woodhouse' (in *Jane Austen: A Collection of Critical Essays*, ed. Ian Watt (Englewood Cliffs, 1963], pp. 98–111). For a more recent treatment of property and propriety as Austenian themes, see D. A. Miller, *Narrative and its Discontents* (Princeton, 1981), esp. pp. 15–50.

21. Paul H. Fry, 'Georgic Comedy; The Fictive Territory of Jane Austen's *Emma*', *Studies in the Novel*, 11 (1979), 129–46. [Reprinted in this volume – see p. 168. Ed.]

22. For an implicitly conventionalising reading of *Emma* in terms of speech-

act theory, see Mary Vaiana Taylor, 'The Grammar of Conduct: Speech Act Theory and the Education of Emma Woodhouse', *Style*, 12 (1978), 357–71.

23. Darrel Mansell, *The Novels of Jane Austen* (New York, 1973), p. 152.

24. Marvin Mudrick, *Jane Austen* (Princeton, 1952), p. 206.

25. Ibid., p. 200.

7

Intimacy in 'Emma'

JAMES THOMPSON

At its most elemental level, Jane Austen's narrative presents its major characters as growing or maturing or developing as separate or distinct or different individuals, who pass from lonely solipsism to intimate union with an other.[1] The historicity of this life story, as opposed to the life story evident in novels of the mid-eighteenth century, for example, is likely to escape readers because it is similar to the life narrative that we envision now. As Philip Slater observes about modern concepts of individuality: 'The notion that people begin as separate individuals, who then march out and connect themselves with others, is one of the most dazzling bits of self-mystification in the history of the species.'[2] Austen is the first English novelist to portray this myth in a fully fashioned form, and this form is in large part the reason for her continued popularity and appeal. In Austen and now, one is not conceived as being born into immanent or pre-existing classes or categories – be these categories natural or divine or social – but instead one is born only into or with or as self or identity.[3]

One consequence of this individualist ideology can be seen clearly in the role of the family in Austen's fiction, in which final separation from the family is not presented as painful, or even as joyful, but finally as immaterial. Marriage is portrayed as the ultimate or final union, rather than as separation or passage – unlike in other cultures, in which a woman's marriage can involve passage from her original or parental family to the family of her husband, sometimes years before the marriage or consummation itself can take place. In

Austen, the man to be married rarely has a family to be reckoned with: in *Northanger Abbey*, *Pride and Prejudice*, *Emma*, and *Persuasion*, for example, the hero has no mother living. Where there is another family, as in *Sense and Sensibility*, they are distant or hostile, as is the case with Mrs Ferrars or Lady Catherine de Bourgh. As the novels progress, even the heroine has an increasingly smaller and less important family to reckon with: Anne Elliot is motherless, as are Emma Woodhouse, Harriet, and Jane Fairfax. With the exceptions of Mrs Weston and Emma's sister, there are no mothers in *Emma*, for all of Austen's late heroines are orphans.[4] *Mansfield Park*, appropriately the only novel to emphasise the importance of family, is the one in which the newlyweds remain in the bosom of the family, for Sir Thomas is 'chiefly anxious to bind by the strongest securities all that remained to him of domestic felicity' (p. 471). But even here the couple must eventually be removed from the park itself, leaving Susan Price to replace Fanny as the surrogate daughter. However much family is to be reckoned with there, none of Austen's novels features a romance plot that turns on the discovery and restoration of parents, as so many earlier eighteenth-century novels had, from *Joseph Andrews* and *Tom Jones* to *Humphrey Clinker* and *Evelina*; indeed, Austen parodies such plots in Emma's grandiose expectations of Harriet's parentage. Along the same lines, Mary Burgan observes that unlike both earlier and later novels that very commonly end by stressing genealogical continuity and female fecundity, Austen never ends her novels with celebrations or even hints of the heroine's future children or a flourishing nursery.[5] Despite Darrel Mansell's observation that the heroine must in the end come to accept her family before she is ready to marry, this acceptance does not involve any form of reintegration with the old family, but rather an abandonment of it at the moment of the new family's creation.[6] Like Cinderella, in *Pride and Prejudice* and *Persuasion*, the worthy heroine is rescued from an abusive family and translated to the prince's palace.

This flight from family in Austen is consistent with the changing shape of the family in the eighteenth century, in the long-term shift toward the nuclear family. Philippe Ariès writes of 'a steadily extending zone of private life' in his history of

> the triumph of the modern family over that of other types of human relationship which hindered its development. The more man lived in the street or in communities dedicated to work, pleasure or prayer, the more these communities monopolised not only his time but his mind.

If, on the other hand, his relations with fellow workers, neighbours and relatives did not weigh so heavily on him, then the concept of family feeling took the place of the other concepts of loyalty and service and became predominant or even exclusive.[7]

The term Randolph Trumbach employs to characterise the emergent eighteenth-century English family structure is *domesticity*: 'in the generation after 1720 privacy and discretion were increasingly emphasised. . . . Marriage had become, as far as possible, an intense and private experience between husband and wife. It was no longer a spectacle nor even a family occasion. It was the hidden pearl of domestic happiness.'[8]

This growing zone of the private is a consequence of the objectification of social relations, the split between work and family, and the general withdrawal of individuals from the public sphere. But we should also note that the size of the household or family did not change very much across this period; according to Peter Laslett in *The World We Have Lost*, the family size in pre-industrial England was both relatively small (4.75 person per household) and relatively constant up to this century.[9] Along this line, Françoise Lautman concludes that the nuclear family is not a consequence of industrialisation: 'the extended family was only found among the ruling or wealthy classes', for they alone had the power or wealth to accumulate, defend, and transfer. 'The real structure and function of the family have not changed. The change lies in the way society views a certain ideal that the ruling classes once practised effectively.'[10] That is to say, what eighteenth-century novels chronicle is not so much a change in the size or shape of the family as a change in attitude and function, and the Bennets, Dashwoods, Woodhouses, and Elliots reflect these changing attitudes. It has been argued that the whole programme of the first great domestic novels is based on 'making the private public'; in the light of the history of privacy, we might want to restate this formula to say that the eighteenth-century novel capitalises on a newly created private zone.[11]

In Austen, the extended family is not seen as a haven in a heartless world, but rather as something suffocating, a mediating stage between the larger public world and the private world of intimacy. The place of privacy in Austen and the narrative pattern that is determined by it can be explored through Austen's use of key terms that represent social and personal relations: *intimacy*, *reserve*, *openness*, and *solitude*. Intimacy is the *summum bonum* of Austen's fiction, her highest value, the reward of her heroines' struggle, and the goal of her narratives. An indication of the importance Austen attaches to intimacy, in her life as well as her work, can be seen in her letter to her niece Fanny, which is uncharacteristically demonstrative and emotional; rarely does one witness Austen struggling as she does here to achieve 'the language of real feeling' (*Emma*, p. 265): 'It is very, very gratifying to me to know you so intimately. You can hardly think what a pleasure it is to me, to have such thorough pictures of your Heart. – Oh! what a loss it will be when you are married' (*Letters*, pp. 478–9). . . .

The process by which false intimacies are exploded and true intimacies are disrupted is most fully worked out in *Emma*, in which Austen appears to be exploring most consciously and carefully the dangers of false intimacy and the value of true intimacy. Here especially, Austen works with a series of contrasts: Emma's former closeness with Mrs Weston is set against her friendship with Harriet Smith; this friendship, or more properly, this patronage of Harriet is set in competition with Mrs Elton's patronage of Jane Fairfax. Through these contrasts, the reader is regularly shown that Emma prefers the insipid company and unequal friendship of Harriet Smith to the more valuable or more equal and thus more challenging friendship expected but spurned between herself and Jane Fairfax. In this particular relationship, the values of intimacy are explicitly contrasted with the repeated accusations of reserve that make Jane so repulsive in Emma's eyes. Overall, the remarkable sense of community that makes this novel so extraordinary at every point suggests both the values of and the constrictions inherent in a tiny community where everyone of the same class is inevitably and necessarily on familiar footings with the others. In this fashion, Frank Churchill can enter into an already established intimacy between the Woodhouses and the Westons, exploiting what already exists and what is expected. The flirtation into which he entices Emma is presented as an especially debased example of intimacy; as he puts it in the last letter to Mrs Weston, 'In order to assist a concealment so essential to me, I was led on to make more than an allowable use of the sort of intimacy into which we were immediately thrown' (p. 438). In obvious contrast, the long-standing friendship between the Woodhouses and Mr Knightley is offered as an exemplum of proper intimacy in almost every fashion. Nevertheless, although Emma spends most of this novel surrounded and almost strangled by intimate friends and acquaintances, she, like all of the other heroines, finds herself very much alone just before the end of the story. Emma's only intimate relations are with unequals, with her former governess and with Harriet, and it is this isolation that leaves her so vulnerable.

The sense of false intimacy or something else such as self-interest or patronage masquerading as intimacy is much more prevalent in *Emma* than any of the previous novels. The whole first volume of the novel focuses on Emma's taking up of Harriet Smith, which Mr Knightley prophesies will bring no good to either. Austen has lifted this plot of dangerous intimacy from Fanny Burney's second novel, *Cecilia*, in which the heroine patronises a woman of a much lower social class, Henrietta Belfield, who turns out to be a rival for Mortimer Delvile, the man Cecilia herself desires; like Emma, Cecilia is able to turn this friend over to another, less threatening lover. In Austen's novel, Harriet plays a similar role to Henrietta Belfield. With her former intimate, Mrs Weston, removed to Randalls, Emma's possibilities for a friend of equal social class are painfully limited by the small size and rigid class structure of Highbury. Jane Fairfax appears to be the only logical choice, but most of the time she does not reside in Highbury. As Mrs Weston points out, Harriet is the only realistic possibility for a friend to Emma. She argues to Mr Knightley,

> how fortunate it was for Emma, that there should be such a girl in Highbury for her to associate with. Mr Knightley, I shall not allow you to be a fair judge in this case. You are so much used to live alone, that you do not know the value of a companion; and perhaps no man can be a good judge of the comfort a woman feels in the society of one of her own sex, after being used to it all her life.

> (p. 36)

Meddlesome though Emma's patronage of Harriet is, this passage highlights Emma's basic need for companionship and friendship with someone other than her idiot father and his ossified circle of friends: 'Mrs and Miss Bates and Mrs Goddard, three ladies almost always at the service of an invitation from Hartfield' (p. 20; Emma herself makes the automatic fifth, of course, night after night with this lively crew).[12] In a passage that is unusually sympathetic for this sharp novel, contact with Mrs Weston is explained as Emma's greatest pleasure, however egocentric Emma's conversation may be:

> there was not a creature in the world to whom she spoke with such unreserve as to [Mrs Weston]; not any one, to whom she related with such conviction of being listened to and understood, of being always interesting and always intelligible, the little affairs, arrangements, perplexities and pleasures of her father and herself. She could tell

nothing of Hartfield, in which Mrs Weston had not a lively concern; and a half an hour's uninterrupted communication of all those little matters on which the daily happiness of private life depends, was one of the first gratifications of each.[13]

(p. 117)

With Mrs Weston gone, Emma's needs might be supplied by the friendship of either Harriet or Jane, but despite the advantages Jane Fairfax presents, it is the very closeness and constriction of Highbury that militate against their becoming close. As Emma tells Harriet of Jane, 'we are always forced to be acquainted whenever she comes to Highbury' (p. 86). Later, in another revealing discussion, Frank Churchill draws Emma out and teases her into making indiscreet remarks about Jane Fairfax:

'I have known her from a child, undoubtedly; we have been children and women together; and it is natural to suppose that we should be intimate, – that we should have taken to each other whenever she visited her friends. But we never did. I hardly know how it has happened; a little, perhaps, from that wickedness on my side which was prone to take disgust towards a girl so idolised and so cried up as she always was, by her aunt and grandmother, and all their set. And then, her reserve – I never could attach myself to anyone so completely reserved.'

'It is a most repulsive quality, indeed,' said he. 'Oftentimes very convenient, no doubt, but never pleasing. There is safety in reserve, but no attraction. One cannot love a reserved person.'

'Not till the reserve ceases towards oneself; and then the attraction may be the greater. But I must be more in want of a friend, or an agreeable companion, than I have yet been, to take the trouble of conquering any body's reserve to procure one. Intimacy between Miss Fairfax and me is quite out of the question. I have no reason to think ill of her – not the least – except that such extreme and perpetual cautiousness of word and manner, such a dread of giving a distinct idea about any body, is apt to suggest suspicions of there being something to conceal.'

(p. 203)

It is inviting and almost too easy to speculate on all the reasons why this friendship never gets off the ground, from the meagre clues of Jane's character, to assumptions of her resentment at Emma's patronage, and on to Emma's reluctance to work at anything, much less an acquaintance. But as was suggested previously, this relationship has all of the signs of having been forced, assumed by others, expected to be so, and thus it is never allowed to develop of its own accord. But Emma appears to want to pick her own friend and not have her only choice dictated by the circle of her father's acquaintance. As Janet Todd has persuasively argued, the undeveloped relationship between Emma and Jane Fairfax is perhaps the most interesting in Austen's novels, a tantalising possibility of what is never allowed to be, a reminder of what Austen never grants.[14] Toward the end of the novel, Emma looks back regretfully at what was never established between them, explicitly comparing her attraction to Harriet and her antipathy to Jane:

> She bitterly regretted not having sought a closer acquaintance with her, and blushed for the envious feelings which had certainly been, in some measure, the cause. Had she followed Mr Knightley's known wishes, in paying that attention to Miss Fairfax, which was every way her due; had she tried to know her better; had she done her part towards intimacy; had she endeavoured to find a friend there instead of in Harriet Smith; she must, in all probability, have been spared from every pain which pressed on her now. – Birth, abilities, and education, had been equally marking one as an associate for her to be received with gratitude; and the other – what was she?
>
> (p. 421)

Emma's intimacy with Jane never develops, and that with Harriet is destroyed, like that between Elizabeth Bennet and Charlotte Lucas: 'The intimacy between her and Emma must sink; their friendship must change into a calmer sort of goodwill; and fortunately, what ought to be, and must be, seemed already beginning, and in the most gradual, natural manner' (p. 482). What was unnaturally forced at the beginning is allowed to decay naturally at the end.

Like Elizabeth, Emma is taken from intimacy to solitude, from companionship to a state of estrangement. In this movement, Emma becomes more like Jane Fairfax, learning something of the reserve that she has found so repulsive. *Reserve* is a word tied to Jane in this novel, as in the phrase 'coldness and reserve – such apparent indifference whether she pleased or not' (p. 166):

> She was, besides, which was the worst of all, so cold, so cautious! There was no getting at her real opinion. Wrapt up in a cloak of politeness, she seemed determined to hazard nothing. She was disgustingly, was suspiciously reserved.
>
> (p. 169)

Austen's most suggestive and extended discussion of reserve occurs in *Sense and Sensibility*, when Edward Ferrars is so startled by

Marianne's accusation of reserve, which arises in a discussion of general civility. Just as in *Emma*, reserve is invested with all manner of pejorative connotations:

> 'I never wish to offend, but I am so foolishly shy, that I often seem negligent, when I am only kept back by my natural awkwardness. I have frequently thought that I must have been intended by nature to be fond of low company, I am so little at my ease among strangers of gentility!'
> 'Marianne has not shyness to excuse any inattention of hers,' said Elinor.
> 'She knows her own worth too well for false shame,' replied Edward. 'Shyness is only the effect of a sense of inferiority in some way or other. If I could persuade myself that my manners were perfectly easy and graceful, I should not be shy.'
> 'But you would still be reserved', said Marianne, 'and that is worse.'
> (p. 94)

In *Emma*, Mr Knightley also remarks on Jane Fairfax's reserve: 'Her sensibilities, I suspect, are strong – and her temper excellent in its power of forbearance, patience, self-controul; but it wants openness. She is reserved, more reserved, I think, than she used to be – And I love an open temper' (p. 289; in the end, Emma declares, 'I love every thing that is decided and open' [p. 460], suggesting that she has begun to adopt Mr Knightley's language as well as his values). As is typical in *Emma*, the distinctions that Mr Knightley draws are more careful and judicious than those that Emma draws in a moment of indiscretion with Frank Churchill. Where Emma's vocabulary is emotional, the words that Mr Knightley uses here are moral, and by them he suggests that there is both a private and a public openness. Similarly, Emma observes, 'There is an openness, a quickness, almost a bluntness in Mr Weston, which every body likes in *him* because there is so much good humour with it' (p. 34). Mr Weston's geniality may be regarded as a species of openness, but this geniality is not to be confused with the openness possible in private intimacy – openness as a kind of public intimacy, and intimacy as a kind of private openness. The two can be collapsed, as in Emma's desire toward the end of the novel: 'Emma grieved that she could not be more openly just' with Mr Knightley (p. 463). Both public and private forms of reserve are the opposite of these forms of openness, but as with intimacy, openness has both negative and positive connotations. Often Jane Fairfax's reserve contrasts favourably with the indiscretion of Emma, who lacks the 'forbearance, patience, self-controul' that Mr Knightley praises. Jane Fairfax's reserve also serves to contrast with the 'ease' or vulgar familiarity of Mrs Elton, who is said to have 'ease, but not elegance' (p. 270); she is 'pert and familiar' (p. 272); and 'self-important, presuming, familiar, ignorant, and ill-bred' (p. 281). Just as with Catherine Morland, Marianne Dashwood, and Elizabeth Bennet before her, Emma has to be taught the necessity of some reserve. The term does not necessarily mean cold, secretive, and suspicious, as Emma implies to Frank Churchill of Jane Fairfax, for reserve can also be a sign of prudence or discretion.

Emma's learning the necessity of some reserve inevitably involves her learning not to speak, and her becoming more private, more distant, and more enclosed, in short, more like Jane Fairfax. At one point Emma concludes, 'Plain dealing was always best' (p. 341), yet this remark occurs just after she has committed her most serious interference with Harriet, which suggests that plain dealing is *not* always best. Emma's reserve, which is learned so late, is predicated on her abandonment of the intimacy with Harriet, the disruption of all of her previous intimacies. Emma has none of the confidants at the end whom she had at the beginning, as all her confidences with both Harriet and with Frank Churchill turn into mortifications, or, in the word Austen uses most often, *blunders*. After the secret engagement has been revealed, Emma is constrained from voicing to Mrs Weston her disapproval of Frank Churchill, limiting for the first time Emma's principal source of confidence and intimacy. And after Mr Knightley's proposal, Austen again and again underscores Emma's restraint, and the way her reserve on the subject of Harriet Smith stands as a barrier between her and Mr Knightley, even at the occasion of his proposal, at which point the narrator concludes: 'Seldom, very seldom, does complete truth belong to any human disclosure; seldom can it happen that something is not a little disguised, or a little mistaken' (p. 431). Later, 'Emma grieved that she could not be more openly just to one important service which his better sense would have rendered her, to the advice which would have saved her from the worst of all her womanly follies – her willful intimacy with Harriet Smith; but it was too tender a subject. – She could not enter on it' (p. 463). It is only after Harriet is safely re-engaged to Robert Martin that Emma can begin to be open with Mr Knightley:

> High in the rank of her most serious and heartfelt felicities, was the reflection that all necessity of concealment from Mr Knightley would soon be over. The disguise, equivocation, mystery, so hateful to her practice, might soon be over. She could now look forward to giving

him that full and perfect confidence which her disposition was most ready to welcome as a duty.

(p. 475)

Emma's history is narrated as a series of succeeding intimacies, from Miss Taylor, who stands in the place of a mother; through Harriet Smith, the female friend; to Mr Knightley, the husband, just as in all of Austen's novels she must separate the heroines from female friendship in preparation for marriage. This path leads the heroine through stages of increasing separation and loneliness, as if she must be made unhappy before she can be removed from her previous state. For the bulk of the novel Emma is presented as the very pattern of self-satisfied efficiency, yet in the end she is made to feel inadequate and insufficient.[15] At the opening of the novel, Emma feared that 'she was now in great danger of suffering from intellectual solitude' (p. 7), but what she comes to by the end is real solitude. The chapter that contains Mr Knightley's proposal starts by evoking, through dreary, rainy weather, a striking sense of angst and ennui from which Emma suffers: 'The weather continued much the same all the following morning; and the same loneliness, and the same melancholy, seemed to reign at Hartfield' (p. 424). The submerged metaphor in *reign* is particularly suggestive because for four hundred pages Austen has conveyed the impression that it was Emma who 'seemed to reign at Hartfield'. Mr Elton's rather apt charade had complimented Emma with the line, 'And woman, lovely woman, reigns alone' (p. 71); if Emma ever did reign, she did so all by herself, an imaginary monarch. The novel, in fact, is full of rulers, from Mrs Churchill, who, Mrs Weston says 'rules at Enscombe' (p. 121); to Frank Churchill, whom Mr Knightley refers to as 'the practised politician' (p. 150); to Mrs Elton, whom Miss Bates calls 'the queen of the evening' (p. 329).[16] The power of these others is more obviously illusory, but Emma too has far less power than she thinks she has, for quite plainly, she thinks of herself as the queen of Hartfield and Highbury as well. But in the end, it is not Emma but loneliness that reigns. . . .

Yet more dangerous than loneliness are the implications of solipsism. Much like Elizabeth Bennet, Emma has prided herself on her penetration, and in both cases this understanding is really a form of imagination; Emma is called an 'imaginist' (p. 335), because she thinks that she can foresee and thus create a match before anyone else, just as she can invent for Jane Fairfax or Harriet life histories, loves, disappointments, rich parentage, all the essentials of a romantic heroine.[17] The impropriety of such inventions is always made clear to us by Mr Knightley, but the danger they represent is rather a different matter. Harriet prefaces her declaration of love for Mr Knightley to Emma with a compliment on her insight:

> 'You (blushing as she spoke), who can see into everybody's heart; but nobody else – '
> 'Upon my word,' said Emma, 'I begin to doubt my having any such talent.'
>
> (p. 404)

In the ensuing chapters, Emma comes to understand that seeing into others' hearts is not a talent, that it is not possible. As she has admitted earlier in a conversation with Frank Churchill, 'Oh! do not imagine that I expect an account of Miss Fairfax's sensations from you, or from any body else. They are known to no human being, I guess, but herself' (p. 202). At this point, however, which is early in the novel, Emma assumes that she can guess Jane Fairfax's feelings. By the end, she is forced to see that it is difficult to know one's own feelings, more difficult to express those feelings to another, and impossible, finally, to know the other's sensations.

The twin threats of loneliness and solipsism serve to emphasise the value of true intimacy: if Emma can never know the inside of Jane Fairfax, the novel is constructed so as to lead us up to the expectation that she can, eventually, know Mr Knightley. Closing the pattern of false, failed, and broken intimacies, the final marriage serves to mark the expectation and the hope that true intimacy can exist. Austen nowhere examines happy marriage within her novels proper, but her novels are constructed so as to lead up to the hope that such happiness is possible, lying just on the other side, as it were, of the last page of the novel. In this sense, Austen's are novels of courtship but not of marriage, for they always end on the threshold of marriage, where intimate happiness is indicated in the future tense, as something about to be experienced, but not experienced and verified quite yet. True intimacy does not exist within the novel proper because Austen indicates that it cannot be portrayed. This failure to portray suggests less that she does not finally believe in it or that she herself does not know how to express it than that she believes it is not expressible. Language begins to falter in the proposal scene and thereafter is replaced by physicality – facial expression, looks, gestures, and touch, hints of sexuality – all extralinguistic forms of communication and union. True intimacy is quintessentially private, and so to represent it is to violate it, to provide just another false or partial intimacy. The last sentence of *Emma* conveys this sense of intimacy as always expressed in futurity, a condition predicated on hope: 'the wishes, the hopes, the confidence, the predictions of the small band of true friends who witnessed the ceremony were fully answered in the perfect happiness of the union' (p. 484; the fact that the description of the marriage is reported to us by one excluded from the ceremony furthers the sense of an enclosing privacy). In Austen's novels, marital happiness is dependent upon knowledge of the other, and full knowledge of the other is another word for intimacy. . . .

The deepest fear in these novels, as is so common in late eighteenth-century literature from Sterne to Cowper to Blake to Wordsworth, is of solipsism, but true intimacy, Austen suggests, breaks out of the circle of self-enclosure, the epistemological self-referentiality embodied in her quotation from William Cowper, 'Myself creating what I saw' (p. 344). The narrative of the 'romantic' love story is the perfect antidote to solipsistic enclosure, for it mythologises a perfect and lasting fulfilment, not just a temporary supplement to essential desire.[18] This need is distinctly different from the family structure of Elizabethan romance and from stage comedy; it is significantly narrower, narcissistic vision, which does not culminate in a reconstituted society, but rather involves finding or creating one other who is like the self, a double who understands, a replication of the inner in the outer world, which provides validation by holding off or deferring solipsism, self-enclosure, coldness, reserve, distance, and loneliness, defeating these within intimacy, in which the two are merged into one.[19]

If all this vision of intimacy seems natural and appropriate, history and anthropology show that it is not. According to Alan Macfarlane,

> one of the major lessons to be learnt from the anthropological discussions of marriage is that the Western concept of 'companionate' marriage is unusual. Elsewhere marriage is not entered into for the sake of companionship; it is not the marriage of true minds, it is not the joining of two halves, it is not the completion of a search for someone before whom one can reveal one's inner soul, a companion in life, a mirror. Usually the worlds of men and women are separate, and this is the case after marriage as it was before. A wife will remain much closer to her female kin and neighbours than to her husband; a man will spend his time and share his interests with other men. The couple will often eat apart, walk apart, and even, for most of the time, sleep apart. They may even dislike each other intensely and yet both honestly

proclaim that it is a satisfactory marriage because the economic, political and reproductive ends have been satisfied. The blending of two personalities, two psychologies, is not involved. Often the couple did not know each other the day before they were married and see relatively little of each other for years afterwards, perhaps even being embarrassed to be left alone together. This does not mean that the relationships in such societies are shallow and that affection is absent, but merely that love and affection run towards kin by blood.[20]

This is a far cry from the notions of love and marriage that we find implicit in Jane Austen's novels, a notion of romantic love perfectly stated in Olive Schreiner's letters:

> The one and only ideal is the perfect mental and physical life-long union of one man with one woman. That is the only thing which for highly developed intellectual natures can consolidate marriage. All short of this is more or less a failure, and no legal marriage can make a relationship other than impure in which there isn't this union.[21]

To read Austen correctly, we need to see the essentially historical nature of this notion of romantic love. Mary Poovey observes very shrewdly of love in Austen:

> As we have repeatedly seen, romantic love purports to be completely 'outside' ideology. It claims to be an inexplicable, irresistible, and possibly biological attraction that, in choosing its object, flouts the hierarchy, the priorities, and the inequalities of class society. Romantic love seems to defy self-interest and calculation as completely as it ignores income and rank; as a consequence, if it articulates (or can be educated to articulate) an essentially unselfish, generous urge toward another person, it may serve as an agent of moral reform. . . . But it is crucial to recognise that the moral regeneration ideally promised by romantic love is as individual and as private as its agent. In fact, the fundamental assumption of romantic love – and the reason it is so compatible with bourgeois society – is that the personal can be kept separate from the social, that one's 'self' can be fulfilled in spite of – and in isolation from – the demands of the marketplace.[22]

That is to say, intimacy, morally corrective union, functions to efface the ideological contradiction between social responsibility and private withdrawal, for intimacy serves as the private 'solution' to alienation and the objectification of social relations – romance and reification are two sides to the same coin or two sides of an ideological contradiction. As Lukács writes, 'the man [or the woman] who now emerges [under capital] must be the individual, egotistic bourgeois isolated artificially by capitalism and ... his consciousness, the source of his activity and knowledge, is an individual isolated consciousness à la Robinson Crusoe.'[23] In *Emma*, Hartfield is a type of Crusoe's island, and for Emma herself, markets, production, classes, family, community, language, all social structures, relations, and functions, exist outside, removed and objectified from her, whereas feeling is the only authenticity that lies within. Emma's hope for happiness comes to depend upon validating the one authentic sign of her being by investing in the one true other, Mr Knightley, who will validate her feelings, and thus her authenticity.

From James Thompson, *Between Self and the World: The Novels of Jane Austen* (Pennsylvania, 1988), pp. 159–62, 166–73, 174–8, 208–10.

NOTES

[As a Marxist James Thompson takes it as a central article of faith that Austen's fiction should not be viewed as correct or natural but rather as time-bound and historical. His specific concern in *Between Self and the World*, as he states it in his introduction, is to historise Austen's attempts to create a 'language of real feeling'. An analysis of this language of real feeling – and therefore of the distinction between public, social language and private, interior feeling – reveals, Thompson argues, a central contradiction at the heart of Austen's fiction introduced by the presence there of elements of both conservative and bourgeois ideology. For an operative definition of bourgeois ideology, which is actually his book's main focus, Thompson turns to Georg Lukács (particularly his *History and Class Consciousness: Studies in Marxist Dialectics*, trans. Rodney Livingstone [London, 1971]). According to Lukács bourgeois ideology is constructed on a series of antinomies, the most important of which develops from the way in which the bourgeois mode of existence simultaneously endows the individual with an unprecedented importance and annihilates individuality through the economic conditions to which it is subjected. The individual thus experiences a sense of alienation and turns within for 'true authenticity'. In Thompson's view this Marxist analysis brings a totalising explanation to the study of Austen's novels, which he reads as being amongst the first in English to treat marriage as a private intimacy set against the threat of loneliness and solipsism. The core topics of marriage and intimacy are the subjects of the last two chapters of *Between Self and the World*, and the extract reprinted above is taken from the last chapter, 'Intimacy'. All quotations in the essay are from *The Novels of Jane Austen*, ed. R. W. Chapman, 5 vols (Oxford: Clarendon Press, 1932–4) and *Jane Austen's Letters to Her Sister Cassandra and Others*, ed. R. W. Chapman, 2nd edn (London: Oxford University Press, 1952). Ed.]

1. In psychoanalytic terms, this narrative is essentially a vision of maturation from narcissism to object-love, a 'transcendence' or breaking through or out of self-enclosure or self-referentiality to closure with the beloved.

2. Philip Slater, *Earthwalk* (Garden City, 1974), p. 49, quoted from Lawrence Stone, *Family, Sex and Marriage in England, 1500–1800* (New York, 1977), p. 683.

3. Louis Althusser argues in 'Ideology and the State' that the individual is always a subject: 'Thus ideology hails or interpellates individuals as subjects. As ideology is eternal, I must now suppress the temporal form in which I have presented the functioning of ideology, and say: ideology has always-already interpellated individuals as subjects, which amounts to making it clear that individuals are always-already interpellated by ideology as subjects, which necessarily leads us to one last proposition: *individuals are always-already subjects.' Lenin and Philosophy and Other Essays*, trans. Ben Brewster (New York, 1971), pp. 175–6. Marx puts it this way: 'human beings become individuals only through the process of history', *Grundisse*, trans. Martin Nicolaus (Harmondsworth, 1973), p. 496.

4. On the subject of motherless heroines, see Susan Peck McDonald, 'Jane Austen and the Tradition of the Absent Mother', in *The Lost Tradition: Mothers and Daughters in Literature*, ed. Cathy N. Davidson and E. M. Broner (New York, 1980), pp. 58–69. See also Nina Auerbach, 'Incarnations of the Orphan', *ELH*, 42 (1975), 395–419.

5. Mary Burgan, 'Mr Bennet and the Failures of Fatherhood in Jane Austen's Novels', *JEGP*, 74 (1975), 551. The reasons for this omission are many, among which Burgan quite rightly numbers Austen's own hostile and fearful attitude toward children and particularly toward childbearing. However, I want to emphasise that the conspicuous absence of the promise of children is but a further sign of the collapse or constriction of the family in Austen's narrative. Edward Copeland suggests that, unlike the heroines of earlier novels, Austen's heroines have no homes to return to. Edward Copeland, 'The Burden of *Grandison*', in *Jane Austen: New Perspectives*, ed. Janet Todd, *Women and Literature*, NS 3 (New York, 1983), 98–106.

6. Darrel Mansell, *The Novels of Jane Austen: An Interpretation* (New York, 1973), pp. 90–1.

7. Philippe Ariès, *Centuries of Childhood*, trans. Robert Baldick (New York, 1962), pp. 398, 375.

8. Randolph Trumbach, *The Rise of the Egalitarian Family: Aristocratic Kinship and Domestic Relations in Eighteenth-Century England* (New York, 1978), pp. 114, 116.

9. Peter Laslett, *The World We Have Lost: England before the Industrial Age* (1965, rpt. New York, 1973), p. 93.

10. Françoise Lautman, 'Differences or Changes in Family Organisation', in *Family and Society. Selections from the Annales,* ed. Robert Forster and Orest Ranum, trans. Elborg Forster and Patricia M. Ranum (Baltimore, 1976), p. 253.

11. I borrow the phrase 'making the private public' from Lennard Davis, *Factual Fictions. The Origins of the English Novel* (New York, 1983), p. 187. See also Ian Watt, 'Private Experience and the Novel', chapter 6 in *The Rise of the Novel* (Berkeley, 1957), pp. 174–207.

12. *Idiot* is Marvin Mudrick's term, *Jane Austen: Irony as Defense and Discovery* (1952, rpt. Princeton, 1962), p. 196.

13. Kenneth Moler observes that much of the criticism of *Emma* centres on the question of how Austen can 'make such a wrong headed girl so very engaging', *Jane Austen's Art of Allusion* (Lincoln, 1968), p. 171. I would suggest that Emma is made engaging by passages such as these that reveal Emma's manipulation to be but cover for some familiar needs and vulnerabilities; after all, it is easy to forget with such a lively character that, at the opening of the novel, Emma has, in effect, just lost her mother for the second time. Austen is obviously much less successful at evoking similar needs and vulnerabilities in a character like Fanny Price, and in consequence, *Mansfield Park* as a whole suffers.

14. Janet Todd, *Women's Friendship in Literature* (New York, 1980), pp. 274–301.

15. The rebuke to Emma's sense of independence can be seen as a kind of secularised version of the rebuke Raphael delivers to Adam in *Paradise Lost*, after Adam has ominously admitted his sense of Eve's perfection in herself:

> yet when I approach
> Her loveliness, so absolute she seems
> And in herself complete.
>   (VIII, 546–8)

16. I owe this suggestive observation and its neat formulation to my colleague Charles Edge.

17. I would like to credit Katrin Burlin's acute observations about Charotte Heywood's fantasy of Clara as exploitation in *Sanditon*, in her essay 'Sanditon and the Art of Advertising', forthcoming. Such points, as Professor Burlin observes, have important implications for the novelist's art and the way in which Austen invents life histories for others, in her letters as well as in her novels.

18. It is not just Emma's fault or her pride and vanity with which Austen is concerned here, but rather this novel follows a common pattern of socialisation, in the form of the feminocentric novel: Women are forced to grow up and leave their childish friends. See Nancy Miller, *The Heroine's Text* (New York, 1980), 155–6.

19. This pattern has affinities with the interiorisation of the sublime as analysed by Thomas Weiskel, which works by introjection; novelistic portrayals of romantic love constitute a domesticated, thoroughly secularised bourgeois form of the sublime. *The Romantic Sublime: Studies in the Structure and Psychology of Transcendence* (Baltimore, 1986), p. 93. We might also note that this form of sublimity, in effect, represents a privileging of idealising narcissism, with its assumption 'You are perfect, but I am part of you'.

20. Alan Macfarlane, *Marriage and Love in England: Modes of Reproduction* (Blackwell, 1986), p. 154.

21. *The Letters of Olive Schreiner, 1876–1920* (Boston, 1924), pp. 151–2, quoted from LeRoy Smith, *Jane Austen and the Drama of Women* (New York, 1983), p. 43.

22. Mary Poovey, *The Proper Lady and the Woman Writer: Ideology as Style in the Works of Mary Wollstonecraft, Mary Shelley and Jane Austen* (Chicago, 1984), p. 236.

23. George Lukács, *History and Class Consciousness: Studies in Marxist Dialectics*, trans. Rodney Livingstone (London, 1971), p. 135.

8

Interrupted Friendships in Jane Austen's 'Emma'

RUTH PERRY

In his Preface to *The Ambassadors*, Henry James asserted with his customary assurance that in every novel two stories are simultaneously told: the story of one's hero and the story of one's story. This second story, a self-reflective commentary on the narrative always parallel to the plot, records the writers' self-consciousness about the creative process.

And what of women writers? Is their awareness of process and authorial stance encoded in their texts in the same manner? Is the second story that women tell and retell compulsively the same story of process to which mainstream writers have recourse? Do women reflect on the nature of their creative experience in the same manner when their place in the culture – and its literary traditions – is so different from that of men?

Perhaps the second story that women tell is the story of what it is like to be a woman in a culture that devalues women. For it stands to reason that in her imaginative projections, a woman writer would respond to this fact, or deal with it in some way.[1] Moreover, insofar as the conventions of the novel define and reinforce women's place in the culture by consigning the heroine either to marriage or to death, many women novelists have felt the need to subvert or disarm certain crucial narrative elements of the genre. The story of *their* story is thus very different from that of Henry James.[2]

Critics interested in the problem, following Kate Millett's early example, have usually proceeded by examining the sexual politics between male and female characters – their economic relations, their different forms of power,[3] the silencing or expressiveness of one gender or the other.[4] I want to suggest that another manifestation of women's feelings about themselves as writers and as women is to be found in their literary representation of social relations among women: the complicated feelings of women characters for one another as they recognise one another's powers and identify with each other as women. Women's friendship, so essential to psychic survival, and so often the most significant mirror for the self – yet constantly undermined, conditioned, distorted, and discouraged in patriarchal culture – *that* is perhaps the subject of the second story, the subtext that chronicles a woman's reactions to her society's prejudices about her as a woman.

Psychoanalytically-oriented theorists have suggested that the psychic origin of writing is an attempt to repair the split occasioned by an identification with the father – the child's first serious break with his or her earliest affectional ties, which are with the mother. If storytelling or conscious manipulation of narrative is an attempt to heal this division, to return to the originary edenic relation with the mother – to a time before the eruption of the father – then there is a psychosexual warrant, as well as the obvious economic one, to look at the effects of the traditional heterosexual expectations on relations among women.[5]

If we assume that women's friendship is a natural outgrowth of shared experience and interests – and especially of early years spent in the company of women – then whatever blocks, distorts, or interrupts that friendship might be seen as symptomatic of the way the culture undercuts women's power and self-sufficiency. Women's friendship tests the power of women within a culture. Where women are weak, friendship among them is inhibited; and where they are strong, it flourishes. Such relationships offer another venue to the complex problems of women's anomalous position in the culture. Indeed, the model of 'interrupted friendships' may prove useful in more than the analysis of individual texts. It may be a fruitful metaphor for understanding the relation of the woman to her literary predecessors and thus to women's literary tradition embedded within a predominantly phallocentric literary culture. The temptation to identify with the ongoing (male) literary culture and to deny continuities with sister writers, to see one's work as part of the primary rather than an alternative tradition, must motivate the literary relations among women just as the pressure to marry distorts their social relations. Writerly affinities, the friendship of minds, are 'interrupted' by literary politics.

Jane Austen's *Emma* is a good text within which to explore how a woman writer understands the determining nature of gender and inscribes it in her text – and how it affects her heroine in relation to the other women characters. Austen lived in a women's enclave within a patriarchal system and understood the effects of such doubled loyalties. She wrote from her life and heart with such clarity and classical symmetry that the layers of her novels come away neatly.

Reviewing the novel in the *Quarterly Review* (October 1816), Sir Walter Scott remarked that *Emma* had even less story than its predecessors. The plot, such as it is, recounts the relationship of Emma, the happy and much-loved daughter of a well-to-do valetudinarian, with a pretty younger girl, Harriet Smith, whom she tries to manœuvre into a romance, first with the local vicar, and then with Frank Churchill. However, Churchill's stepmother, Mrs Weston, who is also Emma's closest friend, has designated him for Emma herself. Despite their tacit plans for him, Frank Churchill turns out to have his own plot and to have been engaged secretly all the while to a fine, accomplished, but poor young woman – Jane Fairfax – who has just returned to the neighbourhood to live with elderly female relatives. The complications of friendship and dependence among these women are distorted by their absorption in the various marriage plots they imagine, illustrating my main points: (1) that Austen uses the marriage plot to comment on the situation of women in her society and not merely to reinscribe it and (2) that the essentials of that commentary are contained in the story of the relations among the women.

LOVE AND FRIENDSHIP

The sexual politics of Austen's novel are usually understood as an odious big brotherism. Emma must be brought down a peg, must be cured of her vanity and arrogance, and by a man – Mr Knightley – who has watched over her, corrected her faults, and given her advice and guidance since she was a little girl. Emma must be taught not to manipulate people, not to interfere in their lives, not to think she knows what is good for them better than they do. Critics have varied in their assessments of Knightley's priggishness and Emma's culpability, but everyone recognises that he keeps reining in Emma's imagination and criticising her romantic scripts for Harriet from his more realistic vantage point, one founded in economic realities and due appreciation of rank and status. Emma imagines that Harriet, with her blonde beauty and a sweet temper, might aspire – like the heroine of some sentimental novel – to a match far above her station. As Austen has taken care to point out in the case of Mr Weston, a man of financial independence may choose an amiable woman without money or connections. But Mr Knightley, the ranking man in town, thinks Emma's romantic schemes for Harriet unrealistic and insists on the importance of birth and breeding. When Emma tells him pertly, 'I am very much mistaken if your sex in general would not think such beauty, and such temper, the highest claims a woman could possess',[6] Austen gives the authoritative Mr Knightley a reply favouring the still higher claims of women's reason, education, and lineage.[7]

Although there is truth in this cliché of male correction and improvement with its easy ironies, it is only the most obvious level of meaning. A more sensitive index of the effects of patriarchal values on women is to be found in an examination of the problematic relations among the women themselves in this novel – and their self-relations – as affected by their need to successfully negotiate hetero-sexual relationships and thus to secure places in society.

To begin with, Austen sets up Emma as a woman who does not have to get married. Among Austen's heroines she is unique: handsome, clever, *and* rich. The cards are stacked in this game; Emma's situation cannot be improved materially by marriage. As she laughingly tells her naïve young friend Harriet, 'I have none of the usual inducements of women to marry. . . . Fortune I do not want; employment I do not want; consequence I do not want: I believe few married women are half as much mistress of their husband's house, as I am of Hartfield; and never, never could I expect to be so truly beloved and important; so always first and always right in any man's eyes as I am in my father's' (p. 104). Yet finally, at the end of a series of misguided and failed female friendships, Emma realises that she too must marry, with no less inevitability than Austen's other heroines.

What, then, was Austen's own attitude toward marriage and toward friendship with other women? Does the biographical information furnish any orienting clues about her relation to these matters? Let us recall that Jane Austen lived her adult life essentially with women.

True, she often enjoyed the society of her brothers and nephews as well, and she was especially fond of the younger, adventurous ones. But she shared a bedroom with her sister Cassandra all her born days, and Cassandra was her first, last, and most constant love. When Jane died, Cassandra wrote to their niece Fanny: 'I *have* lost a treasure, such a Sister, such a friend as never can have been surpassed, – she was the sun of my life, the gilder of every pleasure, the soother of every sorrow, I had not a thought concealed from her, & it is as if I had lost a part of myself.'[8] Their shared life, as seen in the letters they wrote when apart, centred in a world of domestic concerns. They wrote to one another of gowns and flounces, the price of muslin, the details of housekeeping, and the illness of their relatives. In 1805, to the household made up of their mother and themselves, they added Martha Lloyd, whose own mother had just died and who had grown up with them in the neighbourhood of Steventon. Wrote Jane to Cassandra, 'I am quite of your opinion as to the folly of concealing any longer our intended Partnership with Martha' (21 April 1805, p. 157).

There were no second thoughts about the plan; such partnerships were not especially unusual in eighteenth-century England. It was a common enough arrangement for single women to pool their resources and to make a family of friends. A favourite niece, either Anna Austen or Fanny Knight, was occasionally added to the Austen circle. As Jane once wrote to Cassandra, Fanny was 'almost another Sister, – & could not have supposed that a niece would ever have been so much to me. She is quite after one's own heart' (7 October 1808, p. 217). In the novel, Emma says gaily to Harriet of her intended spinsterhood: 'I shall often have a niece with me' (p. 110).

In her own life, then, marriage was not to Jane Austen a sovereign good, nor the lack of it a determining disappointment. In 1808, at thirty-three, she reported to Cassandra the events of a ball she had just attended: 'It was the same room in which we danced 15 years ago! – I thought it over – & in spite of the shame of being so much older, felt with thankfulness that I was quite as happy now as then' (9 December 1808, p. 236).

Critics have often noted the intensity of family feeling in Austen's texts, and a few feminist critics have directed our attention more recently to the relations among the women.[9] When we examine *Emma* in this light, we find many testimonies to the pleasures of women's friendship. The most obvious of these is the relation between Emma and Mrs Weston. Early in chapter five, Mrs Weston tells Mr Knightley, 'perhaps no man can be a good judge of the comfort a woman feels in the society of her own sex, after being used to it all her life' (p. 65). In her own unstinting fondness for Emma, in her idealised motherliness, Mrs Weston is described as 'well-informed, useful, gentle, knowing all the ways of the family, interested in all its concerns, and peculiarly . . . interested in [Emma's] every pleasure, every scheme of her's; – one to whom she could speak every thought as it arose, and who had such an affection for her as could never find fault' (p. 38). Emma could tell 'nothing of Hartfield, in which Mrs Weston had not a lively concern; and half an hour's uninterrupted communication of all those little matters on which the daily happiness of private life depends, as was one of the first gratifications of each' (p. 138).

Indeed, the precipitating cause of the action in the novel, such as it is, is the separation of these friends, because of Mrs Weston's marriage, a marriage that leaves Emma in need of companionship. The story of Emma and her governess is as old as the story of the separation of Demeter and Persephone, the first of many pairs of women divided by marriage. By the end, we have lamented the separation of four sets of friends: Jane Fairfax from Miss Campbell, the inevitable cooling of the friendship between Emma and Harriet, and the double estrangement of Emma from Mrs Weston when the latter has a baby girl to engross her care.

But the great unfinished business of the novel is the never-quite managed friendship of Emma and Jane Fairfax, the two superior young ladies whose association we wait for, whose conversation promises the most delightful equality of tastes and interests, but who are parted on the eve of their mutual good-will by their marriage. All through the novel we long for an improvement in their relations, for the sake of each differently-deprived young woman. Austen scarcely misses an opportunity to emphasise how desirable this friendship is, not only for the two principals, but in the eyes of their various friends and relatives. If the first half of the novel is devoted to the misuse of friendship – exemplified by Emma's manipulation of Harriet's romantic feelings and marital expectations – the second half adds pressure upon pressure for a properly warm bonding between Emma and Jane. Isabella assumes it a most eligible connection, and Knightley urges Emma several times to befriend Jane Fairfax. In the end, Emma does move closer to Jane, making three symbolic overtures only to have them rejected: she invites Jane to Hartfield, she puts her carriage at her disposal, and she sends her some arrowroot. But in spite of everything, the narrative repeatedly – pointedly – evades the looked-for friendship.[10]

THE MARRIAGE PLOT

Emma's exclusive attention to marriage plots of her own devising is consistent with her inability to enter into a relation of equality with other women. Her obsession with arranging marriages blinds her to other relational possibilities – including the possibility of friendships in which one is neither patron nor dependent. Grateful as she is to her governess/friend Mrs Weston for her guidance and education, this connection was never based on equality. And the great attraction of Harriet Smith, beyond her blonde beauty and pliant temper, was that 'everything' could be done for her. Emma's subsequent failure to connect with Jane Fairfax (her exact equal in age, abilities, and sense) taken together with her enthusiasm for these other unequally-structured relationships, might be interpreted in the light of her preoccupation with the marriage plot.

Friendship between women is necessarily problematic in a genre destined to fulfil the marriage plot. That plot must justify a woman's submission to the authority of a husband, either by demonstrating his worthiness as an authority or else by proving her need for his power, his money, or those equivocal substitutes – his moral and spiritual guidance. Destined ultimately to play the heroine in her own marriage plot, Emma *must* be made to acknowledge her dependence on Knightley. The relationhips she has with other women in the meantime must prepare her for the unequal one that she must enter. Determined by that ultimate necessity, the deformations of women's friendship can be read as a running commentary on the marriage plot.

In the first place, Emma's marriage scenarios for Harriet distort their relationship. Harriet, sweet seventeen, is herself a conventional heroine of fiction: guileless, true, and passionate, with beautiful blue eyes. Emma's mistake is to confuse her with a character in a book – to write romantic scripts for her and to paint an idealised portrait of her. Austen's appreciative reading of Eaton Stannard Barrett's burlesque *The Heroine* (1813) at a time when she returned to work on *Emma* may have heightened her satiric sense of the effects of novel-reading on life.[11] In Barrett's novel, Cherry Wilkinson, misguided by her novel-mesmerised governess (who has just run off with the wine-bibbing butler), pretends that she is the heroine of a melodrama. She runs away from home, scorning those aspects of her life that do not conform to the conventions of gothic and romantic fiction. Emma's fantasy that Harriet is the illegitimate daughter of a nobleman is like Cherry Wilkinson's assertion that she is the natural daughter of an Italian count. It is a parodic device as old as the novel itself – a genre that assimilates the variety of human relations to certain stylised, symbolic forms.

Despite the satire, Austen was probably closest to Emma when plotting for Harriet. She meant it when she said that she was creating a heroine whom no one but herself would like very much.[12] Her letters to her family frequently burst into amusing exaggerated narratives, which simultaneously satirised the mind that could imagine them, the humdrum reality so different from these stories, as well as the novels that invented such 'impossible contingencies'. As late as December 1816 Austen wrote to her nephew Edward in the broad burlesque strokes most familiar from her juvenilia: 'I give you Joy of having left Winchester. – Now you may own, how miserable you were there; now, it will gradually all come out – your Crimes & your Miseries – how often you went up by the Mail to London & threw away Fifty Guineas at a Tavern, & how often you were on the point of hanging yourself – restrained only, as some illnatured aspersion upon poor old Winton has it, by the want of a Tree within some miles of the City' (16 December 1816, pp. 467–8). Cartoons like these may have been refined out of her later novels, but ridiculing the melodramatic formulas was always part of Austen's consciousness. She and Cassandra between themselves playfully married off friends and acquaintances, in little scenarios of parodic invention. 'I have got a Husband for each of the Miss Maitlands', wrote Jane to Cassandra in 1808, 'Colonel Powlett & his Brother have taken Argyle's inner House, & the consequence is so natural that I have no ingenuity in planning it' (1 October 1808, p. 209). In response to Cassandra's report of the death of the wife of the much-admired but entire stranger the poet Crabbe, Jane replied brightly, 'Poor woman! I will comfort *him* as well as I can, but I do not undertake to be good to her children. She had better not leave any' (21 October 1813, p. 358).

Emma, who takes 'credit' for having engineered the marriage between Mr Weston and her governess and who imagines several different endings for Harriet Smith's story, also conceives marriage plots for Jane Fairfax that take the place of any real association with her. She convinces herself of an entanglement between Jane and Mr Dixon all the while Jane is living out a romantic scenario undetected by Emma, a scenario as improbable and emotionally sensational as any in a novel. And the dissembling and reserve required of Jane Fairfax to play her part in that drama effectively bar the possibility of any intimacy from her side.

FRIENDSHIP AND FICTIONAL FORM

Austen's message at this level would seem to be that women who imagine themselves and one another only in the marriage plot – as the romantic novel teaches one to do – will miss the possibilities of friendship with other women. Both Emma-the-author and Austen herself are restricted by the novel's standard romantic script. It is from this point of incompatibility between the marriage plot and the friendship plot that we can begin to unravel the subtext of this remarkable novel. The pull towards friendship with Jane Fairfax is very strong, considering that there is no consummation. Austen would seem to be self-conscious about the ways in which the story of women's friendship has no place in the novel of marriage. The repeated frustration of women's friendships in a novel that emphasises the importance of friendship, and the book's emotional unsatisfactoriness on this central crux (for Emma never does find a proper friend to 'replace' Mrs Weston) – these ellipses must alert us to suggestions about the limitations of the form itself.

Certainly all of Austen's novels are concerned with the limits of her chosen genre and all chafe at the imposed boundaries as keenly as her characters feel the limits of their circumstances. From the parodic gothicism of *Northanger Abbey* or the corrected romanticism of *Sense and Sensibility* to the unlikely heroine of *Mansfield Park*, Austen explored the disjunction between the realities of women's lives and the romantic conventions of the novel. *Persuasion* begins where most novels end – the youthful romance over and the protagonist settling into premature spinsterhood at twenty-seven. And in *Emma* she put thwarted friendship at the centre of her three marriage plots, both to forestall any early éclaircissement and to signal that which is lost by women's complicity in the marriage plot.

At every turn marriage is inimical to women's friendship. The friendship between Emma and Jane, which we continually expect and even come to long for, is not only blocked by their respective involvements in their own marriage scenarios, but is further confounded by competition and mutual envy. Emma resents Jane's superior discipline and accomplishment because it spoils her self-idealisation; and Jane is hurt by Frank Churchill's open flirtation with Emma. Competition between Emma and Jane is possible to the same extent as their friendship and for the same reason: because Jane Fairfax is Emma's only real peer. But ultimately the novel evades their mutual recognition of equality, whether in friendship or in competition.

As with other manifestations of the relations among women, the terms of women's competition in this novel serve as a reminder of the patriarchal structures within which women live. Mrs Elton's marriage puts her into competition with all other women in her society and gives her precedence even over Emma Woodhouse. Throughout most of the novel, Emma imagines that she competes with other women only for intellectual or artistic distinction. In these elegancies of mind and manners she recognises that she is better than Harriet but less disciplined than Jane. (Indeed, it is Jane Fairfax as much as Knightley who sets in motion Emma's recognition of her shortcomings.) On the other hand, Jane and Harriet, each in her own way, are aware from the start that, despite the self-referential nature of Emma's perception of their competition, they are all in fact competing for men – for husbands – for Mr Elton, for Frank Churchill, and for Mr Knightley. Emma's eventual recognition of this common object simultaneously precipitates her entry into 'womanhood' and definitively cuts her off from these other women. Furthermore, her moments of jealousy of Jane and Harriet finally function in the plot to lead her to her 'true' good – Knightley. Her competitive feelings for them – and her admiration – are turned to account for the marriage plot.

Jane's desperate dependence on marriage foreshadows the finale of Emma's story, since, inevitably, Emma must stop being an author and submit to becoming a heroine in someone else's script for the book to end.[13] In that sense, too, the imperatives of the form dictate the marriage between Knightley and Emma. Self-conscious about how overdetermined that ending is, Austen ironically undercuts her own authorial hand as Cupid in describing the immediacy of Emma's recognition: 'It darted through her, with the speed of an arrow, that Mr Knightley must marry no one but herself' (p. 398).

Emma's first intimations of the harsh imperative of the marriage plot come when she sees Jane's prospects narrowing in. Then she relents in her dislike and empathetically puts herself in Jane's place; fellow feeling supersedes all earlier reactions. But just as the possibility of friendship between them emerges, it is foreclosed by marriage.

As in the case of Harriet, the marriage plot inhibits the friendship plot.

EMMA AND JANE

There is a historical reason for sensing a close identification between Emma and Jane and for reading their missing connection as symptomatic. In the first version of the novel, in *The Watsons*, they were combined in a single character – Emma Watson, a heroine with Emma Woodhouse's healthy blooming looks and openhearted manner, but with the constricted financial and material circumstances of Jane Fairfax. Her nephew Edward said that Austen never finished *The Watsons* because she had 'placed her heroine too low, in a position of poverty and obscurity, which, though not necessarily connected with vulgarity, has a sad tendency to degenerate into it; and therefore, like a singer that has begun on too low a note, she discontinued the strain.'[14]

Emma Watson, living with difficult, garrulous relatives in a house too small, on the brink of going into service as a governess, has no dowry and no prospects; her family cannot afford to keep her indefinitely. Marriage was, of course, the best advancement to be hoped for in such a position, where if a woman were lucky she might make £30 a year beyond room and board. Although *The Watsons* was never finished, one can guess that Emma was to be saved from service by a marriage with the genteel and intelligent clergyman, Mr Howard. 'Single Women have a dreadful propensity for being poor', remarked Austen in a letter to her niece Anna, '– which is one very strong argument in favour of Matrimony' (13 March 1817, p. 485).

Splitting the character into Jane Fairfax and Emma Woodhouse, she who has little and she who has everything, permitted Austen to use these women to comment on one another and on the destiny they share. Emma Woodhouse, in no need of marriage, has health, wealth and a comfortable house. On the other hand, Jane Fairfax, living in cramped quarters with her grandmother and maiden aunt, determines that she must hire herself out to an office 'for the sale – not quite of human flesh – but of human intellect' (p. 300). Though Emma and Jane represent the poles of wealth among women of the gentry, in fact their situations are merely opposite sides of the same coin. Jane's story is a darker version of the truth that both women must face: women are insufficient by themselves to face the world alone. The unwritten story of Jane's relationship with Frank Churchill casts its shadow on the written novel and is a grim reminder of how dependent women are on men, how vulnerable they are, and how subject to men's values and pleasure – no matter how intelligent, gifted, or disciplined these women may be. This is the real condition of women, not the fairy tale version of the spoiled rich, pampered girl who is the apple of her father's eye and has no need of men.

The analysis of Austen's nephew, Edward Austen, was wrong. Jane Austen did not divide this character merely to provide herself with a suitably well-to-do heroine. The socioeconomic force of this narrative move is to show precisely that class is not everything – that gender is the primary determinant of status for women.

More than *Mansfield Park*, this is a novel of ordination. By the time *Emma* is finished, every woman in the novel is cured of her vanity, and every man is confirmed in his right to choose and be accepted. At twenty-one years of age, the age Jane Fairfax designates as the age of sacrifice, Emma Woodhouse too must learn to forego authorial control and play, to temper her self-love, and to submit to the will of her betters – in this case Mr Knightley; that is, she must accept her portion as a woman. Structured like a fugue, in which the themes of marriage, independence, friendship, service, and sub-mission rise and mingle and subside, the novel also twins Jane Fairfax with Mrs Weston, about whose life before she was Emma's governess we know nothing and who is also saved from service by marriage.

Unmarried women parade through these pages, as counterpoint and corroboration of the marriage theme. All three of the younger women – Emma, Jane, and Harriet – declare at one time or another that they will never marry. Miss Bates, Jane's maiden aunt, is the perennial reminder of the social helplessness of an old maid. Like a dependent child, she is a burden at best despite her sterling character and cheerful disposition. Carriages must be sent for her, she must be fed – with hampers of apples and loins of pork – and her endless repetitive chatter must be patiently listened to.

As everyone knows, the turning point in Emma's moral develop-ment – her apotheosis of self-disgust – comes from Knightley's rebuke when she insults Miss Bates for being tiresome, when she says what everyone knows is true. As usual, Mr Knightley is the agent of Emma's moral growth – her recognition that she has acted badly. The form of his chastisement is instructive: once again, it reminds Emma of the realities of rank and station. 'Were she a woman of fortune, I would leave every harmless absurdity to take its chance. . . . Were she your equal in situation – but, Emma, consider how far this is from being the case. She is poor; she has sunk from the comforts she was born to; and, if she lives to old age, must probably sink more' (p. 368). As in Austen's other novels, the humiliation of the heroine precedes her capitulation. Emma must learn to accept the world as it is before she is fit to be a wife. She must sort out the conventions of fiction from those of society and from the self-indulgence of youth.

There is another insult, unwritten and unheralded in the submerged novel, which only dawns on us upon a second reading or on second thoughts. It is the insult offered Jane Fairfax on this same occasion by her secret fiancé, Frank Churchill, and that unwitting flirt, Emma Woodhouse. Their chatter about marriage, in Jane's helpless presence, is cruel beyond the explicit denigration of Miss Bates. It is no less a reminder of the dependence and vulnerability of single women. On the contrary, to Jane herself this chatter is the sternest of reminders and is what drives her to accept servitude in Mrs Smallridge's establishment as governess to three small girls.

This then is the lesson learned on that most disagreeable of days: that women must marry, that they must not be old maids, if they want to protect themselves from insult and social scorn. This social pressure effectively divides women from one another even if they are not in direct competition for economic subsistence – for it directs women to find their comfort in submission to a benevolent husband rather than in equal intercourse with others of their own sex.

LEARNING ONE'S PLACE

Literally, too, *Emma* is a novel of education. Mrs Weston educates Emma, Emma 'improves' Harriet, and Jane Fairfax contracts to teach Mrs Smallridge's daughters. This daisy chain illustrates another source of strain on women's relationships with one another, insofar as women are expected to be agents of their own socialisation in patriarchal society. It is women's task to socialise and to be socialised. Whether as governesses or wives, to women falls the training of the next generation of women. But first they must learn to submit themselves to the will of others. However much Jane Fairfax may prefer the one over the other, the interchangeability of these roles is the point of Mr Knightley's opening remarks to Mrs Weston. 'But you were preparing yourself to be an excellent wife all the time you were at Hartfield,' he says. 'You might not give Emma such a complete education as your powers would seem to promise; but you were receiving a very good education from *her*, on the very material matrimonial point of submitting your own will, and doing as you were bid' (p. 66). Their roles reproduce themselves: Mrs Weston marries and turns teacher again. The teacher is trained to matrimonial docility; and the wife/mother becomes a teacher for the sake of her children.

In this case, the narrative ends with Emma's marriage. Her future is foreshadowed in Mrs Weston's absorbed attention to her infant daughter. The narrator remarks of this happy development: 'It would be quite a pity that any one who so well knew how to teach, should not have their powers in exercise again.' Emma says: 'She has had the advantage, you know, of practising on me . . . like La Baronne d'Almane on La Comtesse d'Ostalis, in Madame de Genlis' *Adelaide and Theodore*, and we shall now see her own little Adelaide educated on a more perfect plan' (p. 444).

Mme de Genlis's novel of education is more than a gratuitous reference here, for it too is a novel of marriage and friendship and the preparation of girls for their roles as women in society. Ostensibly a series of letters about the elaborate process by which M. and Mme d'Almane instil virtue and impart universal learning to their son and daughter along lines demarcated by gender, the narrative tension is provided by Mme d'Almane's relationship with her epistolary friend the Countess de Nimours, who misses her tenderly and resents the imperatives of the nuclear family that so abruptly separated them. The first volume opens with the reproaches of the Countess de Nimours to the Baroness d'Almane, who disappeared to the country under the cover of night upon the orders of her husband, without even telling her best friend. Like *Emma* itself, this French novel would seem to delineate a process in which women are divided from one another by marriage, their losses partially redressed by daughters and pupils, until they too transfer their primary loyalties to their husbands.

As with the Baroness d'Almane in the country, devoting herself to her beloved daughter, so the relational model in *Emma* is one of unequals – older and younger, teacher and pupil, whether Mrs Weston and Emma, or Emma and Harriet. The constraints of the genre, whose overt ideological purpose must be to reinforce rather than subvert the claims of the nuclear family, preclude such an egalitarian friendship as could be conceivably projected between

Jane and Emma. Mme de Genlis cannot replenish her narrative with anything other than an obsessive reproduction of this mother–daughter, mentor–student relationship first in one generation and then in another.[15] Friendship here would be intrusive, incompatible with the 'real' plot.

A note at the beginning of the 1796 English edition of *Adèle et Théodore* (probably the text Austen read)[16] deepens our sense of the economic pressures on women that made inevitable their roles as educators of their own sex – and hence reproducers of their subservient status.

> This Translation was undertaken by some Ladies, who, through misfortunes, too common at this time, are reduced from ease and opulence, to the necessity of applying, to the support of life, those accomplishments which were given them in their youth, for the amusement and embellishment of it.

Prohibited from the varieties of gainful employment available to men in an inflationary capitalist economy, women who could not secure their subsistence in marriage became the socialisers of younger women, whether as governesses or as writers of conduct books, children's literature, novels of education, or other didactic forms. The maternal role became professionalised, so to speak, with the consequence that other kinds of relationships between women tended to be assimilated to that model. Not only does this relation duplicate the hierarchy of gender in the culture, preparing women for the unequal roles they will assume, but it makes them complicit in the process. In *Adèle et Théodore* as in *Emma*, education is a two-way street. As Miss Taylor schooled herself to compliance in the Woodhouse household, teachers are taught in the process of educating their pupils.

AUSTEN AND HER CRITICS

In this essay I have been arguing that although the marriage plot provides the frame for *Emma*, certain elements of the action call attention to the ways in which compulsory heterosexuality disrupts and distorts the relationships between women. The novel structurally protests the overdetermination of the marriage plot by repeatedly raising and then undercutting our romantic expectations and by locating the real romantic story offstage where we cannot indulge ourselves in it. What romance there is, played out where we can see it, turns out to be illusory – whether it is the romance that Emma offers Harriet with Mr Elton or the romantic flirtation carried on between Emma and Frank Churchill.

Why then has the meaning of this strategy eluded the critics who have read and commented on this novel for the past 150 years? Part of the answer, of course, is that most critics have not interested themselves in the issue of relationships between women. Women's friendship has not been seen as a possible counterplot because patriarchal ideology has informed critical premises at least as much as novelistic assumption. But the misreading has also been deliberate, permitted by the author, even set up by her, partly because she had no radical vision of social change and partly as her own special way of triumphing. All of Austen's best characters excel in just this manner, in speaking simultaneously to several audiences at once. It is an obvious strategy for survival adapted to her position in the world as a dependent and a woman.

D. W. Harding noted long ago that Jane Austen's books are, 'as she meant them to be, read and enjoyed by precisely the sort of people whom she disliked: she is a literary classic of the society which attitudes like hers, held widely enough, would undermine.'[17] Her unexpected astringencies, her bitter clauses, are easily overlooked, he pointed out, passed over by those who do not want to face the satiric intent. Those who retain 'the conventional notion of her work' – that is, as charming and innocuous, 'must always have had slightly to misread what she wrote at a number of scattered points'. Without considering how this strategy might be determined by Austen's gender, Harding has nevertheless shown us that Austen's intermittent satire was related to her necessity to stay on good terms with the people around her. 'As a novelist', he wrote, 'part of her aim was to find the means for unobtrusive spiritual survival, without open conflict with the friendly people around her whose standards in simpler things she could accept and whose affection she greatly needed.'

The critics' misreading then – including Harding's underreading – is as much a sign of Austen's skill in evading confrontation as it is a sign of their inability to imagine an interpretation that would undermine male dominance. Thus Lionel Trilling writes that the degree of Emma's self-love is unusual in a woman – and that it is necessary to moral life. He also comments on her sexual coolness. But he never puts the two together: he never sees the sexual coolness as emanating from her self-love or as a way of preserving it. Accordingly, he accepts the marriage of Emma and Knightley without irony.[18]

Other critics are equally revelatory in the ways in which they miss this aspect of the novel. Edmund Wilson writes that 'Emma is not interested in men except in the paternal relation'. Moreover, he says, she is inclined to infatuation with women. And certainly the erotic attraction between Emma and Harriet is as strong as that between Emma and any of the male characters. Emma wants to take this lovely, pliant, adoring young thing and mould her – to be a hero to her heroine. She is flattered by her and soothed by her. Harriet accommodates to her in everything. Emma is permitted here the male role, Knightley's role, of dominating and improving. Although Wilson is aware that this relationship between Harriet and Emma imitates the affect (and the power relations) of the heterosexual model, he does not read it as a parody of that model, still less as a genuine sexual alternative, but only as another one of Emma's mistakes in need of correction. In the end, he dismisses the homoerotic dimension with a biographical (rather than political) explanation. He gestures toward the strong bond with her sister and her father – and Austen is made safe again, because Emma's lack of interest in beaux and the energy of her feeling for Harriet only prove after all that she was unfailingly loyal to her family.[19]

Taking another tack with regard to this complex novel, Mark Schorer analyses the vocabulary of business, banking, and property in the book to locate it squarely in its capitalist context. But he insists only on the ironies of a 'society whose morality and values are derived from an economics of class', and never thinks about the particular implications of capitalism for women like Jane Austen.[20] W. J. Harvey refers to the unwritten novel about Jane Fairfax and Frank Churchill, but never notices the unwriteable story of the friendship between Jane Fairfax and Emma.[21] He sees the point of the unwritten Fairfax–Churchill novel as being a demonstration that we are affected by the invisible contingencies of others' lives. He does not read that double plot as a reflection on the condition of women.

All critical readings are necessarily partial. But I am suggesting that these essays, which represent perhaps the most imaginative and lucid attempts among the previous generation of critics to interpret the novel, share a common blind spot. They do not take Austen seriously *as a woman*; they do not imagine the implications of what they see to a woman living in a culture that restricted and subordinated women. Thus they are satisfied that Emma needs to be made vulnerable, whether it be to economic realities, to her own sexuality, or to male authority. But they never suspect that a woman writer might feel differently about that 'necessary' vulnerability.

For all of Austen's consciousness of the power relations between the sexes, the polite surface of her text accommodates this critical obliviousness. She permits the appropriation of her text by those who choose to ignore the commentary on marriage, friendship, and women's self-sufficiency just as she permits the appropriation of Emma herself, who marries Knightley in the end and submerges her consciousness in his. All that is left for the critics to explain is the uncommonly independent spirit of the heroine – what Lionel Trilling termed Emma's 'sexual coolness' and Marvin Mudrick deemed her 'lack of tenderness'.

But feminist criticism, whether practised by men or women, re-positions us as readers to see the world from the vantage of women, allowing us to imaginatively reconstruct that social, economic, and psychological reality. When Austen sketched women in their relations to one another, she made visible a dynamic of women's frustrated need for one another. If one takes seriously both that need and its disappointment, another pattern of meaning emerges from the juxtaposition of this narrative about friendship with the various marriage plots.

This meta-narrative, the story of the story of *Emma*, reveals how much the imperative to marry costs women – how it inhibits their range of possible relationships with other women, makes them dependent on male approval, and limits their imaginative and social autonomy. As a writer, Austen was aware of the limitations of that story in a formal, literary sense too. Her resistance to the marriage plot – in fiction as well as life – can be felt in our discomfort with Knightley's unremitting paternalism, the serious lack of beaux in Highbury, and in Jane Fairfax's match with a man clearly her moral inferior. Trapped as an author as her characters are trapped as women, Austen underscores the inevitability of their narratives in the claustrophobia of Highbury, in the discussions within the novel of the limited possibilities for women outside of marriage, and in Emma's marriage – a marriage in which she never even leaves home. None of Austen's women characters, not Emma, nor Jane Fairfax, nor Mrs Weston, can outwit her destiny. Their stories only loop back to repeat themselves as these women become wives, mothers, and teachers, preparing the next generation for its parts in the marriage plot.

I have argued that Austen's ironic undercutting of romance in this novel, together with the unresolved but repeated plea for friendship between women, constitutes her subversive message. In the separation of Emma from Mrs Weston, from Harriet, and finally from Jane Fairfax herself, Austen provided – for those disposed to see it – a critique of her society and of the conventions of the novel of manners that developed to reflect that society. She may not have invented a new story for women, but she knew, more profoundly than perhaps we have understood, what was wrong with the old story.

From *Tulsa Studies in Women's Literature*, 5 (Fall 1986), 185–202.

NOTES

[The approach adopted by Ruth Perry owes a great deal to Sandra M. Gilbert and Susan Gubar's influential study, *The Madwoman in the Attic*. In the nineteenth century, according to Gilbert and Gubar, creativity was considered to be masculine, with the result that female writers experienced an 'anxiety of authorship'. Gilbert and Gubar identify several tactics employed by women to overcome this anxiety, one of which was to revise male genres so that they could be used to record their own stories in disguise. In Perry's reading of *Emma*, this is precisely what Austen achieves by introducing a subplot of authentic female friendships which, because they are sacrificed in order for the main 'male' marriage plot to be terminated, call into question the value of the patriarchal model of marriage. Since it seeks to deconstruct masculine authority, this kind of feminist criticism can properly be termed poststructuralist. However, as Toril Moi points out in *Sexual/Textual Politics*, the deconstructive force of Anglo-American feminist criticism, including Gilbert and Gubar's version, is limited because it tends to immobilise the play of meaning by substituting the authority of the female author for the masculine authority which has been called into question. This criticism can be extended to include Perry since she refers repeatedly to Austen's intentions. Nevertheless, while she might have benefited from the insights of French feminists, such as Hélène Cixous, Lucy Irigaray and Julia Kristeva, who have thoroughly immersed themselves in the work of Derrida and Lacan, Perry does make an important contribution to our understanding of *Emma* by correcting the failure of other critics to 'take Austen seriously as a woman'. The nature of Perry's contribution can be judged by comparing her treatment of female friendships with those of Stove (essay 2) and Thompson (essay 7), neither of whom finds anything worthy of comment in the failure of such relationships. Ed.]

My grateful thanks to Taylor Stoehr and Amy Lang for their improving suggestions.

1. Gilbert and Gubar, for example, found the signs of rebellious anger in the nineteenth-century English texts they examined. Sandra M. Gilbert and Susan Gubar, *The Madwoman in the Attic: The Woman Writer and the Nineteenth-Century Literary Imagination* (Chicago, 1979).

2. Nancy K. Miller has discussed this resistance to the conventions of the genre in 'Emphasis Added: Plots and Plausibilities in Women's Fiction', *PMLA*, 96, 1 (1981), 36–48.

3. Judith Lowder Newton argues that women novelists grant their heroines forms of power in their intelligence and abilities that differ significantly from instrumental or dominating power. See *Women, Power and Subversion: Social Strategies in British Fiction, 1788–1860* (Athens, Ga, 1981).

4. Terry Castle's brilliant analysis of the power relations between Clarissa and those who restricted her – whether Lovelace or her family – includes the observation that Clarissa's attempts to communicate are always being silenced, distorted, misinterpreted, interrupted. See *Clarissa's Ciphers: Meaning and Disruption in Richardson's 'Clarissa'* (Ithaca, 1981), especially chapter 2.

5. See Margaret Homans, *Bearing the Word: Language and Female Experience in Nineteenth-Century Women's Writing*, especially the first chapter, 'Representation, Reproduction, and Woman's Place in Language' (Chicago, 1986), pp. 1–39.

6. Jane Austen, *Emma* (New York: Penguin, 1966), p. 90. Subsequent references will be cited parenthetically in the text.

7. Wayne Booth argues in a splendid reading of *Emma* that despite the ostensible sexual politics of the novel, in which every reader is reinforced in the belief that 'women are indeed the weaker sex, that unlike men they cannot be whole, cannot find maturity, without the protective instruction and care from the right kind of man', there are the seeds of a critique in our resistance to Knightley, however mild, and in the other ironies of the ending. See 'Emma, *Emma*, and the Question of Feminism', *Persuasions* (December 1983), 29–40.

8. *Jane Austen's Letters to Her Sister Cassandra and Others*, ed. R. W. Chapman, 2nd edn (London, 1952), 2 July 1987, pp. 513–14. Subsequent references will be cited parenthetically in the text by date of letter and page number.

9. This essay owes much to earlier feminist work done on Austen by Deborah Kaplan, Susan Lanser, Janet Todd, Jane Lilienfeld, Judith Wilt, and, of course, Nina Auerbach, all of whom have contributed significantly to the project of reinterpreting the relationship between Austen's life and her writings.

10. Janet Todd's treatment of women's friendship in *Emma* was the first extended examination of the issues I discuss here. See *Women's Friendship in Literature* (New York, 1980), pp. 274–301. Todd argues there that the failure of friendship between Emma and Jane Fairfax is due to Emma's wilful evasion of what is expected of her, and her narcissistic jealousy of Jane's accomplishments.

11. Q. D. Leavis proposes the view that the basis of *Emma* was *The Watsons*, drafted when Austen was living in Bath. As will be clear later in my argument, I subscribe to this view of the literary history of *Emma*. Q. D. Leavis, 'A Critical Theory of Jane Austen's Writings', *Scrutiny*, 10 (1941–2), 61–87. For Austen's reading of Barrett's *The Heroine*, see *Jane Austen's Letters* (London, 1952), 2 March 1814, pp. 376, 377. For a fuller treatment of Barrett's influence on Jane Austen's novel, see Margaret Kirkham, *Jane Austen, Feminism, and Fiction* (New York, 1983), chapter 18.

12. J. E. Austen-Leigh, *A Memoir of Jane Austen*, 2nd edn (London, 1882), p. 148.

13. Many critics have analysed the inevitability of death or marriage as endings for the novel. I understand these endings as alternatives for neutralising the individual consciousness that has been the occasion for the narrative, whether by ending it or resolving it into a social (rather than private) entity.

14. William Austen-Leigh and Richard Arthur Austen-Leigh, *Jane Austen, Her Life and Letters: A Family Record* (London, 1913), p. 175.

15. Both of the Baroness d'Almane's pupils, the Countess d'Ostalis and Adèle (Adelaide), put the finishing touches on their education as women in caring for and training their 'own' little girls. This is particularly conspicuous in the case of Adèle. Just as she reaches maturity and the story of her own education is finished, she discovers six-and-a-half year old Ermine, an Italian orphan, and the cycle begins again – with Adèle, 'The youngest and most lovely of mothers'.

16. Jane Austen was reading Mme de Genlis's *Les Veillées du Château* in 1800 (*Jane Austen's Letters* [London, 1952], 8 November 1800, p. 82) and a bad translation of *Alphonsine* in 1807 (ibid., 7 January 1807, p. 173).

17. D. W. Harding, 'Regulated Hatred: An Aspect of the Work of Jane Austen', *Scrutiny*, 8 (March, 1940), 346–62.

18. Lionel Trilling, 'Emma', originally published as an introduction to the Riverside edition of *Emma* (Boston: Houghton, Mifflin, 1957), pp. v–xxiv.

19. Edmund Wilson, 'A Long Talk About Jane Austen', *The New Yorker*, 13 October 1940.

20. Mark Schorer, 'The Humiliation of Emma Woodhouse', *The Literary Review*, 2: 4 (Summer 1959), 547–63.

21. W. J. Harvey, 'The Plot of *Emma*', in *Essays in Criticism*, 17 (1967), 48–63.

9

The Self-Contained: 'Emma'

NANCY ARMSTRONG

In the following exchange between Frank Churchill and Emma, the twin problems of suppression and disclosure overlap; there is at once too much and too little information revealed. His speech approaches the point of exposing his true feelings, whereupon hers intervenes and stifles his confession:

> He looked at her, as if wanting to read her thoughts. She hardly knew what to say. It seemed like the forerunner of something absolutely serious, which she did not wish. Forcing herself to speak, therefore, in the hope of putting it by, she calmly said . . .
>
> (p. 265)

At this point, the problem with language in the novel, despite what Emma surmises, is not a matter of how to prevent the male in question from indiscriminate speech. The capacity to unleash asocial desire was the basis on which conduct books so strenuously objected to novels. It is therefore historically significant when a novel such as this no longer seeks authorisation by opposing the seduction of other fiction, but calls upon fiction for a more complete representation of desire. Were Emma to let it happen in the instance cited above, the mediation of speech would provide an instrument for establishing polite relationships where they do not already exist. Where Frank Churchill is concerned, her moments of stress and embarrassment arise strictly out of ignorance of his emotional attachment to Jane Fairfax, information that Emma suppresses by silencing him. It is as if, having condemned fiction-making as the source of unruly desire, Austen's novel can call upon fiction as a means of solving the

148

problem that fiction itself has produced. Given its nature, this problem calls for linguistic reform.

It is worth noting how writing comes under suspicion in the process of such reform. Mr Elton's preciously penned charade characterises him as a man of class pretensions and mercenary concerns. To communicate love in highly figurative terms as he does is, in Austen's terms, to offer the signs of passion with a lack of emotional depth. Although Emma describes it as 'A very proper compliment!' she does not concur with Harriet that Elton's poem is, 'without exception, the best charade I ever read'. Instead, she claims she 'never read one more to the purpose, certainly' (p. 51). In saying this, Emma contradicts herself, for she also confesses that she does 'not consider its length as particularly in its favour. Such things in general cannot be too short' (p. 52). I would like to take note of the procedures that, despite such observations, allow Emma so to misconstrue Mr Elton's meaning. Emma interprets Elton's poem allegorically, creating a personal sentimental meaning to complement general political terms. Such an allegorical reading is perfectly in keeping with the conduct book's suggestions about the proper use of classical mythology and history within a female curriculum. But Elton's verse refuses to be nudged and coaxed into a sentimental meaning despite the fact the charade itself invites such usage. Although Emma confidently translates the first and second verses into 'court' and 'ship' respectively, these terms remain stubbornly affixed to a political motivation. To lend them any other meaning is to misconstrue not only the true object but also the very nature of Elton's desire:

To Miss—
CHARADE
My first displays the wealth and pomp of kings,
    Lords of the earth! their luxury and ease.
Another view of man, my second brings,
    Behold him there, the monarch of seas!

But, ah! united, what reverse we have!
    Man's boasted power and freedom, all are flown;
Lord of the earth and sea, he bends a slave,
    And woman, lovely woman, reigns alone.
(p. 48)

As a component of this novel, the poem is the more brilliant for being composed entirely of clichés. It represents sexual relations as a power struggle, and in claiming that 'woman' makes of sovereign 'man' a 'slave', it dramatises a refusal of meaning to be feminised. Although Emma considers herself to be 'quite mistress of the lines', her sentimental interpretation simply conceals their meaning, which is all on the surface. Elton is hardly enthralled by the lowly Harriet but means to rise to the station of Emma herself. In the lines of this benighted man, sexual desire has not been sufficiently detached from power to be love, and no amount of interpretive ingenuity on Emma's part can make it be so.

But this sentimental misreading of Elton's poem is one part of a twofold error that also entails her failure to understand the sincere feeling displayed in Robert Martin's letter. It is a mark of Emma's ignorance as a reader, then, that she fails to discern the superior self-worth in Robert Martin's plain style or to understand how its ability to communicate emotion so clearly to Harriet designates him as the right man for her to marry. For such writing suggests that it is Harriet herself – distinct and apart from any social identity – that he values. Again, the traditional categories of writing prove misleading, for just as men supposedly use grandiloquent expression to persuade, tradition would have it that they use the plain style for purposes of logical argument. Thus when Harriet asks if Robert's is 'a good letter? or is it too short?', Emma replies 'rather slowly',

> – so good a letter, Harriet, that every thing considered, I think one of his sisters must have helped him. I can hardly imagine the young man whom I saw talking with you the other day could express himself so well, if left quite to his own power, and yet it is not the style of a woman; no, certainly, it is too strong and concise; not diffuse enough for a woman. No doubt he is a sensible man, and I suppose may have a natural talent for – thinks strongly and clearly – and when he takes a pen in hand, his thoughts naturally find proper words.
>
> (p. 33)

I dwell on the analyses of style contained within Austen's novel because they are her means of raising the whole question of writing and what constitutes the polite style.

In his discussion of John Ward's lectures on rhetoric, Wilbur Howell calls attention to an interesting corruption of classical categories that occurred in many eighteenth century treatises on rhetoric. Of Ward's lectures on the plain, middle, and high styles, Howell contends, 'These treatises intended the distinction to mean that different subjects require different treatments, and that true excellence in oratory consists not in cultivating the grand style at the expense of the plain but in being always able to command the three styles as the subjects demand.' In borrowing the Ciceronian categories, however, rhetorical treatises such as Ward's – which grew rapidly in number along with female conduct books during the second half of the eighteenth century – adapted that 'part of Latin rhetoric which gave the tropes and figures such an interminable emphasis as to discredit by implication the rhetorical function of plainness'.[1] Without saying so explicitly, Howell's analysis demonstrates how the styles of oratory ranked writing according to its implicit familiarity with Latin texts; written usage of rhetoric maintained a political hierarchy, in other words, quite at odds with the classical principles of rhetoric as eighteenth century theory drew them from Cicero's *Orator*. Thus it is highly significant that Austen should put the most admirable pen in the hand of a man in the 'yeomanry', as Emma calls Robert Martin, rather than in that of a woman, as Richardson does. By means of Elton's charade, she declares the high style to be little more than pretension by attributing it to a man 'without any alliances but in trade' (p. 93). But most telling of all in Austen's subtle critique is the failure of the high style of writing to translate into effective speech: 'for with all his good and agreeable qualities, there was a sort of parade in his speeches which was very apt to incline her to laugh' (p. 56).

By means of Frank Churchill's letters, on the other hand, Austen introduces what Emma's former governess regards as 'one of the best gentleman's hands I ever saw' (p. 202). In this case, Mr Knightley proves a stern critic, however. He regards with suspicion the verbal decorum that comes from an elite education, since the man in question does not carry out his words in other forms of behaviour. 'It is Frank Churchill's duty to pay this attention to his father', Knightley argues, 'He knows it to be so, by his promises and messages; but if he wished to do it, it might be done' (p. 99). On another occasion, Knightley compares the gentleman's hand to 'woman's writing', and only when Churchill's letter arrives to confess finally the extent of his involvement with Jane Fairfax does this suspicion give way to qualified approbation. Knightley feels that at least the young man has begun to subordinate style to truth in his writing: 'Mystery; Finesse – how they pervert the understanding! My Emma, does not every thing serve to prove more and more the beauty of truth and sincerity in all our dealings with each other?' (p. 307). Writing has truth value in Knightley's critique only when it proves consistent with the other modes of an individual's behaviour – particularly speech – rather than with the class that individual comes from or aspires to. Because Austen has introduced all this writing into *Emma* as an agent of social disruption, we must regard such critical commentary as central to the strategic intention of the novel. The novel contains other writing than fiction, I am suggesting, to establish the novel as a new standard for writing. The preferred style of writing has its source in common English and derives its value from its capacity to communicate the author's feelings without inflating or concealing them; it has all the advantages of a stable currency. In terms of the reigning system of values, however, Martin's writing ranks below the styles of both Elton and Churchill. It ranks below theirs because male writing bears the mark of the author's political position and indicates that Martin occupies a lower place in the social world than either Elton or Churchill.

It is no wonder, then, that Austen turns away from writing and from the materials of a male education in order to produce the linguistic reforms that will eventually authorise Robert Martin's style of writing. Nor is it any wonder that she turns to gossip and conversation, which are speech modes identified with the female, when she wants to put forth a kind of writing that reveals the true qualities of the individual. It is important to mention that, in addition to making fiction, Emma is less than conscientious in observing the strictures of female education. As a girl, she drew up 'a great many lists . . . at various times of books that she meant to read regularly through – and very good lists they were', according to Knightley, 'very well chosen, and very neatly arranged – sometimes alphabetically, and sometimes by some other rule' (p. 23). Like her inability to complete a painting, her failure to read may be initially regarded as a flaw, but because of Austen's apparently critical attitude toward written culture, Emma's lack of diligence in this respect proves a virtue, a refusal to be written by culture.

By the end of the novel, literacy is no longer represented in such (conduct-book) terms. It is not acquired from writing at all but through mastery of the rules for polite speech. In renouncing the figures of fiction that invariably generate desire where none should be, Emma's speech acquires a kind of politeness that represents emotional truth more accurately than writing presumably ever could. The model for this kind of speech is none other than that which unfolds with the novel's first asseveration: 'Emma Woodhouse, handsome, clever, and rich, with a comfortable house and happy disposition, seemed to unite some of the best blessings of existence; and had lived nearly twenty-one years in the world with very little to distress or vex her.' Such a statement appears to constitute writing that derives from speech rather than from writing. The speech is the speech of the parlour where behaviour is observed and regulated, and the writing derived from that speech is a form of writing that uses gossip with all the force and precision of a diagnostic instrument. The novel's second major pronouncement on Emma's situation illustrates such use of this language: 'The *real* evils indeed of Emma's situation were the power of having *rather too much* her own way, and a disposition to think *a little too well* of herself; these were disadvantages which threatened to alloy her many enjoyments' (p. 1, italics mine). How different these fine anomalies in an otherwise comfortable life are from the perils to body and soul which Pamela has to encounter.

If the hierarchy among styles of masculine writing creates a gap between writing and speech in this novel, then the hierarchy among styles of feminine speech effaces these differences between speech and writing. The writing that is closest to speech places an author low in a hierarchy of writing, but it is precisely the kind of English modelled on speech that identifies the well-educated woman. We might say that Austen attaches gender to writing in order to create a disjunction between writing and speech. Such disjunction always constitutes a serious crisis in the organisation of her fictive communities. Producing this crisis allows her not only to valorise a new kind of writing based on polite speech, but also, and more importantly, it enables her to situate speech logically prior to writing. In this way, she uses speech to authorise her preferred style of writing on grounds that the source of speech, unlike that of writing, resides in the individual. And as she establishes this as the basis for the truth value of writing, Austen also grants priority to the verbal practices of women, women who may never carry out programmes of reading literature, but who are nevertheless essential to maintaining polite relationships within the community.

To have the authority of language that comes straight from the heart, however, women's speech must be purified of all traces of writing. Thus it is early on in the novel that Austen has Emma renounce her novelistic practices:

> It was foolish, it was wrong to take so active a part in bringing any two people together. It was adventuring too far, assuming too much, making light of what ought to be serious, a trick of what ought to be simple. She [Emma] was quite concerned and ashamed, and resolved to do such things no more.
>
> (p. 83)

There is a special element of irony in this statement. For even as she has Emma renounce the strategies of fiction-making, Austen condemns her heroine to think out social relationships over and over again in terms of imaginary narratives. It is by this process that Emma develops a language that will enable her not only to express but also to know her own feelings, and such knowledge is the precondition for avoiding the pitfalls entailed in misrepresenting the feelings of others. Thus the novel produces a reliable language of the self by the curiously backward process of allowing its heroine to repeat her misreading of sexual relations until she knows her own feelings. Accordingly, Mr Knightley recognises two spirits in Emma, a 'vain spirit' that prompts her fiction-making and a 'serious spirit' that understands the violations of truth as they occur. 'If one leads you wrong, I am sure the other tells you of it', he explains (p. 225). It is in such a dialectic with fiction-making that the self-regulating voice is produced, a voice, paradoxically, that becomes virtually indistinguishable from the voice of the novelist by the end of the novel.

In drawing this relationship between gender and truth, I want to isolate a political move that distinguishes Austen from Richardson. Like Richardson, Austen represents the struggle between various modes of representation as a struggle between male and female, but for Austen the female requires reform at least as much as – often more than – the male. In view of the fact that this struggle is all about language, it is fair to conclude that Austen is not out to seize cultural authority, as Richardson was when he put Pamela in charge of Mr B's country estate. Emma is already too much in charge of the house when the novel opens. Left with too much leisure time on her hands, Emma naturally inclines toward matchmaking. With the influx of the Eltons and the Churchills and the decline of the Bates, the power to regulate sexual relations, Austen suggests, is quite as complex as it is powerful, and it requires a far more subtle means of standardisation than Richardson offered by means of his dialogue between male and female. In those instances when fiction is allowed to proceed unrestrained, words behave promiscuously, and the power Emma inherits as the woman of the house proves disruptive. On the other hand, whenever she renounces the power of speech to constitute desire, she acquires another form of power, which influences even Mr Knightley. Of Emma's long-withheld approval of Harriet's engagement to Robert Martin, he remarks, 'You are materially changed since we last talked on this subject before'. But upon Emma's admission, 'I hope so – for at that time I was a fool', he accedes to her former interpretation of Harriet's character: 'And I am changed also; for I am now very willing to grant you all Harriet's good qualities' (p. 327). Thus, as in Pamela, male and female echo one another in a mutually authorising relationship.

In Emma, however, the transformation is a double one whereby he acknowledges the value of an unextraordinary woman such as Harriet and she understands the uncommon value of the common man. The conflict between male and female did not require the conversion of the one to the other's system of values after all; it simply required finding the right kind of currency to represent what was in the interest of both. Knightley's speech is a renunciation of the conventional language of love: '"I cannot make speeches, Emma", – he soon resumed; and in a tone of such sincere, decided, intelligible tenderness as was tolerably convincing – "If I loved you less, I might be able to talk about it more. But you know what I am. – You hear nothing but truth from me"' (p. 296). However faltering the terms in which she has Knightley confess his true feelings for Emma, Austen proves yet more withholding when it is Emma's turn to reply. On this occasion, the voice of the novelist completely supplants that of the lover: 'she spoke then, on being so entreated. – What did she say? – Just what she ought, of course. A lady always does. She said enough to show there need not be despair – and to invite him to say more himself' (p. 297). At this moment in the novel when there seems to be an absence of words, one has the sense of language reborn, not borrowed and used, as it emerges directly from the individuals in question, word by word, each loaded at last with real meaning, because each is fixed to a feeling that already exists before the individual finds words and occasion to pronounce it. This is the language of pure desire uncoloured by any form of value other than its own. It discloses the core of the individual, at least of individuals who have such a core, and the core of the novel as well, that is, the motivations that all along have been silently shaping behaviour.

Although Austen suggests that writing should imitate speech because speech comes straight from the self, the novel itself operates according to an entirely different principle. To ground desire in a self that exists prior to language, Austen has to disclose areas in the self that have not yet been spoken. To be present before it is spoken, desire has to be inscribed within the individual. That is to say, it has to be written.

As the reader first encounters her, Emma feels no sense of deficiency, even though, as the narrator says, she has 'the power of having rather too much her own way, and a disposition to think a little too well of herself' (p. 1). The novelist grants Knightley authority to read the human character – authority that is nearly equal to her own – on grounds that he 'was one of the few people who could see faults in Emma Woodhouse, and the only one who ever told her of them' (p. 5). But it is only the novelist who can turn Emma's self-sufficiency into a deficiency that instigates desire independent of a social origin. If early on Emma speaks of herself as a most complete individual, Austen writes this speech as the lack of a lack, the absence of Emma's awareness that she is missing something as a female. Austen situates the fact of gender prior to speech by making Emma's speech reveal as writing the very truth it denies as speech. As she confesses to Harriet,

> I have *none* of the usual inducements of women to marry. Were I to fall in love, indeed, it would be a different thing! but I *never* have been in love; it is *not* my way, or my nature; and I do *not* think I ever shall. And, without love, I am sure I should be a fool to change such a situation as mine. Fortune *I do not want*; employment *I do not want*; consequence *I do not want*: I believe few married women are half as much mistress of their husband's house as I am of Hartfield; and so always first and always right in any man's eyes as I am in my father's.
>
> (p. 58, italics mine)

By giving her heroine such perfection through the possession of every material thing and every social prerogative that ever a polite person could want, Austen creates deficiency on another level. It is the same order of deficiency that prompts Emma to insult Miss Bates and thereby inspire Knightley's harshest indictment: 'How could you be so unfeeling to Miss Bates?' (p. 258). In similar fashion, Austen attributes the smallest lapse in social decorum to a failure within the individual, a flaw which she identifies as a defect of gender.

When understood as such, each lapse in turn gives rise to some form of subjectivity appropriate to a female. Thus it is by linking Harriet with Mr Knightley in her most socially outrageous act of mismatching that Emma is finally shot through with genuinely monogamous desire. Again, it is by creating an absence that her fiction, like the novel itself, calls forth a desire that is gendered and that therefore, by implication, is genuine: 'Til now that she was threatened with its loss, Emma had never known how much of her happiness depended on being *first* with Mr Knightley, first in interest and affection' (p. 285). From this awareness come the first signs of utterly genuine feeling that establish relations between Emma and Knightley, a union that magically stabilises the community. Why this depends on the production of female desire becomes clear when we examine the impact of such feeling. Emma's desire for Knightley manifests itself in two ways. She becomes her own disciplinarian – far less indulgent than the gently ironic novelist – as she subjects herself to Mr Knightley's standard of conduct: 'She was most sorrowfully indignant; ashamed of every sensation but the one revealed to her – her affection for Mr Knightley – Every other part of her mind was disgusting' (p. 284). As she rises in her own esteem to meet this standard, however, she also grows far more tolerant (as the novelist is) of others' failings.

It is when she turns her critical eye on herself, not when she tries to regulate the feelings of others, that Emma becomes the very figure of politeness. As the essential quality of the new aristocrat – so closely akin to charity, on the one hand, and to condescension, on the other, yet utterly unlike them in the complex of emotions from which it springs – politeness hangs in the balance of Emma's gravest crime, a nearly imperceptible act of rudeness toward the tiresome Miss Bates. As Mr Knightley explains the nature of this crime to Emma, politeness emerges as the model for feelings, speech, and social behaviour:

> Her situation should secure your compassion. It was badly done indeed – You, whom she had known from an infant, whom she had seen grow up from a period when her notice was an honour, to have you now, in thoughtless spirits, and the pride of the moment, laugh at her, humble her – and before her niece, too – and before others, many of whom (certainly *some*) would be entirely guided by *your* treatment of her.
>
> (p. 257)

It is more than a little interesting to note that in order to fill the model Mr Knightley sketches out for her, Emma must not only learn that she desires, but must also suppress the aggravation she feels towards women she cannot absolutely control. That Emma is so transformed in the course of the novel suggests that the acquisition of this form of literacy is the same as the formation of a nineteenth century individual. The individual is, by her very nature, unformed and in want of perfection.

To work this modification upon the Richardsonian model is to put a double edge to the power of example. If to be real is to deviate from the type, then to perfect oneself is to modify the type in aspiring to fulfil it. For one can observe the shift in Austen's emphasis away from natural virtue as the quality a woman exemplifies to a more complex understanding of subjectivity and the part example plays in shaping it. Emma's problem, as the narrator notes in the second statement of the novel, originates in her absent mother. Because her 'mother had died too long ago for her to have more than an indistinct remembrance of her caresses', she was raisèd by a woman who 'had fallen little short of a mother in affection', but who allowed Emma to have 'rather too much her own way' and 'to think a little too well of herself' (p. 1). While there is no lack of nurturant figures in her world (if anything, there are too many), it is the self-regulatory function missing along with the mother that is significant, and it is this which Emma acquires in learning that she loves Mr Knightley. It is also in taking on this particular feature of gender that her example will maintain polite relations within the community rather than breed disrespect and induce mutability.

Austen's novel castigates behaviour that has been prompted by social motivation – Emma's low regard for Martin, Knightley's for Harriet, Elton's for Harriet, as well as Emma's for Miss Bates. It makes such motivation, which dominates the behaviour of the new Mrs Elton, into the distinctive feature of the nouveaux riches and a false basis, therefore, for genteel behaviour. By allowing the linguistic surface of relationships to be misread on repeated occasions, however, the novel inscribes the traditional signs of status within a domestic framework where they obey a new principle of political economy. That is, both men and women acquire status within an economy of conduct in which verbal behaviour – their use of these signs – is paramount. The more prolifically they spend words, the less concealed and thus the less misinterpreted their feelings become, which is to say that the true nature of the self becomes more exposed. This is as true of Augusta Elton as it is of Harriet Smith and Miss Bates, even though the latter two ladies expose a self more benign and genial. Yet despite the sense of innocence generated by Miss Bates's redundancy, she is all on the surface, her meaning too readily apparent. That she leaves nothing for one to interpret is confirmed by a glance through any edition of *Emma*, which identifies the places seamlessly filled with her speech as pages one can afford to skim over quickly. The relative value of signified to signifier is just the reverse in the case of Jane Fairfax whose self-containment requires elaborate strategies of reading. On her behaviour in respect to Frank Churchill, for example, Mr Knightley muses,

He could not understand it; but there were symptoms of intelligence between them – he thought so at least – symptoms of admiration on his side, which, having once observed, he could not persuade himself to think entirely void of meaning, however he might wish to escape any of Emma's errors of imagination.

(p. 234)

For all the aesthetic value that seems to accompany the withholding of feelings, however, Jane's manner of conduct no more represents the ideal than Miss Bates's. '"Jane Fairfax has feeling," said Mr Knightley – "I do not accuse her of want of feeling. Her sensibilities, I suspect, are strong – and her temper excellent in its power of . . . self control; but it wants openness"' (p. 195). Just because her true feelings are barely discernible, Jane, like Harriet, gives rise to impolite fictions. These narrative possibilities indeed break into the novel and destabilise the exchange of information that constitutes social relations themselves. Polite speech is not simply a psychological function – that point where candour meets discretion – but a medium of exchange, a form of currency that alone ensures a stable community.

I use these terms in an effort to lend the novel's self-enclosure a materiality it cannot achieve within conventional literary classifications. I use the notion of economic exchange to suggest that this novel dramatises a linguistic exchange which it reproduces outside the framework of fiction as the conditions for reading the novel. Austen uses the traditional signs of social status to show how they wreak havoc among the members of her community if they have the power to define individuals. But communication is confused and the community disrupted just as surely when status signs are ignored. In this way, Austen demonstrates that these signs do not operate effectively within traditional rhetorical categories or within the reigning grammar of social identity. She slips signs of status into a new system of meaning, and by such usage, detaches them from a context. Through a plot consisting of repeated errors to the one (male) side and the other (female), Austen creates rules based on her usage. This grammar falls into place as such with the perfection of communication between Knightley and Emma:

While he spoke, Emma's mind was most busy, and, with all the wonderful velocity of thought, had been able – and yet without losing a word – to catch and comprehend the exact truth of the whole; to see that Harriet's hopes had been entirely groundless, a mistake, a delusion, as complete a delusion as any of her own – that Harriet was nothing; that she was everything herself; that what she had been saying relative to Harriet had been all taken as the language of her own feelings.

(p. 296)

Thus, one can argue, Austen allies herself more with Jeremy Bentham than with Samuel Johnson.

By saying this, I mean to refute the idea that Austen was an ardent little Tory who sought to make fiction justify a traditional notion of rank and status. But in opposing this position, I do not subscribe to the view of Austen as a proto-feminist rebel who thrashed against the constraints that bound an author of her sex unwillingly to convention. These, I would rather argue, are alternatives by which literary criticism rewrites the past because they are alternatives that authors such as Austen wrote into fiction, making it possible for fiction to do the work of modern culture. I have drawn upon the distinction between grammar and usage to represent the thematic opposition of personal desire to social constraint that criticism uses to figure out Austen's politics, and I have used the notion of economy, too, in an effort to lend Austen's writing a materiality it tends to lose in critical discussion. If nothing else, this chapter has attemped to demonstrate that writing, for Austen, was a form of power in its own right, which could displace the material body of the subject and the value of those objects constituting the household. In helping to establish the semiotic organisation of nineteenth century England, in other words, the novel helped to create the conditions theorised by Bentham – a world largely written, one in which even the difference between words and things was ultimately a function of discourse.[2] . . .

With a kind of self-awareness rivalled, in my opinion, only by Jeremy Bentham, Austen proposes a form of authority – a form of political authority – that works through literacy rather than through traditional juridical means to maintain social relations. If, by Austen's time, sexual relations are assumed to be the specialised knowledge of the female, and if it is in female writing that the terms of such relationships are figured out, then fiction fulfils its discursive function by exemplifying the conduct of relationships between men and women. Novels do not have to launch elaborate self-defences anymore, for they have appropriated the strategies of conduct books to such a degree that fiction . . . instead of conduct books . . . can claim the authority to regulate reading. More often than not, those conduct books that do not aim their wisdom specifically at children or members of the aspiring social groups turn a critical eye on the genre and deplore the limitations of educational programmes meant only for women. I am suggesting that with Austen, if not with Burney before her, the novel supplants the conduct book as that writing which declares an alternative, female standard of polite writing.

Rather than perform the psychologising function that conduct books by now presumed to be the purpose of female education, Austen's fiction set out to discover those same truths as the private reality underlying *all* social behaviour, even that which belonged to the domain of the public and masculine, i.e. political, world. As architects of the new educational curriculum were also in the process of deciding, it was not enough to cultivate the hearts of women alone. It was now time to consider how social institutions might be changed. In the words of the Edgeworths:

> without depreciating or destroying the magnificence or establishments of universities, may not their institutions be improved? May not their splendid halls echo with other sounds than the exploded metaphysics of the schools; and may not learning be as much rewarded and esteemed as pure *latinity*.[3]

So, too, on the fictional front, where the battle for representing the woman had already been won, once can see the entire matter of relative social position – or in other words, the ranking of men – undergoing translation into linguistic features. The Edgeworths' question of whether an aristocratic education provided the entire basis for male knowledge is simply recast to consider which style of writing best represented the relative value of men. No longer, by implication, was the aristocratic tradition of letters, of 'latinity', necessarily privileged in this regard. To say this would seem to contradict the argument that identifies Austen's place in history with her formulation of strategies of containment.

To read *Emma*, we must not only equate language with power. We must also equate the language of power with prose that imitates the word spoken by an elite minority of country gentlefolk quite removed from the centres of power. And if it seems dangerous to make the first equation because it empowers the Eltons and the Churchills of the world and introduces a certain fluidity into the closed and stratified world of Austen's fiction, then the second of these equations offers a way of limiting the destabilising effects of the first. This peculiar capability on the part of her communities to be both permeable and restrictive is one that also characterised the

English country gentry at the turn of the century. How the fluidity of its membership translated into a question of language is explained in Lawrence and Jeanne Fawtier Stone's *An Open Elite? England 1540–1880*. The fact that for a century the gentry was a rank to which people belonging to different social groups could ascend and from which individuals could as easily decline was inscribed upon the English countryside:

> In the eighteenth century, upwardly mobile purchasers might change the old name of a seat, because they found it insufficiently genteel or imposing to suit their aspirations. In Hertfordshire, Pricketts became Greenhill Grove, Tillers End became Coles Park, and Cokenhatch, at least for a time, became Earlsbury Park.[4]

In quite literally effacing the history of the house, the turnover of country property destabilised the signs of personal identity, a historical process recorded most obviously in *Mansfield Park* but resonating throughout all of Austen's fiction. 'Since continuity of the "house" – meaning the patrilinear family line – was the fundamental organising principle to which these families subscribed', the Stones continue, 'the prime object was to keep together the . . . component elements which made it up'.[5] Among these were not only the land, the family name, and a title, if there happened to be one, but also – and of equal importance – the household objects which preserved the family's history. If it was primarily nostalgia for the iconicity of such household objects that animated her representation of a community in crisis, we would have to place Austen with the liberal Tories of her day. But this, I feel, would be to adopt too simplistic a view of her understanding of the medium in which she thought out the dynamism of the ideal community. I am quite certain that Austen understood as well as anyone could the power of fiction to constitute things, truth, and reality. It was not the country gentry and their specific interests that she promoted as the best life for everyone to live. The ways of the town and the city and their connection with commerce abroad always hover at the borders of the elite community to remind and reassure us of its limitations. It was not this particular segment of society that she idealised, then, but rather the language that constituted the nuances of emotion and the ethical refinements that seemed to arise from within to modify the political meaning of signs, a new language of kinship relations capable of reproducing this privileged community on a personal scale within society at large. It is in this respect that Austen's writing implies the presence of a new linguistic community, a class that was neither gentry nor nobility as the eighteenth century knew them, yet one that was clearly a leisure class and thus a paradoxical configuration that can only be called a middle-class aristocracy.

From Nancy Armstrong, *Desire and Domestic Fiction: A Political History of the Novel* (New York, 1987), pp. 145–60, 279.

NOTES

[Nancy Armstrong's *Desire and Domestic Fiction* is heavily influenced by Michel Foucault's idea that, since nothing exists prior to its written representation, the struggle for the status of truth and thus power is a struggle between different discourses. The discourse of particular concern to Armstrong is the domestic novel, which she treats in a Foucauldian manner as a document and an agent of cultural history. The domestic novel is important, Armstrong argues in her introduction, because, beginning with Samuel Richardson's *Pamela* (1740), it took over the conduct-book project of disentangling the language of sexual relations from the language of politics. As a consequence it created a new form of political power which emerged with the rise of the domestic woman who controlled private life and who emphasised personal virtue as opposed to the status considerations which were all important to the eighteenth-century aristocratic establishment. By disseminating this new female ideal the domestic novel contributed to the empowerment of the middle classes and, by the mid-nineteenth century, transformed the self into the dominant social reality. Armstrong thus attributes considerable influence to female functions and challenges Gilbert and Gubar's view, echoed by Perry (essay 8) in this collection, of women as an oppressed and silent minority excluded from history. According to Armstrong, Richardson's *Pamela*, which is discussed at length in chapter three of *Desire and Domestic Fiction*, 'The Rise of the Novel', was so successful in establishing the female subject as an object of knowledge and in redirecting male desire to a woman who embodied domestic virtue that, by Austen's time, fiction could acquire the status of truth simply by limiting itself to the topics of courtship and marriage (thus achieving the self enclosure referred to in the subtitle Armstrong gives to her discussion of *Emma*). This left Austen free to concern herself with the finer points of conduct needed for a good marriage. In the extract reprinted above – which is preceded by a discussion of how Emma, for all her mistakes, makes gender matter more than social signs of identity – Armstrong argues that Austen's particular contribution to the development of the domestic novel resides in the equation she establishes between the formation of an ideal community and the formation, as a polite standard of English, of a precise language of sexual relations from the speech of an elite group of country gentlefolk who adhered to domestic norms. All quotations in the essay are from Jane Austen, *Emma*, ed. Stephen M. Parrish (New York: Norton, 1972). Ed.]

1. Wilbur Samuel Howell, *Eighteenth-Century British Logic and Rhetoric* (Princeton, 1971), p. 115.

2. Jeremy Bentham, *Bentham's Theory of Fictions*, ed. C. K. Ogden (New York, 1932).

3. Maria Edgeworth and Robert L. Edgeworth, *Practical Education*, (London, 1801), II, 383–4.

4. Lawrence and Jeanne Fawtier Stone, *An Open Elite? England 1540– 1880* (Oxford, 1984), p. 71.

5. Ibid., p. 72.

10

Georgic Comedy: The Fictive Territory of Jane Austen's 'Emma'

PAUL H. FRY

Sir Walter Scott welcomed *Emma* in 1816 as a healthy return to the land of the living from that never-never 'land of fiction' where, as he said, both readers and writers of popular romances insist on sequestering themselves.[1] But Scott and more recent critics who have praised Jane Austen for her lifelike renderings have not always seen that she has her own ways of keeping reality at a distance. She anticipates and at the same time undermines the viewpoint of Scott in approaching *all* fiction, not just Romance, as a territory that is radically distinct from the land of the living.[2] Her famous metaphor for her fiction is even more aptly chosen than may first appear: the 'little bit of ivory' is a working surface, and not a slice of life 'two inches wide'.

That Jane Austen disapproves of Romance as a model world is of course true and has often been argued; this essay is intended in part to show once more, from several perspectives, how that disapproval informs her fiction. But it will also be insisted here that when she reacts against Romance, she does not simply choose life instead. Rather she designs a new milieu, a preferred model world which does not in fact banish Romance but moves it from the centre to the border of her narrative. Romance for Jane Austen is not so much an implausible as an undesirable pattern of expectation. The plot of *Emma* acknowledges the accidents of Romance, and allows them to occur, but only at a safe distance from the sort of accident that is morally to be desired. The centre of her territory requires another name, and the one proposed here is 'Georgic Comedy'.

Emma is clearly comic, no matter what one's definition of comedy may be, and it is almost as apparent that the novel has georgic qualities, if we understand 'georgic' to mean the teaching of useful and sociable skills against the backdrop of a farm.[3] In proper balance, man and landscape everywhere in Jane Austen are mutually supportive, as on a farm: the brief misanthropy of Elizabeth Bennet – 'What are men to rocks and mountains?'[4] – is as imbalanced as Mary Crawford's too urbane declaration that she is 'something like the famous Doge at the court of Lewis XIV; and may declare that I see no wonder in this shrubbery equal to seeing myself in it' (III, pp. 209–10). Jane Austen's values are without a doubt communally centred, but they are still rural values that the community discovers by locating itself firmly in the nature it cultivates, reaping as it sows. This is a key theme of *Emma*, in which marriage and becoming the mistress of a farm are interdependent signs that the expansive egoism of Romance has been modified by a moral expansion of territory, a georgic extension of village and estate.

TOWARD AN OPEN CARRIAGE: ROMANCE AS FALSE EXPENDITURE

The 'gentleman-farmer' Robert Martin (IV, p. 62) merits the unstinting approval of the gentleman (Knight) and farmer (George) Mr Knightley. The difference between them is that Mr Knightley is a gentleman as it were by definition – although Emma has no very clear idea wherein the definition lies. It is not, of course, his arriving at the Coles' in his carriage 'as [he] should do' that makes him 'like a gentleman' (IV, p. 213), but his having unobtrusively offered his carriage to the Bateses. Later, 'The mistake' has by no means 'been slight' (IV, p. 320) when the Eltons forget to send their oft-promised carriage to those same ladies. For 'carriage' in this set of relations one may read 'conduct'. Like a farm, a gentleman is to be valued chiefly by the standard of utility, by the grace of *means*, of 'dealing' and being dealt with. Carriage of any kind, including gentility of bearing, is beyond the present means of Robert Martin, within the recent means of Mr Cole, and soon to be 'set up' (IV, p. 345) by Mr Perry.

Character is assessed in Jane Austen by a standard that hovers between economic and aesthetic metaphors, a standard according to which innate qualities and social position are equally determining but not always separable graces. The causal ambiguity of this standard makes the socioeconomic freedom-to-become of Jane Austen's characters seem genuine, even though in *effect*, in the narrative sense of a just ending, that freedom is very limited.[5] As an ambiguous principle, the grace of means smooths the transition between the economic basis and the narrative freedom of Jane Austen's analysis of life's daily transactions. When Mr Knightley affirms 'the *beauty* of truth and sincerity in all our *dealings* with each other' (IV, p. 446; italics mine), he is making an aesthetic judgment in favour of a transparent or open commerce, and opposed to the love of mysterious dealings that markedly influences the course of the novel.

Among Jane Austen's juvenilia there is a skit entitled 'THE MYSTERY: An Unfinished Comedy'.[6] The mystery is that although much is intimated nothing happens and no information whatever is disclosed during the entire skit. The point is well taken. It is the moral and narrative bad faith of mystery and its heroes to promise much and provide nothing, like the Eltons with their carriage. Emma realises this, though she fails to learn from her perception until later, when she says that 'Mr. Knightley does nothing mysteriously' (IV, p. 226). Romance presumes that the undisclosing allure of mystery is more beautiful than 'the beauty of truth'. Thus one of the main attractions of Harriet for Emma is her conventional foundling-status, or what Mr Knightley indignantly calls 'the mystery of her parentage' (IV, p. 64).

It is mystery that promotes false 'interest':

> 'Charming Miss Woodhouse! allow me to interpret this interesting silence. It confesses that you have long understood me.'
> 'No, sir', cried Emma, 'it confesses no such thing.'
>
> (IV, p. 131)

Emma is obliged to notice here that there is nothing interesting about a silence that can be misinterpreted; she has allowed Mr Elton a usurous *self*-interest. Hence she will break silence as quickly as she can at the parallel moment of Mr Knightley's declaration of love, when he says, 'You are silent . . . absolutely silent: at present I ask no more' (IV, p. 430). He asks for no interest, but happily he is given more than he bargained for. Emma has learned that reticence, the evasive tactic of Jane Fairfax, may be as mysterious, as false a capital, as the diplomatic persiflage of Frank Churchill.

Measured according to the beauty of truth, genteel carriage is neither too sparing nor too lavish with words, for both excesses are riddling, like the glib charade offered almost speechlessly by Mr Elton 'To Miss——', or like the diversionary Alphabets volubly suggested by Frank Churchill. This latter diversion is refused by Jane Fairfax, whose need for secrecy has made her an habitual hoarder even of irrelevant disclosures. Frank Churchill's opposite stratagem, here and always, is to subvert the relevant enigma with a false one that is diverting and reassuringly decipherable. Hindsight regarding the secret lovers' awkward coalition of caution and risk shows them to resemble thieves falling out among themselves.

Such 'enigmas, charades, or conundrums' (IV, p. 70) are fictions that mislead under a borrowed cloak, yet they are always transparent to the clear-sighted. In volume III, chapter 5, Mr Knightley replaces Emma in sharing the narrator's *erlebte Rede*, and one is therefore privy to his perception that the circumstances of the Alphabets game are mysterious: 'These letters were but the vehicle for gallantry and trick' (IV, p. 348).[7] He knows that the mystery may place him in the condition of 'Cowper and his fire at twilight, "Myself creating what I saw"' (IV, p. 344), but in fact his ease in guessing the truth about Frank Churchill and Jane Fairfax is nearly equal to his ease in unjumbling the letters of the game.

Emma, on the other hand, who is not clear-sighted but an 'imaginist' (IV, p. 335), has been able to interpret Mr Elton's charade only half correctly. The solution is indeed 'courtship', but the solution of the charade's riddling rhetoric is Power (court) and Wealth (naval commerce) – the status and fortune, that is, that prove to the unblindered eye that Mr Elton will never marry Harriet Smith. Unwittingly, though, Emma explains what it is necessary to understand: that the charade is 'a sort of prologue to the play, a motto to the chapter; and will soon be followed by matter-of-fact prose' (IV, p. 74). What is to follow in Emma's case is the prose of comic denouement, the unravelling of the mystery, both mute and verbose, of false properties.

TOWARD A HEALTHY NARRATIVE: ROMANCE AS VESTIGIAL INTERPOLATION

Sham in *Emma* always borrows a posture from Romance. At her least credible, Jane Fairfax, having spurned Emma's finally wholehearted bid for her friendship, 'had been seen wandering about the meadows, at some distance from Highbury' (IV, p. 391). This is an 'interesting silence' beyond the outskirts of the communicable knowledge that should inform village life. Jane Fairfax's false choice, her decision for a secret enagement, forces her to appear in the attitude of a Heroine. (' "For as to secrecy",' says Mary Crawford in *Mansfield Park*, ' "Henry is quite the hero of an old romance, and glories in his chains"' [III, p. 360]. Jane Fairfax is suppressing her story, which is – in her case inadvisedly – a tale not told, a reticence akin to the narrator's reticent handling of interpolation.

Many rejected plots linger in the plot of *Emma*, as if pointing to their own unsuitability. At the demise of the first Mrs Weston there was talk, Emma says, of 'a promise to his wife on her death-bed', shown by subsequent events to have been 'solemn nonsense' (IV, p. 12). The pining away of the first Mrs Weston, the death of Lieutenant Fairfax, and the pining away of *his* wife – these are Interpolated Tales summarily dismissed in matter-of-fact prose. They are tales not told precisely because they are 'interesting' in Mr Elton's sense of the word, and from this sort of affectivism the narrator recoils with ironic disrelish: 'Human nature is so well disposed towards those who are in interesting situations, that a young person, who either marries or dies, is sure to be kindly spoken of' (IV, p. 181). The interest the narrative of *Emma* invests in marriage has the air of being brought to bear on deserving young persons, and not, as in Romance characterisation (especially as it is truncated in interpolation), upon persons whose character is merely their fate.

Romance interpolation is also apt to be the vehicle of illness and death, like the tale that Nelly Dean tells the convalescent Lockwood in *Wuthering Heights*, a tale which turns on the venerable convention of the consumptive heroine. *Emma* suppresses real illness in favour of a pervasive hypochondria that is vindicated only once, appropriately offstage, by the death of Mrs Churchill. Illness in Romance hypersensitises consciousness and redirects the plot; hypochondria in *Emma* is the channel of all exposure-anxieties,[8] and points, not to the dying fall or consumption of plot in Romance, but to the converse norm of health, the expansion of plot in comic generation. Little Anna Weston is born on cue, 'Mrs Weston's friends were all made happy by her safety' (IV, p. 461), and Mr Perry is *not* consulted about the child's slight indisposition. Here, then, there is none of the morbid 'interest' of sensibility. (' "Confess, Marianne",' Elinor has said in *Sense and Sensibility*, ' "is not there something interesting to you in the flushed cheek, hollow eye, and quick pulse of a fever?"' [I, p. 38]).

The second Mrs Weston belongs to Highbury as the first Mrs Weston belongs to Romance with Lieutenant Fairfax and his wife, the younger Miss Bates. These latter three characters are altogether peripheral, on the border of things in space and time, because the issues of their lives belong to the territory of Lachrymose Interest. To remain in Highbury is to belong to the main plot in ethos as well as in circumstance. Even Frank Churchill and Jane Fairfax, for all the restitution the finale allows them, can never live in Highbury. To understand them as thieves, as threats against the cognitive property of the community, helps to explain their departure under narrative sentence. 'Happy those, who can remain at Highbury' (IV, p. 260), Frank Churchill has said, but secrecy leads to exile, and they depart for Enscombe, heroine and *pĭcaro*,[9] in an aftermath of Jane's virtual illness, her pining away in interesting secrecy. Enscombe is not an unhappy fate, to be sure, but Yorkshire is pointedly a long way from Surrey. There is a fine aptness in Emma's motto upon the star-cross'd Jane Fairfax when the secret engagement has been revealed: 'Of such, one may almost say, that "the world is not their's, nor the world's law"' (IV, p. 400). We shall return at last to consider the preconditions of banishment from the territory of *Emma*.

Unlike the parody-heroine Harriet Smith, the above-mentioned peripheral characters, including the onstage secret lovers, are not merely parodic of Romance; Harriet's cold and her 'tooth amiss' (IV, p. 451) underline the triviality of her recurrent bad health, and contrast her with the consumptive heroine that Jane Fairfax very nearly becomes. The pathos freely evoked by the peripheral characters (or at least not withheld from them) occupies a necessary outer region of the plot, from which the moral norms but not the symmetrical patterns of Romance have been removed: the narrative of *Emma* discredits Romance without discounting it.

It is indeed crucial to see why a mysterious reticence improper in a character is proper for the narrator. The plot of *Emma* depends, as Wayne Booth has complained, on the mystery of Jane Fairfax and Frank Churchill, yet the denouement disapproves of it.[10] This is not narrative duplicity, however, but an acknowledgement that Romance, while it is incompatible with the 'beauty of truth', is nevertheless in its own way as faithfully repeated and played out in common life as Domestic Comedy is. People *do* get sick, and perhaps they even marry princes; certainly they do embroil themselves in mystery. Perhaps the essential point of *Emma* is, not that such things do not happen, but rather that they are best avoided.

Jane Austen numbers among her trio of heroines a Romance heroine treated for the most part without parody in order to admit the mimetic truth of 'interest' and secrecy while denying their moral value. Jane Fairfax and her story, then, together with the story of the first Mrs Weston (recalling the didactic content of Richardson and Burney) and the story of Lieutenant Fairfax and his wife (recalling the lachrymose content of Sterne and Mackenzie), *are* a part of what fiction calls reality; as moral and narrative *exempla*, they are mimetic but not to be imitated. It will be instructive in light of this tacit theme to consider Emma herself as a reader or interpreter, as well as plot-maker, who fails to make this distinction.

TOWARD MARRIAGE: ROMANCE AS INEXPERIENCE

Perhaps the most notable interpolation in the novel is the 'story' of the gypsies. Staple picaroons and agents of mystery in Romance (where they are especially serviceable in plots of mysterious parent-age, like Harriet's), the gypsies trespass into Highbury to remind us that they do not belong there. Fittingly, it is their romance-counterpart, Frank Churchill, who routs them while on an errand of secrecy about which he is obliged, as always, to prevaricate. This for what it is worth is *Emma*'s Romance of the Forest; it is like the labyrinthine Wilderness of the Rushworth estate into which Fanny is led in *Mansfield Park*. This interpolation is as compressed as possible and wholly unelaborated; Frank Churchill's rescue of Harriet makes up 'the amount of the whole story' (IV, p. 334). Although for Emma the romantic possibilities of the adventure are 'peculiarly interesting' (IV, p. 335), for the other adults of the village this sort of interpola-tion is trivial, a child's fiction: 'the whole history dwindled soon into a matter of little importance but to Emma and her nephews: – in her imagination it maintained its ground, and Henry and John were still asking every day for the story of Harriet and the gipsies, and still tenaciously setting her right if she varied in the slightest particular from the original recital' (IV, p. 336). Emma is herself not *quite* a child in this instance though, for if a child's taste is satisfied simply by the repetition of the exotic, Emma the 'imaginist' would prefer that the exotic be embellished, elaborated into a Romance of the fullest possible proportions.

In saying that Emma is a maker of romance-plots, we should not conclude that she is as limited or mechanical in mind as a Female Quixote. She is not even temporarily addicted to romance-reading. When she magnifies Robert Martin's failure to buy a Gothic novel, she is only thinking of his mercenary preoccupation and not alleging that he has poor taste. In fact, the vagueness of 'the book you recommended' (IV, p. 34) may indicate her awareness that *The Romance of the Forest* is not wholly edifying reading. Emma values books as a sign of good breeding (Robert Martin 'does not read?' [IV, p. 29]); she belongs to 'this age of literature' (IV, p. 69), but she falls well short of 'labouring to enlarge her comprehension' (ibid.; the reference is to Harriet) by reading Romances or anything else with any perseverance. In Mr Knightley's opinion, Emma reads too little, but her 'very good lists' (IV, p. 37), however ironically mentioned, suggest that what she does or would read might be well chosen. Thus Emma's disregarding Harriet's assertion that Robert Martin has read *The Vicar of Wakefield* (he is, as Mr Knightley says, 'very well judging' [IV, p. 59]) is deliberate, and not an indication of her own poor literary judgment.[11]

Emma is not, then, a victim of bad reading. Rather her tendency not to read is a facet of her more subtle sort of quixotism. Like Quixote, and in this regard like Charlotte Lennox's Female Quixote (1752),[12] she lives in isolation, estranged partly by circumstance and partly by preference from suitable company. This is one of the many conditions she shares unwittingly with Mrs Elton: 'all her notions were drawn from one set of people, and one style of living' (IV, p. 272). As is the case with Lennox's Arabella, Emma's mother is dead and her father cannot discipline her. Her real bearing at Hartfield, where she favours frightened girls with her notice, suggests the tempting self-isolation of royalty, and her frustration at Mrs Elton's usurping her function as 'queen of the evening' (IV, p. 329) at the Crown is much too pronounced.[13]

With autocracy comes the habit of overruling words themselves, and of making categorical judgments; both excesses flourish in isolation from experience. Outside the flux of even the simplest village life, evaluation hardens to pure geometry in an imaginary space. Emma's 'second and third rate of Highbury' (IV, p. 155) too closely resembles Mrs Elton's 'first circles, spheres, lines, ranks, every thing' (IV, p. 359). Emma's 'imaginism' should be understood, then, as proceeding from an empirical vacuum; her mind soars without obstacle in a fine empyrean where intelligence without insight is perfectly possible – as it is never possible for the merely fatuous tribe of literary victims of bad literature. Fact and fiction are *both* epistemological mysteries for Emma, and in her inexperience both of text and context she blithely crosses and recrosses the abyss between them. Emma is an author of fantasies who nevertheless possesses what can appear to be a matter-of-fact mind, and her inaccuracy is reflected not least in the pseudo-accuracy of such phrasings as 'You have drawn two pretty pictures – but I think there may be a third – a something between . . .' (IV, p. 13).

Her own knack for drawing pretty pictures is of course remarkable. Her portrait of Mr Elton showing her portrait of Harriet to his parents, or her portrait of Frank Churchill 'Standing up in the middle of the room' (IV, p. 147) to Mrs Churchill – all this shows her to be, again, not a victim of literature but a victim of her own fictions. Mr Knightley, by contrast, is inclined to discredit even truths if they appear to be fictitious, and his conversation is relentlessly empirical. 'Dirty, sir! Look at my shoes. Not a speck on them' (IV, p. 10). Or again: 'He had gone beyond the sweep . . . the snow was no where above half an inch deep . . . He had seen the coachmen' (IV, pp. 127–8).

' "If you were as much guided by nature in your estimate of men and women",' says Mr Knightley to Emma, ' "and as little under the power of fancy and whim in your dealings with them, as you are where these children are concerned, we might always think alike" ' (IV, pp. 98–9). Emma thinks, again, like a very bright and autocratic child.[14] Readers have puzzled over Jane Austen's fondness for a heroine 'whom no one but myself will very much like'. But if we see that even Emma's most disagreeable blunders stem from a single remediable flaw – imaginism in an empty space not wholly self-created, mind without object – then we can see that the remedy awaiting Emma, her discovery of clear-sightedness through the embrace of Experience in the person of Mr Knightley, is not at all an arbitrary or miraculous conversion.

TOWARD MUTUAL SUPPORT: ROMANCE AS INCESTUOUS DEMOCRACY

Emma's marriage is not proposed, of course, as a fusion in which all differences of personality disappear. Here is another crucial distinction between the plot of Romance and the plot of *Emma*. In celebrating a more complete triumph over irreducible differences than the many imperfect marriages of *Emma* will allow, erotic union in Romance carries with it suggestions of incest, of the mysterious affinity of kindred souls. Since comic marriage, on the other hand, is a reconciliation, it is actually threatened by the incest motif, which signifies that there is no difference to be reconciled. In *Emma*, Mr Knightley is already equivocating with his feelings when he says of Emma that 'Isabella does not seem any more my sister' (IV, p. 40). The fraternal incubus arises to be expelled, not fostered:

> 'You have shown that you can dance, and you know we are not really so much brother and sister as to make it at all improper.'
> 'Brother and sister! no, indeed.'
>
> (IV, p. 331)

After they have reached their understanding, Emma has a moment of heroic renunciation when, in determining not to leave her father, she proposes a chaste and fraternal future with Mr Knightley. But this notion clashes with the kind of love that she and he have unwittingly exhibited for each other from the beginning; they are not metaphysical mirrors but attracted opposites. Part of the irony of Jane Austen's 'last word' concerning 'the perfect happiness of the union' (IV, p. 484) is that the union, we know, is less hypostatic than soldered. The same can certainly be said of all the other marriages in the novel, each of which is a yoking together by violence of unequals.

 This difference between erotic union in Romance and in *Emma* also has a political dimension. In Romance, though the pauper may turn out to be the prince, there is nearly always at least a moment in which love conquers class distinctions. In more radical Romances, social classes and exogamous families merge together in the union of such figures as Shelley's Laon and Cythna. By contrast, marriage in Jane Austen's comedy reflects without altering the hierarchical nature of community, in which class relations are conducted at a fixed distance. Emma's charitable sortie with Harriet calls forth the same dispassionate tolerance that is required on the part of the superior partner in most Highbury marriages: concerning the parish poor, Emma 'understood their ways, could allow for their ignorance and their temptations, had no romantic expectations of extraordinary virtue from those, for whom education had done so little' (IV, p. 86). Like marriage, charity is also in part a form of self-gratification: 'These are the sights, Harriet, to do one good' (IV, p. 87). Although it is imperfect, and scarcely selfless, an 'unequal' marriage is the best of all possible arrangements, lacking as it does the subversive symbolism of romantic union, the latent incestuous quality that has as its social equivalent the triumph of Eros, the apocalyptic fusing of *all* persons as next-of-kin in a vision of absolute equality. The strained unity of Tory lovers, their yoke, reflects in a system of mutual benefit the triumph of *Caritas*, of love as charity.[15] Something like this, as we shall see now, is the lesson of georgic marriage.

A GENTLEMAN'S FARM: THE LANDSCAPE OF GEORGIC COMEDY

The exposure of Harriet to the gypsies in a 'very retired' part of her walk, 'Deeply shaded by elms on each side' (IV, p. 333), is one of several exposures of the reader to Jane Austen's ironically diminished version of the State of Nature. It is a secluded extreme of wildness (insofar as the presence of the domestic elm and of Miss Bickerton are compatible with wildness!) against the backdrop of which Emma's fantasy of union between the hero, Frank Churchill, and the heroine, Harriet, might almost seem appropriate in a Romance. It remains to be shown in this essay how the sort of union that is more appropriate to the social environment of Highbury may in turn be located in a natural environment, in a georgic setting that, without ceasing to be rural, nevertheless accommodates itself to a State of Society.

Harriet is blind to the romantic suggestiveness of Emma's tableau, as indeed by this time she is more qualified than Emma is for admission to a comic society. In the confusion of references that follows her adventure with the gypsies, she remains instinctively unmoved by Frank Churchill's romantic rescue, and is sublimely moved, *elevated*, by the comic rescue enacted at the Ball by Mr Knightley: 'It was not the gypsies – it was not Frank Churchill that I meant. No! (with some elevation) I was thinking of a much more precious circumstance – of Mr Knightley's coming and asking me to dance' (IV, p. 406). Mr Knightley champions Harriet against the threat of ostracism, but Harriet champions herself as a member of the dance by admiring him for it.

Harriet has, however, 'elevated' herself too far; the magistrate Mr Knightley (to whom Frank Churchill leaves the task of securing the gypsies' retreat) is no Lord of Misrule, nor is it his purpose to play Leicester to Harriet's Amy Robsart when he might have the Queen. The distance between Harriet and Mr Knightley is the distance between Donwell Abbey, which Emma instinctively hoards, and Abbey-Mill Farm, a threshold that Emma refuses to cross. For Emma, what is signified by this distance must be narrowed extremely, but not cancelled altogether. Jane Austen accomplishes the narrowing, as we shall see, by focusing the contours and actual distances of the landscape itself. In our mind's eye, she brings the Farm to the foot of the Abbey.

While her characters gaze at the view during the 'al-fresco party' at Donwell (IV, p. 357), Jane Austen is at pains to oppose the respective landscapes of both Farm and Abbey to the tastes made popular by the Picturesque tourism and the fey pastoralism of the previous half-century. She appeals to the century-old taste of Pope's *Epistle to Burlington* in describing the practical layout of the Abbey, 'with all the old neglect of prospect' (IV, p. 358)[16] and with 'its suitable, becoming, characteristic situation, low and sheltered ... and its abundance of timber in rows and avenues, which neither fashion nor extravagance had rooted up' (ibid.). Pope decried 'an op'ner Vista ... / Foe to the Dryads', yet in his generation Addison had already associated an open vista with the love of Liberty;[17] and thus in gauging the conservatism of Jane Austen it is important to see that her taste for closed prospects bypasses a century's growing preference for libertarian Sweep.[18]

She was by no means uninfluenced, however, by the Age of Sensibility. In *Mansfield Park*, Fanny Price's Cowperian love of the Picturesque depends on her having discovered in nature a regulating God rather than an analogy for latitude; once her point of closure is explicit, then she can give herself up to picturesque scenes and their softening moral effects. In the passage we have just quoted from *Emma*, the initial decision for closure is only a stationing or anchorage in nature, after which, increasingly during the Donwell expedition, the vista will open out after all.

In rendering Donwell, Jane Austen combines Humphry Repton's standard of genteel Utility with the roughness of picturesque surface admired by the more progressive William Gilpin.[19] The house and grounds of Donwell lack the smoothness that Emma thinks she prefers to the 'unpolished' Martin family, and that Mr Knightley condemns in the tonsured Frank Churchill. 'The house was larger than Hartfield, and totally unlike it, covering a good deal of ground, rambling and irregular, with many comfortable and one or two handsome rooms. – It was just what it ought to be, and it looked what it was' (IV, p. 358). The houses of Gothic fiction, as is often remarked, are symbols of their inhabitants' minds; houses in Jane Austen are symbols of the total person. Mr Knightley himself is 'larger than' Emma, older and more rugged; he rambles daily, covering a good deal of experiential ground; the slight irregularity of his brusque manner ('if any young man were to set about copying him, he would not be sufferable' [IV, p. 34]), the comfortable ease of his social footing in Highbury, his handsome moral nature (manifest only when needed, like a parlour), and finally, the unity of appearance and reality that he recommends and exemplifies – all these qualities complete the portrait of house and man.[20] When Emma says 'Just what she ought, of course' (IV, p. 431) in accepting Mr Knightley's proposal of marriage, her behaviour is 'just what it ought to be', like Mr Knightley's house. Thus Emma's unrecorded response is not really a disappointing evasion or reticence on the part of the narrator (as it is often thought to be), but a sign, rather, that at last Emma has joined Mr Knightley and his house in exemplifying the value of appropriateness.

Beyond the immediate grounds of Donwell there is a vista after all, an appropriate latitude of prospect. It is seen through a pair of 'high pillars, which seemed . . . to give the appearance of an approach to the house, which never had been there' (IV, p. 360). In this there is just enough arbitrarily unapproachable hauteur to point away from the Abbey and toward Harriet's appropriate future Prospect:

> It led to nothing; nothing but a view at the end over a low stone wall. . . . The considerable slope, at nearly the foot of which the Abbey stood, gradually acquired a steeper form beyond its grounds; and at half a mile distant was a bank of considerable abruptness and grandeur, well clothed with wood; – and at the bottom of this bank, favourably placed and sheltered, rose the Abbey-Mill Farm, with meadows in front, and the river making a close and handsome curve around it.
>
> It was a sweet view – sweet to the eye and the mind. English verdure, English culture, English comfort, seen under a sun bright, without being oppressive.
>
> (ibid.)

The low stone wall is the only thing that remains between Emma's prejudices and her potential self; between her sense of the Farm as 'nothing', a nil for Harriet, and her final *gaffe* (a simple inversion of her old distortions) – her fear that all barriers may be torn down and that Donwell itself may be her protégée's future home. But Harriet will in fact live lower in this georgic scene, which is as gently stratified socially as its downward slope is terraced. The sight of the comic rescuer Mr Knightley 'giving Harriet information as to modes of agriculture &c'., (IV, p. 361) will only be misconstrued later on by Emma because she will still fail then to understand the ideology that belongs to this setting. An altogether alien Eros would be required, as we have suggested, to *level* Mr Knightley and Harriet; but Emma is still dislocated enough to confuse Eros with charity.

SEASONAL RETURN AND ROMANTIC DEPARTURE

Ever since *The Seasons*, the Georgic ideal in the English literary imagination had come increasingly to offer a compromise between nature and art. For Jane Austen, art is by far the more prominent feature in the admixture. As Mary Lascelles says, 'Jane Austen's people generally have more to lend the landscape than to borrow from it'.[21] The Abbey-Mill Farm, with its 'light column of smoke ascending' (IV, p. 360), is furrowed as one approaches it by the essential figure of farming, the line or Row: 'the broad, neat gravel-walk, which led between espalier apple-trees to the front door' (IV, p. 186). The Romantic eye, on the other hand, partly though not completely effaces the furrow in scenes resembling Abbey-Mill Farm, and poises its georgic world at the minimum edge of cultivation:

> Once again I see
> These hedge-rows, hardly hedge-rows, little lines
> Of sportive wood run wild; these pastoral farms
> Green to the very door; and wreaths of smoke
> Sent up, in silence, from among the trees!
> Wordsworth, 'Tintern Abbey', ll. 14–18

> a most living landscape, and the wave
> Of woods and corn-fields, and the abodes of men
> Scatter'd at intervals, and wreathing smoke
> Arising from such rustic roofs . . .
> Byron, 'The Dream', ll. 32–5

Here and earlier we have reduced 'Romance' and the 'Romantic' to their common perspective in order to underline the channelling together in the plot of *Emma* of what is on the one hand a genre and on the other hand a world-view. Georgic in Romanticism, as in the two passages above, is a nostalgic projection, an elegiac moment the speaker cannot return to except as a sadly alienated visitor who has at once outgrown it and fallen from it. The comic stage of Jane Austen, by contrast, projects the quietest of green worlds, not as a prelapsarian point of departure but as a postlapsarian goal. Her farm is not grown away from but grown toward. Since the Fall in Jane Austen is a premise, not an initiation, it is never a decisive plunge into the anxiety of homelessness except for those characters who belong to Romance, and whose necessary exile we have already stressed.

Since *Emma* is 'A Hartfield edition' (IV, p. 75) of *A Midsummer Night's Dream*, it is perhaps not surprising that evidence of human frailty is nowhere more plainly exhibited than – 'at almost Midsummer' (IV, p. 357) – on Box Hill, the Athenian Forest of the novel's most precocious Exploring Party. Like the shaded part of the road where Harriet was surprised by the gypsies, Box Hill is *too* picturesque – more so, that is, than Donwell – too open and meandering to encompass the principle of separation' (IV, p. 367) that prevails there, and that Emma has anticipated in conversation with Mrs Elton: 'We are rather out of distance of the very striking beauties which attract the sort of parties you speak of; and we are a very quiet set of people, I believe; more disposed to stay at home than engage in schemes of pleasure' (IV, p. 274). The Box Hill episode recalls the expedition to Sotherton in *Mansfield Park*. The motives for *that* exploring party were equally frivolous and vain, and the ensuing disequilibrium was equally extreme. The characters on Box Hill stray too far apart, and disperse into a State of Nature in which taste and behaviour have a common ground that is, again, excessively picturesque. Highbury's 'very quiet set of people' remains or should remain safely within the georgic world to which Romance, represented in the persons of Jane Fairfax and Frank Churchill (who until now has never been 'home' [IV, p. 191]), can only engineer a tentative and transient return. Emma is enabled, through committed contact with the georgic environs of Highbury, to become a mediate and complete person.

It is the seasonal quality of Georgic – that is, the fitness of things in season – that Jane Austen stresses in presenting Mr Knightley: 'as a farmer, as keeping in hand the home-farm at Donwell, he had to tell what every field was to bear next year' (IV, p. 100). The action of the novel covers the four-part annual cycle of Thomson's and many other georgic poems. Aware of Spring as a probable crisis in her life (q.v. IV, p. 315), as it is for Thomson's lovers, Emma lives in the novel from the onset of winter until the next harvest-time – though the late October date of her wedding, rather beyond harvest-time, is perhaps not the least disturbing element in the lengthy denouement.[22] Meanwhile, the increased social mobility of which

Mr John Knightley reminds her (q.v. IV, pp. 311–12) takes her away from the 'solitary grandeur' of Hartfield and toward a time when she will become the mistress of a gentleman's farm. Mr Knightley, as we have said, is reflected in his house and actions as a total man; Emma becomes worthy of him when, in opening herself to the quiet beauties of the physical world – the green world of comedy reined in by the 'English [agri]culture' of Georgic – she becomes a whole character in her own right.[23]

CONCLUSIONS AND ENCLOSURES: IDYLL AS GEORGIC

Lionel Trilling, citing Schiller's *On Naive and Sentimental Poetry*, has called *Emma* an 'idyll'.[24] This is an accurate term up to a point, but it must be added that Jane Austen's fictive territory is an idyll only of a specific kind. Resembling only the most localised, mimetically undisplaced form of the idyll (e.g. Goethe's *Hermann und Dorothea*), the environs of Highbury are pointedly ordinary. Emma, again, has reminded Mrs Elton that Highbury, only sixteen miles from London and all of seven miles from Box Hill, is not in itself a leading attraction 'of the garden of England' (VI, p. 273; the decay of the Crown Inn confirms this[25]), nor is it even near such attractions, nor indeed has Surrey an undisputed claim to Mrs Elton's epithet. The rarefied affectations of the pastoral idyll are repudiated via Mrs Elton's 'simple and natural' impersonation of a Fair Phyllis misplaced on Mr Knightley's farm. While it is possible for Harriet to have been commendably affected by a pastoral convention on a farm when Mr Martin 'had his shepherd's son into the parlour one night on purpose to sing to her' (IV, p. 28), even this passage shows among other things that in the everyday world shepherds are classed even lower than the 'yeomanry'. Devoid, then, of striking beauty and pastoral simplicity, Jane Austen's idyll also lacks perfection of climate. Although Highbury 'was reckoned a particularly healthy spot' (IV, p. 22), it is only nominally a place whither Jane Fairfax can be sent to recover her health in 'her native air' (IV, p. 161). Emma's wilful declaration that 'There does seem to be something in the air of Hartfield which gives love exactly the right direction' (IV, p. 75) is, as the context shows, only a midwinter day's dream.

Jane Austen's juvenile sketch called *Evelyn*, about a village of that name, is a satire on the gratuitous perfections of both the bounteous physical nature and the charitable human nature that are the themes of most idylls. The border of *Evelyn*'s territory betrays the excess geometry of 'A beautifully-rounded, gravel road without any turn or interruption' (VI, p. 181): 'Every house in this village, from the sweetness of the Situation, & the purity of the Air, in which neither Misery, Illhealth, or Vice are ever wafted, is inhabited' (VI, p. 181). Highbury is too ordinary, certainly, to furnish forth a full-blown idyll of this sort; it exists, rather, in the closer mimetic relation to reality that Georgic bears to farming. The fiction of *Emma* merges with what one takes for Experience; the merger is not so much – or so importantly for students of Jane Austen's art – a triumph of verisimilitude as a discovery of a new narrative region: a 'middle place' that is far more appropriate than the exotic locales of Romance for the middle style of the middle class.

Like her ethics and her politics, Jane Austen's territory is determinate and fixed. Being quite aware that it is potentially stultifying, she is ambivalent about any comic dance that remains disagreeably 'a crowd in a little room' (IV, p. 249). Without the fresh air and 'grown-up health' (IV, p. 39; *re* Emma) of the 'home-farm of Donwell', and without 'the beauty of truth and sincerity' made available to Emma as an acceptably open vista, the absence of Prospect,[26] of the invigorating scope even of mystery and exile, is a depressing condition which the passage of time, in the land of non-fiction, could only worsen. Georgic marriage, with its 'perfect happiness', is a generic solution, an artifice, but unlike the topographically and morally displaced unions of Romance, it finds near at hand, in 'English culture', a familiar and attractive mirror of itself.[27] The unsituated 'Garden of England' is transformed by Jane Austen to a *rus conclusus,* an enclosed farmland ample enough in range to unite adjoining parishes, but firmly immured against outlying fictions.

From *Studies in the Novel*, 11 (Summer 1979), 129–46.

NOTES

[Fry's essay appears at the end of this collection because of the way in which it integrates traditional and poststructuralist approaches to *Emma*. Readers might find it illuminating to consider how Fry differs from the more consistently traditional Stovel (essay 1) in his treatment of Austen's generic affiliations. Ed.]

1. *Quarterly Review*, March 1816; Rpt. in *Jane Austen: The Critical Heritage*, ed. B. C. Southam (London, 1968), p. 60. In the ensuing discussion of the relation between genre and representation, I have borne in mind Darrel Mansell's suggestive phrase explaining *Emma* as 'existing somewhere between Surrey and fantasy' (*The Novels of Jane Austen: An Interpretation* [London, 1973], p. 166). Box Hill, for instance, is rather faithfully copied from life by fiction, and yet the two topographies in which it is situated, cartographic and – as will be shown – moral, cannot be conflated at all.

2. On the selectivity of Jane Austen's descriptive technique in contrast with the greater clutter – for example – of her letters, see especially A. Walton Litz, '"A Development of Self": Character and Personality in Jane Austen's Fiction', in *Jane Austen's Achievement*, ed. Juliet McMaster (London, 1976), p. 64. Litz speaks boldly of 'her created world'.

3. For the purpose of this essay, the genre of 'Georgic' so defined need embrace a tradition no broader or less self-aware as a tradition than the one that spans the *Works and Days*, the *Georgics*, and Dyer's *Fleece* (a poem which, like Gabriel Oak's shearing-barn in *Far from the Madding Crowd* plainly poises its subject on the threshold *between* pastoral and georgic). See Dwight L. Durling, *Georgic Tradition in English Poetry* (New York, 1935).

4. *The Novels of Jane Austen*, ed. R. W. Chapman, 5 vols (London: Oxford University Press, 1932–4), II, 154; henceforth cited in text by volume and page.

5. The failure to notice the selectivity of Jane Austen's discourse, a selectivity that is based, arguably, on an instinct for literary convention, has given rise to studies of character in her work that are rather malapropos. By insisting that Emma and Mr Knightley remain flawed – and most intricately so – J. F. Burrows, for one, deprives *Emma* of its conventionally redemptive structure (*Jane Austen's 'Emma'* [Sydney, 1968]; Burrows would say, of course, that he *redeems* the novel from that structure). Well and good, but this approach ends by depriving the novel of any structure whatsoever. At this extreme, the atomism of close character-ology (performed in the name of verisimilitude) and the *frayages* of deconstruction turn out to coincide. For a recent essay that follows Burrows, see John Hagan, 'The Closure of *Emma*', *Studies in English Literature*, 15 (1975), 545–61 – which title must be read, one supposes, ironically.

6. *The Works of Jane Austen: Minor Works*, ed. R.W. Chapman, 1st edn (1954, rev. London: Oxford University Press, 1965), p. 55. This sixth volume of the Standard Edition will be cited henceforth in the text by volume (VI) and page. Stuart M. Tave shrewdly singles out this moment as a telltale violation of Wordsworthian ethics in 'Jane Austen and One of Her Contemporaries', in *Jane Austen: Bicentenary Essays*, ed. John Halperin (Cambridge, 1975), pp. 61–74.

7. On the relation of games and mystery in *Emma*, see Joseph Wiesenfarth, '*Emma*: Point Counterpoint', in Halperin (above), p. 210.

8. In Jane Austen, as A. Walton Litz has remarked, 'hypochondria is used as an emblem of fear of reality' (*Jane Austen: A Study of Her Artistic Development* [New York, 1965], p. 37).

9. This word does not allude simply to his being attracted to the local Inn. In his role as trickster or 'king of his company' (IV, 150), Frank Churchill is an upwardly mobile saboteur of fixed social order. He is not in fact socially secure by birth; only tangentially a Churchill, he is nearly as much an orphan as Jane Fairfax is. Concerning outsiders and their confused identity in the novel, see Malcolm Bradbury, 'Jane Austen's *Emma*', in *Jane Austen: 'Emma'. A Casebook*, ed. David Lodge (Nashville, 1970), p. 219.

10. Wayne C. Booth, *The Rhetoric of Fiction* (Chicago, 1961), p. 254.

11. For a different view of this issue, see Mary Lascelles, *Jane Austen and Her Art* (1939; rpt. London, 1963), p. 69; and Edward M. White, '*Emma* and the Parodic Point of View', *Nineteenth-Century Fiction*, 18 (June, 1963), 56ff.

12. For a discussion of Jane Austen's use of this text, see Kenneth Moler, *Jane Austen's Art of Allusion* (Lincoln, 1968), pp. 162–4.

13. On this point see Joseph Wiesenfarth, '*Emma*: Point, Counterpoint', in *Jane Austen*, ed. John Halperin (Cambridge, 1975), p. 214.

14. Brigid Brophy, speculating psychoanalytically upon Jane Austen's 'History of England' concludes: 'The *History* shows her deeply susceptible to the equation between one's own infantile history and an infatuation with "history", in which "history" is a throng of people in vivid colours – as if perceived by infant eyes . . . , each in a small feudal way an absolute monarch of himself. . . . Infancy ceases when education has made the individual constitutional monarch of himself' ('Jane Austen and the Stuarts', in *Critical Essays on Jane Austen*, ed. B. C. Southam [London, 1968], pp. 31–2). On Emma's 'imaginism' see Stuart M. Tave, *Some Words of Jane Austen* (Chicago, 1973) pp. 205–22.

15. For another view of the politics of this episode, see Arnold Kettle, '*Emma* (1816)', in *Jane Austen: A Collection of Critical Essays*, ed. Ian Watt (Englewood Cliffs, 1963, p. 122). For the assertion that Jane Austen's emphasis on unequal marriages reflects her social bitterness, see Lloyd W. Brown, 'The Business of Marrying and Mothering', in *Jane Austen's Achievement*, ed. Juliet McMaster (London, 1976), pp. 34ff.

16. Cf. *Northanger Abbey*, V, p. 161 and *Mansfield Park*, III, p. 56 for the other low-set buildings in Jane Austen. In *Sanditon*, she clearly sides against Mr Parker and with 'Our Ancestors', who 'always built in a hole' (VI, p. 380). In *Pride and Prejudice*, because Darcy is himself as

much a sublime object as a character, it is not surprising that the house
on 'his beautiful grounds at Pemberley' (II, p. 373) is elevated rather
than set low.

17. Alexander Pope, *Epistle to Burlington*, ll. 93–4. See also Joseph Addison: 'a spacious horizon is an image of liberty' (*Spectator*, 412).

18. See Marilyn Butler, *Jane Austen and the War of Ideas* (Oxford, 1975), for the skilful placement of *Emma* in the tradition called by Butler the 'conservative' or 'anti-jacobin' novel (p. 150).

19. The Repton whom Mr Rushworth hopes to employ in the improvement of Sotherton defines utility, in his *Sketches and Hints on Landscape Gardening* (1794), as 'everything that conduces to the purpose of habitation with elegance' (*The Art of Landscape Gardening* [incl. the *Sketches*], ed. John Nolen [Boston, 1907], p. 58). At the same time, we know that Jane Austen herself was 'enamoured of Gilpin on the Picturesque' (Mary Augusta Austen-Leigh, *Personal Aspects of Jane Austen* [New York, 1920], p. 29); and it was Gilpin, together with R. P. Knight, Sir Uvedale Price, and ultimately the Kant of the Third Critique, who developed the anti-utilitarian criterion of Disinterestedness as the basis of aesthetic judgement. Very probably, then, in naming Repton, Jane Austen wished to distance herself from the taste of Mr Rushworth. Martin Price, in 'The Picturesque Moment', quotes the ensuing passage about Donwell Abbey in a context somewhat different from this one, but what he says may be read in support of the present remarks (Frederick W. Hilles and Harold Bloom (eds), *From Sensibility to Romanticism* [London, 1970], pp. 267–8). On this subject in general and related issues, see Alistair M. Duckworth, *The Improvement of the Estate: A Study of Jane Austen's Novels* (Baltimore, 1971).

20. On the resemblance of Donwell and Mr Knightley, see A. Walton Litz, 'A Development of Self', in *Jane Austen's Achievement*, ed. Juliet McMaster (London, 1976), p. 72.

21. Mary Lascelles, *Jane Austen and Her Art* (London, 1963), p. 197. See also Joel Weinsheimer, 'Jane Austen's Anthropocentrism', in *Jane Austen Today*, ed. Joel Weinsheimer (Athens, Ga, 1975), p. 138.

22. For the fullest discussion of the seasonal structure, see Edgar Shannon, '*Emma*: Character and Construction', *PMLA*, 71 (1956), 647ff. For the 'shade' of the denouement, see Mark Schorer, 'The Humiliation of Emma Woodhouse', in *Jane Austen*, ed. Ian Watt (Englewood Cliffs, 1963), p. 109.

23. At least this is true in so far as such a transformation can be expected in a *portrait moral*; one must agree with Karl Kroeber's observation that 'In Jane Austen's novels some characters may realise their latent potentials but none truly changes; no character is inherently enigmatic' (*Styles in Fictional Structure: The Art of Jane Austen, Charlotte Brontë and George Eliot* [Princeton, 1971], p. 35).

24. Lionel Trilling, 'Introduction', *Emma*, Riverside edn (Cambridge, Mass: Houghton, Mifflin, 1957), p. xix ff.

25. See G. Armour Craig, 'Jane Austen's *Emma:* The Truths and Disguises of Human Disclosure', in *Emma*, ed. Stephen M. Parrish, Norton Critical Editions (New York, 1972), p. 423.

26. For a recent, phenomenologically tinged discussion of the constricted spaces of *Emma*, see Francis R. Hart, 'The Spaces of Privacy: Jane Austen', *Nineteenth-Century Fiction*, 30 (December 1975), 328ff.

27. Hence the striking truth of Martin Price's observation, that 'Jane Austen presents [her world] for recognition rather than seeks to imagine it anew' ('Manners, Morals and Jane Austen', ibid., p. 262).

Further Reading

My aim in this bibliography is not to survey Austen criticism but to identify some of the essays and books which (in addition to the extracts included in the anthology), have contributed the most to our understanding of Austen's novels and, more particularly, of *Emma* during the last twenty years. Readers who wish to gain a sense of what was happening before the 1970s would be advised to consult David Lodge (ed.), *Jane Austen: 'Emma'. A Casebook* (London: Macmillan, 1968) which offers an historical survey of critical responses to *Emma* and reprints almost all of the most significant essays written on the novel during the 1950s and 60s. For a complete picture of Austen criticism during the period covered by this bibliography, readers should consult David Gilson, *A Bibliography of Jane Austen* (Oxford: Clarendon Press, 1982), Barry Roth and Joel Weinsheimer, *An Annotated Bibliography of Jane Austen Studies, 1952–72* (Charlottesville: University Press of Virginia, 1973), Barry Roth, *An Annotated Bibliography of Jane Austen Studies, 1973–83* (Charlottesville: University of Virginia Press, 1985), and, for the years since 1983, the *MLA Annual Bibliography*. Useful overviews of aspects of modern Austen criticism are offered by Julia Prewitt Brown, 'The Feminist Depreciation of Austen: A Polemical Reading', *Novel*, 23 (Spring, 1990), 309–13; Alistair M. Duckworth, 'Prospects and Retrospects', in Joel Weinsheimer (ed.), *Jane Austen Today* (Athens Ga: University of Georgia Press, 1975), pp. 1–32; David Spring, 'Interpreters of Jane Austen's Social World: Literary Critics and Historians', in Janet Todd (ed.), *Jane Austen: New Perspectives, Women and Literature*, NS 3 (New York: Holmes and Meier, 1983), pp. 57–62; James Thompson, 'Jane Austen and History', *Review*, 8 (1986), 21–32; Joel Weinsheimer, '*Emma* and its Critics: The Value of Tact', in Janet Todd (above), pp. 257–72.

I

Throughout the period under consideration here, many critics have continued to employ traditional critical tools, either ignoring alternatives or writing in defiance of them. Some notable examples include the following.

John Hardy, *Jane Austen's Heroines: Intimacy in Human Relationships* (London: Routledge, 1984).
In his chapter on *Emma*, Hardy offers a character study of the heroine in which he argues that she is initially indelicate and unjust and only comes to know herself when she comes to know her love for Knightley.

Jocelyn Harris, *Jane Austen's Art of Memory* (Cambridge: Cambridge University Press, 1989).
Harris's discussion of *Emma* comprises a painstakingly thorough and sometimes ingenious examination of the ways in which *A Midsummer Night's Dream* serves as a source for *Emma*.

Darrel Mansell, *The Novels of Jane Austen: An Appreciation* (London: Macmillan, 1973).
Mansell's analysis of the familiar topic of Emma's education is more sensitive than most. In his reading Emma has to learn to prefer the world's art to her own and to realise that Mr Knightley, who lives in a workaday world and accepts facts, is the man she really wants.

Tony Tanner, *Jane Austen* (Cambridge, Mass: Harvard University Press, 1986).
Although informed by a poststructuralist interest in writing, Tanner essentially reads *Emma* once again as a novel about the heroine's education. He argues that the reader finds Emma attractive because she has the capacity to learn, a desire to play and is a force against inertia.

Stuart Tave, *Some Words of Jane Austen* (Chicago: University of Chicago Press, 1973).
Tave's close reading of the way in which the word 'imagination' functions in *Emma* is yet another study of Emma's educational deficiencies. For Tave Emma must learn that the truth is much more beautiful than anything she can imagine.

II

Of the many attempts made during the 1970s to add an historical dimension to the interpretation of Austen's novels, the following are particularly worthy of consideration.

Julia Prewitt Brown, *Jane Austen's Novels: Social Change and Literary Form* (Cambridge, Mass: Harvard University Press, 1979).
Brown reads *Emma* as a dialectic between self and society in which the life of the individual must be coordinated internally before it can function externally to maintain the harmony of the Highbury community.

Marilyn Butler, *Jane Austen and the War of Ideas* (Oxford: Clarendon Press, 1975).
Although sometimes accused of being too rigid in its analysis of Austen's ideological affiliations, Butler's study of Austen's place in the jacobin/anti-jacobin debate remains unmatched in its scholarly rigour. Butler reads *Emma* as a novel which sees truth as fixed, permanent and external to the

individual and is therefore sceptical of intuition, imagination and original insight, the qualities of the inner life.

Terry Lovell, 'Jane Austen and the Gentry: A Study in Literature and Ideology', in Diane Laurenson (ed.), *The Sociology of Literature: Applied Studies* (Keele: University of Keele, 1978), pp. 15–37.

Although it is not primarily concerned with *Emma*, this essay will inform a reading of the novel because it has much more sense of the conflict between conservative and capitalist values in Austen's novels than any but some of the most recent studies of her work. Like most critics of the 1970s Lovell views Austen as a conservative.

David Monaghan, *Jane Austen: Structure and Social Vision* (London: Macmillan, 1980).

Monaghan's book focuses on Austen's use of formal social occasions as vehicles for the testing of her characters' manners, and therefore, in a Burkeian reading of polite behaviour, of their morals. The chapter on *Emma* examines how the Highbury community has become moribund because of a failure to maintain its social rituals and the process by which it is regenerated.

David Monaghan (ed.), *Jane Austen in a Social Context* (London: Macmillan, 1981).

This collection is useful because of the range of social contexts its contributors cover.

Elliot Rubinstein, *Jane Austen's Novels: The Metaphor of Rank, Literary Monographs*, vol. 2, ed. Eric Rothstein and Richard N. Ringler (Madison: University of Wisconsin Press, 1969), pp. 101–93, 218–25.

Rubinstein's important but often overlooked study argues that Austen's novels should be understood as fictional microcosms of the England of her time. For Rubinstein the village of Highbury in *Emma* represents Austen's most concentrated use of her microcosmic approach.

Allison G. Sulloway, 'Emma Woodhouse and *A Vindication of the Rights of Woman*', *The Wordsworth Circle*, 7 (Autumn 1976), 320–32.

By identifying the influence of Mary Wollstonecraft, Sulloway is able to posit a subversive Austen in a reading that prefigures much of the feminist criticism of the 1980s. Because marriage to Knightley involves Emma accepting the role of submissive wife, Sulloway argues that we cannot accept the novel's happy ending.

III

The increasing influence of poststructuralist approaches on Austen criticism during the 1980s is illustrated by the group of essays below.

John P. McGowan, 'Knowledge/Power and Jane Austen's Radicalism', *Mosaic* (Summer 1985), 1–15.

Using Foucault's definitions of the terms, McGowan identifies in *Emma* an unresolved conflict between romantic or modern plot and classical ending.

Edward Neill, 'Between Deference and Destruction: "Situations" of Recent
Critical Theory and Jane Austen's *Emma*', *Critical Quarterly*, 29 (1987),
39–54.
Neill seeks to identify how, by reading with what Barthes calls 'an entirely
modern gaze', the critic can reveal the ostentatious anti-jacobinism of
Emma to be gratifyingly ruptured.
Richard F. Patteson, 'Truth, Certitude, and Stability in Jane Austen's Fiction', *Philological Quarterly*, 60 (1981), 455–69.
Austen's novels, according to Patteson's deconstructive reading, are full of
ambiguities, anxieties and inconsistencies which subvert the stability
which characters, most notably Knightley and Emma, and readers seek.
Gregory T. Polletta, 'The Author's Place in Contemporary Narratology',
in Antony Mortimer (ed.), *Contemporary Approaches to Narrative* (Tub-
ingen: Narr, 1984), pp. 109–23.
Following the lead of Roland Barthes, Polletta seeks to undermine the
concept of the author. Thus he argues that there are many voices in *Emma*
and not one privileged authorial voice.
Adena Rosmarin, '"Misreading" *Emma*: The Powers and Perfidies of Interpretive History', *ELH*, 51 (1984), 315–42.
In her combative essay, Rosmarin argues that *Emma* challenges the
explanatory power of mimesis. For her the novel's narrative voice and
dialogue are often misleading. However, she limits the element of indeterminacy thus introduced by suggesting that Austen intended her readers to
make mistakes and be mystified so that they could learn as Emma does.
Thorell Tsomondo, '*Emma*: A Study in Textual Strategies', *English Studies
in Africa*, 30 (1987), 69–82.
Tsomondo's essay is based on the contention that, in *Emma*, Austen has a
modern conceptualisation of art as a discourse about a system of constantly shifting signification. Like other recent critics he concentrates on
those parts of the novel which thematise reading and writing and concludes that *Emma* is a network of interpretations.
Michael Williams, *Jane Austen: Six Novels and their Methods* (London:
Macmillan, 1986).
In his introduction Williams claims to be following the reader-response
theories of Wolfgang Iser and to be concerned with the dialectic between
author and reader. The reader of *Emma*, he argues, must venture his own
explanations for the novel's misunderstandings and confusions and must
match them to the often contradictory explanations offered by the characters. Unlike Davies (essay 5) and Rosmarin, however, Williams does not
believe that the reader can ever resolve all the novel's uncertainties.

IV

Some of the essays discussed above, most notably McGowan's and Neill's,
show an awareness of the historical dimensions of poststructuralist thought.
However, because they place their emphasis on questions of language, struc-

ture and narrative voice, they tend, as a group, to be somewhat ahistorical. Essays more centrally indebted to feminist and Marxist theories are discussed below.

David Aers, 'Community and Morality: Towards Reading Jane Austen', in David Aers, Jonathan Cook and David Punter (eds), *Romanticism and Ideology: Studies in English Writing, 1765–1830* (London: Routledge, 1981), pp. 118–36, 184–6.

Apart from James Thompson, Aers is the only critic to subject *Emma* to a rigorously Marxist analysis. In his reading *Emma*'s major flaw resides in her failure to recognise the capitalist dimensions of Tory ideology. He also argues that Austen's ideology is made extremely vulnerable by its failure to acknowledge the existence of the working class.

Sandra M. Gilbert and Susan Gubar, *The Madwoman in the Attic: The Woman Writer and the Nineteenth-Century Literary Imagination* (New Haven: Yale University Press, 1979).

As part of their analysis of the anxiety of authorship experienced by women artists, Gilbert and Gubar argue that in *Emma* Austen reveals her fascination with the imagination and her anxiety that it is unfeminine. Thus the fate of Emma, who functions as an avatar of Austen the author, is to be initiated into a secondary role of service and silence.

Claudia L. Johnson, *Jane Austen: Women, Politics and the Novel* (Chicago: University of Chicago Press, 1988).

Johnson takes issue with Marilyn Butler's simple conservative/radical model by arguing that, in the late eighteenth and early nineteenth centuries, many apparently conservative women writers, including Austen, employed subversive strategies to undermine conventional views of sexual difference. Thus, in *Emma*, according to Johnson, Austen subtly confirms the propriety of the heroine's power.

Margaret Kirkham, *Jane Austen: Feminism and Fiction* (Brighton: Harvester, 1983).

By placing the novel in the context of contemporary writing about women, Kirkham is able to conclude that *Emma* embodies the essential convictions of enlightenment feminism.

Leroy W. Smith, *Jane Austen and the Drama of Women* (New York: St Martin's Press, 1983).

Like Claudia Johnson, Smith sees Austen's novels as mounting a female challenge to a patriarchial establishment which in many respects she supported. Emma's problem, in Smith's reading, is that she acts like a patriarchal male, a role that she must shed in order to achieve an ideal union with Knightley.

Mary-Elizabeth Fowkes Tobin, 'Aiding Impoverished Gentlewomen: Power and Class in *Emma*', *Criticism*, 30 (Fall 1988), 413–30.

In her Marxist-oriented essay Tobin argues that Emma's failure to respond appropriately to the plight of impoverished gentlewomen threatens to alienate the middle classes from the gentry and drive them into a union with the working classes.

Janet Todd, *Women's Friendships in Literature* (New York: Columbia University Press, 1980).
Todd concludes from her analysis of Emma's relationships with Mrs Weston, Harriet Smith and Jane Fairfax that in *Emma* Austen reveals a strange fear of those very female friendships into which she herself seems to have entered joyfully.

Readers are also referred to two important Marxist-feminist studies of Austen which do not deal to any significant extent with *Emma*. These are Judith Lowder Newton, *Women, Power and Subversion: Social Strategies in British Fiction, 1788–1860* (Athens, Ga: University of Georgia Press, 1981) and Mary Poovey, *The Proper Lady and the Woman Writer: Ideology as Style in the Works of Mary Wollstonecraft, Mary Shelley and Jane Austen* (Chicago: University of Chicago Press, 1984).

Notes on Contributors

Nancy Armstrong is Professor of Comparative Literature at the University of Minnesota. In addition to *Desire and Domestic Fiction* (New York, 1987) and articles on fiction, feminism and theories of history and fiction, she has co-edited *The Ideology of Conduct* (London, 1986) and *The Violence of Representation* (London, 1989). Most recently she has completed a book with Leonard Tennenhouse, *The Imaginary Puritan*.

J. M. Q. Davies is Senior Lecturer in English at Northern Territory University in Darwin, Australia. His publications include *Blake's Milton Designs* (1992), a translation of *German Tales of Fantasy, Horror and the Grotesque* (1989), and a number of scholarly articles and reviews.

Alistair Duckworth is Professor of English at the University of Florida. As might be expected of the author of *The Improvement of the Estate* (Baltimore, 1971), his scholarly activities include lecturing and writing on Jane Austen and the English novel, and on literature and landscape in the eighteenth century. He has been awarded a Guggenheim Fellowship and has been a Visiting Fellow at Magdalen College, Oxford.

Paul H. Fry is Professor of English at Yale University. He is the author of *The Poet's Calling in the English Ode* (New Haven, 1980), *The Reach of Criticism* (New Haven, 1983), and *William Empson* (London, 1991). His articles have covered topics in Romanticism, the history of criticism, and literary theory.

Joseph Litvak is an Associate Professor of English at Bowdoin College in Maine. He has published essays on Charlotte Brontë, Henry James and the New Historicism. His book, *Caught in the Act: Theatricality in the Nineteenth-Century English Novel*, is forthcoming from the University of California Press at Berkeley.

Beatrice Marie is an Assistant Professor of English at George Mason University in Virginia. Her publications are in the areas of nineteenth-century British literature and critical theory. She is presently working on a book about the revolutions of 1848 and Victorian fiction.

D. A. Miller is Professor of English at Harvard University. In addition to *Narrative and its Discontents* (Princeton, 1981), he is the author of *The Novel and the Police* (Berkeley, 1988).

Ruth Perry is Professor of Literature and Women's Studies at Massachusetts Institute of Technology. She is the author of *Women, Letters, and the Novel* (New York, 1981) and *The Celebrated Mary Astell* (Chicago, 1986), and the editor of George Ballard's 1752 *Memoirs of Several Ladies of Great Britain* (Detroit, 1985).

Bruce Stovel is a member of the English Department at the University of Alberta. He has published several essays on Jane Austen and a number of essays on British and Canadian novelists including Fielding, Richardson, Sterne, George Eliot, Mordecai Richler, Brian Moore and Margaret Laurence.

James Thompson teaches at the University of North Carolina at Chapel Hill. Besides *Between Self and the World* (Pennsylvania, 1983), he is author of *Language in Wycherley's Plays* (University, Alabama, 1984) and is currently working on *Representations of Exchange*, a study of the origins of political economy and the novel.

Index